ecpr PRESS

Parties, Governments and Voters in Finland

Politics under Fundamental Societal Transformation

Lauri Karvonen

ecprPRESS

First published by the ECPR Press in 2014

Cover © iStock #6304632

The ECPR Press is the publishing imprint of the European Consortium for Political Research (ECPR), a scholarly association, which supports and encourages the training, research and cross-national co-operation of political scientists in institutions throughout Europe and beyond.

ECPR Press
Harbour House
Hythe Quay
Colchester
CO2 8JF
United Kingdom

Typeset by Lapiz

Printed and bound by Lightning Source

British Library Cataloguing in Publication Data

A catalogue record for this book is available from the British Library

ISBN: 978-1-910-259-33-7
PDF ISBN: 978-1-910-259-44-3
EPUB ISBN: 978-1-910-259-40-5
KINDLE ISBN: 978-1-910-259-41-2

www.ecpr.eu/ecprpress

Policy Making In Multilevel Systems: Federalism, Decentralisation, and Performance in the OECD Countries (ISBN: 9781907301339) Jan Biela, Annika Hennl and Andre Kaiser

Political Conflict and Political Preferences: Communicative Interaction Between Facts, Norms and Interests (ISBN: 9780955820304) Claudia Landwehr

Political Parties and Interest Groups in Norway (ISBN: 9780955820366) Elin Haugsgjerd Allern

The Personalisation of Politics: A Study of Parliamentary Democracies (ISBN: 9781907301032) Lauri Karvonen

The Politics of Income Taxation: A Comparative Analysis (ISBN: 9780954796686) Steffen Ganghof

Regulation in Practice: The de facto Independence of Regulatory Agencies (ISBN: 9781907301285) Martino Maggetti

Representing Women?: Female Legislators in West European Parliaments (ISBN: 9780954796648) Mercedes Mateo Diaz

The Return of the State of War: A Theoretical Analysis of Operation Iraqi Freedom (ISBN: 9780955248856) Dario Battistella

Schools of Democracy (ISBN: 9781907301186) Julien Talpin

Transnational Policy Innovation: The role of the OECD in the Diffusion of Regulatory Impact Analysis (ISBN:9781907301254) Fabrizio De Francesco

Urban Foreign Policy and Domestic Dilemmas: Insights from Swiss and EU City-regions (ISBN: 9781907301070) Nico van der Heiden

Why Aren't They There? The Political Representation of Women, Ethnic Groups and Issue Positions In Legislatures (ISBN: 9780955820397) Didier Ruedin

Widen the Market, Narrow the Competition: Banker Interests and the Making of a European Capital Market (ISBN: 9781907301087) Daniel Mügge

Please visit www.ecpr.eu/ecprpress for information about new publications.

Contents

List of Figures and Tables

Acknowledgements

This book would not have been written had it not been for my participation in the Finnish National Election Study from 2002 on. The scholars who collaborate within this programme have inspired me enormously and I want to thank them all for their ideas, criticisms and collegial support. While the inspiration to write this book was sparked by the collective FNES enterprise, the result would have looked a lot different had it not been for Heikki Paloheimo of the University of Tampere. Both the fundamentals and the details of the book have been influenced by my discussions with Heikki. His contribution to Chapter Five was of a nature and magnitude that he must be seen as my co-author for that chapter. Moreover, an Academy of Finland research project led by Heikki on 'Political Power in Finland' has provided me with both inspiration and economic support; essentially, this book must be seen as part of that project (Academy of Finland Project Grant 138458).

The Department of Political Science at Åbo Akademi University provides an excellent environment for scientific research. The Centre of Excellence 'Democracy: A Citizen Perspective' (D:CE) has created opportunities for long-term research efforts and a continuing scholarly exchange on a daily basis. Åsa Bengtsson, Kimmo Grönlund, Guy-Erik Isaksson and Johan Meriluoto have advised and assisted me in particularly valuable ways. My heartfelt thanks to all of you.

Peter Triantafillou of the ECPR Press and Roskilde University, plus two anonymous reviewers, read the first version of the manuscript and proposed both major revisions and detailed adjustments in the text. This helped me see many flaws and imbalances in it; I have tried to follow their advice as much as possible. I extend my sincere thanks to them for a thorough and professional review that I believe has helped me improve the book considerably.

Lauri Karvonen
Åbo, Finland, November 2014

Chapter One

Introduction

Parties, Governments and Voters

Two themes run through contemporary analyses of political parties in established western democracies. On the one hand, parties are seen as indispensable and unavoidable in a democracy. E. E. Schattschneider's famous words 'modern democracy is unthinkable save in terms of political parties' (1942: 1) are frequently quoted, as is James Bryce's (1921: 119) statement 'parties are inevitable. No one has shown how representative government could be worked without them' (Dalton and Wattenberg 2002b: 3; Webb 2002: 1; Dalton *et al.* 2011: 3). Political parties perform a number of tasks that place them, in a unique way, at a critical nexus in the political process. Parties aggregate individual preferences and propose programmatic or ideological alternatives. They mobilise citizens as voters and party members. They recruit candidates and officeholders. They represent the views of their constituents in elected assemblies. They govern by making decisions and directing government bureaucracy (Dalton *et al.* 2011: 6–7; Merkl 1970: 105–10; Seiler 1986: 60–5). While each of these functions may also be influenced by actors other than parties, only parties combine these tasks continuously. Thereby, parties contribute to the stability of democracy; it is to this that Seymour Martin Lipset refers when he writes that 'democracy in mass polities requires institutionalized parties' (2001: 5).

Parallel to this, a second theme is presented, frequently by the same authors quoted above. This is the 'decline of parties' thesis, according to which political parties are past their prime. Since their golden age two or three decades after WWII, parties have met with increasing difficulties in several of their central tasks. Various explanations have been offered. Ultimately, many of them are founded on the notion that the erstwhile social divisions that gave rise to most contemporary parties have been transformed to an extent that calls existing party distinctions into question. Changing collective identities affect the party-identifications of citizens: ever fewer citizens find it natural to identify with a given party. As the distance between parties and citizens grows, citizens tend to become increasingly critical of party government and, at times, of the representative system itself. Parties are perceived as elite organisations more interested in furthering their own goals than pursuing goals that are important to ordinary citizens (*cf.* Dalton and Wattenberg 2002b: 3–5; Webb 2002: 1–3; Dalton *et al.* 2011: 9–14). In the words of Bernard Manin (1997: 206–35), representative government has moved from 'party democracy' to 'audience democracy'; citizens have become an audience for, rather than collective participants in, the political process.

This book views the case of Finland in the light of these questions. Finland has retained the democratic form of government that it established upon gaining independence in 1917. It clearly belongs to the group of long-standing western democracies. Although not one of the cases most frequently included in comparative surveys, data on Finland have been presented in several of the comparative studies dealing with parties and voters in the OECD countries (Dalton 2004; Strøm *et al.* 2006). Similarly, empirical evidence on Finland is increasingly included in comparative survey databases available for research (Dalton and Anderson 2010). Why, therefore, a book specifically on the Finnish case?

It would be inaccurate to argue that Finland is a deviant case in a broad western comparison. The main trends that can be documented in the Finnish case are parallel with those found in most comparable countries. The argument, rather, is that Finland stands out as an *extreme* case. The modern, technologically advanced welfare state that Finland is today is, in fact, a fairly recent creation. The social changes through which these advanced post-industrial structures were introduced occurred much later than elsewhere in the west; but once they got under way they took place with unprecedented rapidity. The basic aim of this book is to tell the story of what happens to parties, governments and voters when the fundamental features that conditioned party-formation and voter-alignment undergo a rapid transformation. It is this perspective that makes the Finnish case interesting in an international comparison. To the largest extent possible, this book will therefore examine Finland in a comparative perspective.

The order of presentation of three of the main analytical components – parties, governments and voters[1] – is based on a deliberate choice. In many ways, of course, it might seem natural to start with the voters; this would, indeed, reflect the ideal democratic chain of governance. In other words: a) social change affects b) citizens' identities, values and views of politics, which creates pressures on c) parties who must adapt their messages, campaigns and organisations to match voters' expectations, which, in turn, has effects on the way parties d) govern or act in opposition.[2] This fundamentally democratic way of looking at the relationship between parties, governments and voters is *demand-centred*; change in citizens' needs and preferences is the driving force. One can, however, also view the relationship from the *supply-side*. People's view of politics is not only guided by their perceived needs but by what is 'on offer' in the political sphere. How parties present themselves and how they act in government and opposition has a powerful effect on voters' political behaviour and choices. This is what Seymour Martin Lipset and Stein Rokkan mean when they write: 'Parties do not simply present themselves *de novo* to the citizen at each election; they each have a history and so have the constellations of alternatives they present to the electorate' (1967: 2). It is a central theme and a crucial point in the present analysis that citizen reactions to

---

1. Throughout this study, terms such as 'voting', 'voters', 'elections', etc. refer to *parliamentary* elections, unless otherwise indicated. Local, presidential and European elections remain outside the scope of the book.

2. For an important analysis that is organised according to this logic, *see* Dalton and Wattenberg 2002a, vii–viii.

politics in Finland cannot be explained without considering the change in coalition politics from the 1980s on. Thus, patterns of voter behaviour are best understood against the background of change within parties, plus the transformation of government coalitions. That the voters are the focus of the final part of the empirical analysis is therefore not only a matter of the technical organisation of the volume; it also reflects how the analysis views the fundamental chain of causality between parties, governments and voters.

The next sections of this chapter will highlight previous research on each of the main themes covered in this book. Besides summarising main findings, the discussion aims to pinpoint features that makes Finland a potentially interesting case for comparative analysis.

The Social Roots of Parties

[…] the party structures of the 1960s reflect, with few but significant exceptions, the cleavage structures of the 1920s.

This oft-quoted sentence from Lipset and Rokkan's analysis (1967: 50) has long constituted a given point of departure when contemporary parties are analysed with reference to their historical roots. An overarching theme in the literature has been the astonishing stability of parties and party systems, despite fundamental transformations in those social structures and political conflicts that originally gave rise to political parties (Mair 1997; Gallagher *et al.* 2011: 288–302). From the 1980s on, however, the notion of 'frozen party systems' (Mair 2001: 27–44) has come under attack from scholars who point to, *inter alia*, the emergence of new values and issues that cut across traditional partisan divides, to heightened electoral volatility and to the appearance of new party alternatives in the electoral arena (Pedersen 1983; Inglehart 1997; Dogan 2001).

The core element of Lipset and Rokkan's analysis is the notion of deep-seated structural *cleavages* that divided the population into politically relevant segments. Centre–periphery, state–church, land–industry and owner–worker stand for the main divisions that were fundamental for the emergence of European parties. The configuration of these factors interacted with a number of *critical junctures* in European history. The Reformation and the settlement at Westphalia was the first such juncture, creating varying politically relevant divisions within European countries. The National Revolution of the post-Napoleonic years was particularly pertinent to the issue of mass education and the relationship between the church and the secular state. The Industrial Revolution brought the tension between rural/agricultural and urban/industrial interests to the fore and elevated the owner–worker cleavage to a national scale. The International Revolution (the Russian revolution and its aftermath) was of decisive importance to the development of the working-class movement and, consequently, to the prospects of national consensus and international alliances (Rokkan 1970: 112–31; Flora *et al.* 1999: 304–5).

These divisions account for the characteristic set of parties that have dominated the politics of west-European countries throughout the democratic era. The variations in the position and character of conservative, liberal, religious, regional, ethnic, agrarian, socialist and communist parties are largely explicable in terms of the Lipset-Rokkan model. The validity of the model up until the 1970s seems not to be questioned very much in the international literature (*cf.* Rose and Urwin 1970). As to the effects of structural change on the party system and on voter-alignments more recently, the issue is not definitely settled. Writing in the late 1990s in a major summary of comparative research, Peter Mair (1997: 76–90) finds strong support for the continued relevance of the cleavage-based model. A decade later, he is echoed by Martin Elf (2007: 277–94) when it comes to the continued relevance of the class cleavage; Elf, however, finds that the relevance of religious cleavages has declined. Mattei Dogan (2001) and Wouter van der Brug (2010: 586–607) document a more general decline in the importance of structural factors. Summing up the discussion in 2011, Gallagher and others find clear evidence of the weakening of collective identities and in the distinctiveness of social bases of party support. On the other hand, they find that 'the overall balance between the broad left bloc and the broad centre-right bloc is remarkably constant [...] The principal political protagonists [...] have proven very resilient'. However, the social structure is, in their view, but one of the factors that have protected the traditional party system. The structure of party competition in itself goes to protect established parties (Gallagher *et al.* 2011: 314–15).

Basically, we know that the structural foundations of societies look entirely different from the years after WWI that witnessed the consolidation of the basic party-divisions in western Europe. Also, the extent of attitudinal change among the citizens is well documented and seems to reflect this structural transformation. On the other hand, the picture is less clear-cut when it comes to the development of party-systems and fundamental voter-alignments.

Research on Finland has largely confirmed the general features found in comparative studies. In an article published in 1999, Jan Sundberg finds that, despite diminished class-voting and increased electoral volatility, Finnish and Scandinavian party-systems still comply with the model of 'frozen party systems'. A couple of years later, Pertti Pesonen (2001: 115–37) finds considerable evidence for the persistence of cleavage-based politics, but also notable change. In Heikki Paloheimo's analysis a decade later (2009: 15–61), these conclusions are largely supported, although the effect of more recent issues such as the environment and internationalisation is found to be considerable. Most recently, David Arter asks whether the 'Big Bang' elections in Scandinavia, including the 2011 Finnish election, have altered the party systems of the Nordic countries. He, too, appears to regard the core of the systems as stable (2012b: 842–3).

The fact remains that Finland stands out as a highly interesting case simply because of the extent, timing and pace of social transformation itself. It is clearly pertinent to look for special features related to the lateness and rapidity of this change. The first empirical analysis in this book will, therefore, devote considerable space to an analysis of the transformation of the pillars on which the Finnish party system and voter alignments have traditionally rested.

Coping with pressures

Although research points to a rather surprising degree of continuity in west European party systems, considerable change in the structure of inter-party competition has taken place since the heyday of cleavage-based parties. As Bonnie Meguid (2010: 257) puts it: 'The electoral grasp of the once oligopolistic mainstream parties has weakened. Adding to their insecurity, and in some cases causing it, is a set of new political competitors'. Indeed, there has been a cumulative growth in the vote-share of new parties in western Europe. By the first decade of the 2000s, a little under a third of the vote was mustered by parties that started to contest elections in 1960 or later (Gallagher *et al.* 2011: 308). In some cases, notably Italy, the change was much more dramatic; one can speak of an entirely new party system (D'Alimonte 2008). The effect on the structure of party competition is anything but uniform, however. Many countries display high levels of party-system fragmentation; in others there has been a successive bipolarisation of the system, meaning that electoral competition is increasingly a race between two dominant parties or blocs (Bengtsson *et al.* 2014: 30; Gallagher *et al.* 2011: 197).

Finland is interesting in the light of two opposing pressures. On the one hand, the attenuation of the international importance of the communist movement as well as the accelerating decrease in the agricultural population would seem to make for a more coherent left and right wing in the Finnish party system. On the other hand, the fairly early breakthrough of 'new politics' in the form of an environmental party and the recurrent waves of populist challenge complicate the picture in Finland (Arter 2012b: 840–2). Moreover, the open-list proportional system in use allows for a peculiar form of two-level competition, in which parties and candidates may forge their campaigns fairly independently of each other.

Parties can cope with social change by adjusting their messages to fit the new reality. Contemporary analyses of the ideological positions of parties point in two different directions. On the one hand, there are those who argue that the fundamental ideological contradictions which marked politics until the end of the Cold War have brought most political actors closer to each other (Fukuyama 1992). On the other hand, research also attests to the continued relevance of the left-right dimension (Klingemann *et al.* 2008: 27; Jahn 2011: 760). Contemporary comparative research has access to an invaluable longitudinal dataset provided by the Manifesto Research Group.[3] A comparison focusing on Finland is especially promising, given the traditionally high degree of polarisation of the Finnish party system (*cf.* Sartori 2005: 129). Finland long had one of the strongest communist parties in western Europe;[4] this party could not help but be affected decisively by the demise of the communist bloc. What have these changes entailed for party ideology in general?

Parties are organisations. Like any other organisation, a party has a natural tendency to safeguard its existence and, preferably, expand its scope, domain and

---

3. https://manifesto-project.wzb.eu

4. However, as David Arter aptly points out, 'there have never been anti-system parties of left *and* right concurrently represented in the Finnish legislature' (1987: 71, emphasis in original).

resources. And like other organisations, a party's internal life is affected by the pursuit of these goals. Ever since Robert Michels (1915) formulated his classic 'iron law of oligarchy', political scientists have held that there are innate tendencies towards centralisation and institutionalisation in political parties. Party leaders, professional party functionaries and delegates will, given time, inexorably come to dominate local branches and individual members. Angelo Panebianco's (1988) work is very much a continuation of this line of research; Panebianco argues that the traditional mass party has given way to an electoral-professional party. Of course, such developments have had profound effects on party *membership*. Together with the effects of structural transformation, the perception of a widened gap between the elite and the rank and file of parties has caused a rather dramatic drop in party membership throughout western Europe (van Biezen *et al.* 2012; Gallagher *et al.* 2011: 331). In a way it is increasingly unclear what the role of the individual member in a modern professionalised party organisation should be.

One of the central features of contemporary party theory is the notion of the *cartel party* (Katz and Mair 1995). Cartel parties share the interest of keeping potential new competitors out. In this endeavour, parties use their position in the state as a means of paramount importance. The introduction of public party subsidies clearly favours incumbent parties economically over potential newcomers. Incumbents can also, for example, regulate access to government broadcasting so as to favour themselves. Party legislation is decided by parties in parliament and they are not likely to shape these laws so as to endanger their own positions.

Finland undeniably displays several features of the typical cartel party system. Public party finance has existed for decades and a Party Law has codified the special position of political parties since 1969. However, it would not be correct to interpret this development as part of a general attenuation of internal party democracy. Quite the contrary: Finnish legislation is fairly unusual in imposing standards of internal democracy – including member-influence over candidate nominations – on the parties (Hazan and Rahat 2010: 4, 49). Together with the candidate-oriented electoral system, this feature makes Finland an interesting case for comparison (Arter 2006: 26–43). To what extent have these features created deviations from the pattern of 'incumbent advantage' found in the comparative literature (Somit *et al.* 1994)?

Parties and governance

In the world of stable democracies, western Europe has long stood out as the home of parliamentarism, multi-partyism and coalition cabinets. Save for Great Britain and, although not consistently, France, west European countries have had proportional elections basically throughout their democratic history. Proportional elections enable several parties, frequently including fairly small ones, to gain representation; the degree of proportionality displays a well known correlation with the degree of fragmentation of the party system (Farrell 1997: 146–50). Parliamentarism makes the cabinet dependent on the will of the parliamentary majority for its continued existence. The surest way to ensure the backing of this majority is to include enough parties in the cabinet to correspond to a majority in parliament. Again with the exception of the United Kingdom, the single-party-majority cabinet has only rarely been a viable option. Coalition cabinets have been the most common cabinet type in western Europe in the period after WWII (Gallagher *et al.* 2011: 434).

For formal coalition theory, the reality of European cabinet politics has posed a challenge. In the simplest terms, coalition theory states the following. Parties are office-seeking creatures; they aim for executive power in order to be able to realise their policy goals. If they cannot reach a majority on their own, they will form coalitions with other parties. However, they seek to retain as much government power as possible. Therefore, they will not ally themselves with more parties than necessary for attaining majority status; they aim at forming *minimal winning coalitions* (MWCs). This view of parties as rational and utility-maximising actors is often associated with William Riker (1962). As an explanation of government-formation in Europe it was long viewed with scepticism. For one, Klaus von Beyme, a well respected specialist in comparative European politics, held that the assumption of formal coalition theory had little relevance for Europe (1985: 323). Up until the early 1990s, the empirical study of government coalitions in Europe and formal coalition theory had largely separate existences (Laver and Schofield 1990: 7–11).

The empirical reality of politics in contemporary western Europe indicates that the MWC hypothesis offers a partial explanation but not much more. Roughly a third of west-European cabinets since WWII have been of this type (Mitchell and Nyblade 2008: 207; Gallagher *et al.* 2011: 434). Other common cabinet-types have been surplus (or oversized) majority coalitions, single-party-minority cabinets and minority coalitions. The question from the point of view of the theory is whether a third is a small or considerable portion of all cabinets; the fact remains that this type has been more common than the alternatives.

Finland is an extreme case in a European comparison; no other country has had a higher proportion of oversized coalitions than Finland. This observation certainly merits detailed attention in the present volume. Moreover – and this is a central point in Chapter Four – Finnish coalition politics displays a change from the 1980s onwards that has had important effects on inter-party relations and voter responses. A factor of fundamental importance was the process of constitutional reform that transformed the institutional power relations concerning government-formation. Chapter Four contains an account of the constitutional change that, in fact, meant that Finland abandoned its semi-presidential form of government to become a parliamentary system.[5]

As for the allocation of cabinet portfolios, it is hardly surprising that research has found a proportionality norm to be of paramount importance. In other words: large parties get more portfolios, and portfolios of greater political importance, than do small ones. When no party has a clear strategic advantage over others,

---

5. Relatively recent international sources (De Winter and Dumont 2008: 151; Müller and Strøm 2008) still mention Finland as an example of semi-presidentialism. By contrast, Rasch (2011: 50) notes that Finland has become 'fully parliamentarised'.

this rule applies to a great extent. When there is a party that does have such an advantage, the allocation of portfolios is more disproportional (Verzichelli 2008: 237–65; Isaksson 2011: 230–5; Isaksson 2013: 65–73). Finland largely offers an illustration of the first situation. However the marked change between the period after the 1980s and earlier decades again makes the Finnish case an intriguing one.

Stability is an important key to government power. Cabinets need to have sufficient longevity in order to be able to implement their policies. Short-lived and transient governments can scarcely carry out major reforms. Cabinet-stability has long been a phenomenon that political scientists have sought to explain with the aid of large sets of comparative evidence (Taylor and Herman 1971; Warwick 1994; Saalfeld 2008). Structural factors, such as the party system, the cabinet's status (majority/minority), cabinet type (MWC or not) and the number of parties have been found to be of importance. Constitutional provisions such as positive *versus* negative parliamentarism place varying requirements on cabinets. Critical events that take place during a cabinet's reign may have strong effects on cabinet durability, fairly independently of structural attributes (Browne *et al.* 1986). The ideological diversity of cabinets and the bargaining environment may complicate or alleviate a cabinet's chances of survival (Saalfeld 2008).

As will be shown in some detail in Chapter Four, the periods prior to and after the 1980s in Finland represent two different worlds in terms of governmental stability. Again, this change is so pronounced that it places Finland in a fairly special position in a west-European comparison. Arguably, the markedly heightened stability of Finnish parliamentarism can be seen as the basic political precondition of Finland's successful transition to a post-industrial society.

Citizen responses

'Parties are nothing if not survivors. They represent continuity in democratic politics and they are central to the successful operation of a representative democracy. The ubiquity of parties in old and new democracies confirms their role as the main organising principle of modern government.' Thus write Dalton, Farrell and McAllister (2011: 230–1) in a cogent analysis of the role of parties as organisers of democracy. The authors argue that parties have managed to adapt to changing circumstances much more successfully than an all-out decline of parties thesis might suggest.

Comparative researchers probably tend to agree, as long as the discussion is about *parties in government* and parties and the state. However, when it comes to the role of citizens, many scholars would be likely to paint a more sombre picture. A large number of empirical studies, many presented in the form of broad cross-national comparisons, have documented and analysed the changing relationship between parties and citizens. Although considerable cross-national variance does exist, the basic message is that the distance between parties and voters is increasing. Turnout at elections is declining; since turnout peaked in western Europe in the 1960s it has dropped nearly ten percentage points (Gallagher *et al.* 2011: 306). Trust in parties and politicians is clearly lower than citizen confidence in institutions such as the legal system (Grönlund and Setälä 2012: 528).

Citizens increasingly switch parties from one election to another. Sweden, with its time-honoured electoral research, provides a vivid illustration. In the fifties and sixties, around half of the Swedish voters said that they strongly identified with a given party. In the two latest elections, only 15–17 per cent said the same thing (Oscarsson and Holmberg 2013: 384). Calls for alternative forms of citizen influence are both voiced and put into practice in an increasing number of countries (Smith 2011). Several well publicised political science book titles convey a vivid impression of how this development is viewed: 'disaffected democracy' (Pharr and Putnam 2000) is increasingly marked by 'parties without partisans' (Dalton and Wattenberg 2002a), which has given rise to calls for a 'transformed democracy' (Cain *et al.* 2003) throughout the west.

How these trends are interpreted depends to a large extent on whether parties and elections are seen as entirely decisive for the viability of democracy or whether alternative forms of citizen-activity and influence are brought into the picture. In the former case, the conclusion is clearly more pessimistic: 'The trends paint a somewhat gloomy picture of the state of the old, party-based form of electoral democracy' (Holmberg and Oscarsson 2004: 277). A statement like this puts emphasis on factors such as electoral turnout, party-identification, trust in parties and politicians and party membership. If however, factors such as alternative forms of participation (petitions, demonstrations, political consumerism, contacting politicians and other decision-makers), fundamental democratic values and attitudes and political interest are stressed, a much more varied and positive impression emerges. There has been a steady growth in alternative forms of participation (Christensen 2011: 42; Dalton 2008: 60). Overwhelmingly, citizens in stable western democracies view democracy as better than alternative forms of government.[6] When World Value Study data for western Europe in the 1980s and 1990s are compared with surveys in 2005–7, self-reported political interest has risen or at least remained stable. There is no widespread citizen apathy and heightened levels of education have, in fact, improved citizens' capacity to make independent judgments in political matters. The most optimistic interpretations see a process of 'reshaping of democracy' through a new generation of 'good citizens' (Dalton 2008), therefore. Add to this the expanded institutional opportunities in modern democracies (Cain *et al.* 2003) and the promise of democratic innovations (Smith 2011) and the optimistic interpretation does not appear altogether illusory.

Interpretations of the findings vary, and we can hardly expect the dust to settle on this debate any time soon. Scholars will continue to stress either the party and electoral aspects of democracy or a wider array of channels of citizen activity and influence. Few if any scholars seem, however, to view the trends discussed in this section as something temporary, which will be replaced with 'business as usual'. Hardly anyone seems to envisage a return to the routines of political life half a century or so ago. Looking into a case such as Finland, with its late and rapid patterns of social transformation, may lead to observations of interest for a wider comparative analysis.

---

6. *See* http://www.worldvaluessurvey.org

Country and people[7]

Vast in terms of territory and small in terms of population, Finland is a sparsely inhabited country. The nearly 340,000 square km of its territory place it in the top third of the world's states in terms of geographic size. With a population of nearly 5.3 million, however, it ranked 117th among the 193 independent nations in 2013. Stretched in a north-south direction, the distance between its geographical extremes from northerly Utsjoki to the capital Helsinki on the south coast is – as the crow flies – over 1000 km. Basically all of Finland lies north of the 60th latitude, making it one of the northernmost countries in the world. The vast majority of the Finnish population resides in the southern third of the territory. Two-thirds of the population live in urban areas. Consequently, large parts of the Finnish territory, especially in the north and east, are extremely sparsely populated.

The demographic structure of Finland is typical of a post-industrial state. The share of persons under fifteen years of age is slightly less than 17 percent, a drop from about 35 per cent since 1900. Persons aged 65 or more also make up 17 per cent of the population, to be compared with about 5 per cent in 1900. Life-expectancy is high in an international comparison, around 80 years; for women it is as high as 83. All of this means that Finland faces similar demographic pressure to the rest of the west. An ever smaller share of the population is expected to shoulder the burden created by an ever larger proportion of senior citizens. One possible solution lies in increased immigration. The share of foreign nationals is still low in a west-European comparison, around 4 per cent.

The level of education is high. Of persons aged 15 or more, 68 per cent had qualifications over and above the nine-year comprehensive school in 2011. The share of college or university graduates was nearly 30 per cent. In terms of basic cultural features, Finland is a fairly homogeneous country. More than 90 per cent of the population has Finnish as their native tongue; among the languages of Europe, Finnish is related only to Estonian and (remotely) to Hungarian. Swedish is a recognised national language that is constitutionally equal to Finnish. Swedish-speakers make up slightly less than 6 per cent of the population and reside along the south and west coasts as well as in the large archipelago in the south-west. In religious terms, Finland is also highly homogeneous: Seventy-six per cent of Finns are members of the Lutheran Established Church. Twenty-one per cent are religiously non-affiliated, largely people who have left the Lutheran church; the rate of withdrawals from church membership has increased during recent years.

---

7. The remainder of this introductory chapter presents facts necessary for an understanding of the background and setting of parties and electoral politics in Finland. Those who are familiar with basic facts about Finland may well omit these sections. Readers who wish a more thorough presentation of Finnish history and Finland as a society should consult alternative sources (Arter 1987: 3–38; Kirby 2006; Pesonen and Riihinen 2002).

In a global comparison, Finland is a wealthy country. GDP per capita (PPP) in 2012 was US $36,500, making Finland the 34th wealthiest nation in the world. In terms of income distribution, Finland is one of the most equal countries. The occupational structure is similar to that in other advanced western economies, with around 70 per cent of the economically active population employed in the tertiary sector. The historical development of the economic structure of Finnish society will be highlighted in Chapter Two.

Highlights of Finnish history

Starting around the middle of the twelfth century, the vast territory that is now Finland was gradually incorporated into the kingdom of Sweden. The eastward extension of Swedish rule came at a decisive moment. East of Finland, the growing Russian realm had begun to extend its attempts to introduce Christianity of the Orthodox variety to Finland as well. As Finland was extremely sparsely populated during this time – there were possibly no more than 50,000 people in its entire territory – it basically constituted a strategic vacuum between the two neighbouring powers. If the Swedish push eastwards had occurred just a few decades later it is quite possible that Russia might have gained a decisive foothold in Finland.

Finland remained an integral part of Sweden for six and a half centuries, all the way up to 1809. Finland was not a Swedish colony in the modern sense of the word, however. For much of the long era of Swedish rule, south-western Finland, with the city of Turku (Åbo), belonged to the core of the Swedish kingdom. Some other areas of what is now Finland were more peripheral, but so were many regions of present-day Sweden as well. The historical legacy of the Swedish period is massive and accounts for most of the fundamental features of Finnish society and culture. As part of Sweden, Finland was incorporated into western Christianity, first Catholicism and then Lutheranism. The early introduction of basic freedoms and rights, including the right to representation, concerned the Finnish population in a manner equal to the population of Sweden proper. Most importantly, the limited role of the landed aristocracy and the prominent position of the independent peasantry constituted a historical heritage of far-reaching importance for the subsequent evolution of Finnish politics and society. *In short, the long history that Finland shares with Sweden accounts for the west-European and Nordic character of Finnish society.*

From about 1700 on, the growing Russian presence along the east coast of the Baltic created increasing pressures towards the eastern part of the Swedish kingdom. In the course of the eighteenth century, several wars were fought between Russia and Sweden. Finland was a main battlefield of these wars and extended periods of Russian occupation of Finland occurred during the eighteenth century. It was not until 1809, however, that Russia secured final control over Finland. Having lost the 1808–9 war, Sweden was forced to cede Finland to Russia.

The nearly eleven decades of Russian sovereignty over Finland are frequently regarded as a main precondition for Finnish statehood. Having conquered Finland, Czar Alexander I solemnly promised to honour the laws, privileges and social order that Finland had inherited from Sweden. In fact, he declared that the transfer to Russia 'elevated Finns to the family of nations'. Far from being simply amalgamated into Russian territory, Finland became a highly autonomous Grand Duchy, in many ways a special territory only loosely connected to Russia at large. The first seven or eight decades under Russian rule were a period of relative calm, both internally and in relation to Russia. Gradually, the Finnish economy started to profit from access to the enormous Russian markets. As for internal political development in Finland, the first half of the Russian era was a period of stagnation. The Diet, the Finnish representative body, was not assembled until 1863 by the fairly liberal Czar Alexander II. Its real powers remained limited, however. The year 1863 marks another reform of far-reaching importance. The Czar ordained that Finnish, the language of the vast majority, should attain an equal status with Swedish in the course of twenty years. This decision gave a boost to the Fennoman movement, whose goal was to make Finnish the predominant official language of Finland.

From the late 1880s on, pressure on the autonomous position of Finland started to increase. The Pan-Slavic movement was gaining momentum in Russia and it directed strong criticism against what it depicted as the undue privileges of the Finns. The liberal years of Alexander II had been succeeded by a period of reactionary politics in Russia. A series of decisions limiting Finland's autonomy followed, giving rise to an organised movement in Finland to defend the country's position. The growing workers' movement gradually began to regard Russian rule as the main obstacle to social and political reform in Finland. The Social Democratic Party, founded in 1903, therefore emerged as perhaps the most outspoken proponent of Finnish independence.

The Russian defeat by Japan in 1905 and the ensuing internal turmoil in Russia created the conditions for major reform in Finland as well. Finns were allowed to carry out a radical representative reform in 1906. Basically overnight, the last system based on the four estates in northern Europe was replaced by the first parliament based on universal suffrage in the whole of Europe. When the first elections to the new parliament were held in 1907, the Finnish Social Democrats emerged as the strongest socialist party in Europe; they won no less than 80 of the 200 seats in parliament. Other parties were compelled to create organisations around the country to be able to match the socialist appeal to common people. The 1906 representative reform was therefore an important factor behind the emergence of the Finnish party system.

The problem with the new democratic parliament was that it was not matched by similarly democratic executive institutions. Cabinets were appointed and dismissed by the Czar at will. The social democratic representatives in parliament could therefore not achieve any major reforms. Their main concern, the plight of crofters and landless rural workers, was endlessly debated and investigated by parliamentary commissions but remained unsolved.

Continued Russian repression gave rise to an armed independence movement during WWI. The Russian revolutions of 1917 provided a chance for Finland to declare its independence in December of that year. The political polarisation of Finnish society had, however, proceeded so far that a civil war between socialist

Red Guards and bourgeois White Guards broke out in January 1918. Led by legendary general Mannerheim and aided by German intervention, the latter emerged victorious in May 1918.

The defence of Finland's autonomy and the social order inherited from Sweden prepared the country for national sovereignty. On the other hand, Russian rule held back the gradual process of democratisation and the emergence of an organised civil society typical of the rest of Scandinavia. Once the barriers to mass mobilisation were removed, the development was unprecedentedly rapid.

The young Republic of Finland that emerged from the settlement after WWI was a politically polarised society. The 'White' bourgeois side that had won the civil war viewed the working-class movement with a high degree of suspicion. The left itself had split into a reformist social democratic wing and a revolutionary wing. The latter was directed from Moscow and became dominant in the labour-union movement. It instigated a series of politically motivated strikes and provoked a strong anti-communist popular movement known as the Lapua Movement. Lapua gradually took on an increasingly clear fascist character.

Against this background, it may seem surprising that Finnish democracy survived the turmoil of the interwar years. A combination of factors lies behind this outcome. Lapua's initial successes – most importantly, legislation banning all communist organisations – along with its increasing radicalisation turned many of its erstwhile supporters against it. After what looked like an attempted *coup d'état* in 1932, Lapua was outlawed, along with its auxiliary organisations.[8]

The struggle against the extreme right and against economic depression had brought the social democrats and the Agrarian Union[9] closer to each other. The 'Red–Green' coalition cabinet between these two parties in 1937 signified the definite defeat of political extremism in interwar Finland. At the same time, it marked the beginning of a development towards a welfare state.

The interwar period in Finnish history is marked by political conflicts that might have led to the collapse of the democratic order. Democracy was saved thanks to the collaboration of moderate forces in politics and society, notably social democrats and the Agrarian Union. The late 1930s were characterised by the central role of 'Red-Green' agreements in Finland as well as elsewhere in Scandinavia.

The Soviet Union attacked Finland at the end of November, 1939. The secret pact between Stalin and Hitler concerning their respective spheres of influence in north-east Europe was the strategic precondition for the Soviet campaign. Contrary to what Stalin apparently believed, Finland was neither militarily feeble nor politically divided. The defence that the Finns put up in this 'Winter War' led to massive Soviet losses and brought about a tidal wave of goodwill for Finland throughout the democratic world. This did not, however, materialise in the form of direct military assistance on the part of the western powers. Finland had to settle for an armistice in March 1940 that meant the loss of important territories in the south-east.

---

8. Ironically enough, using the same legislation that Lapua had forced Parliament to adopt against communist organisations.

9. The farmers' party.

The Winter War was followed by sixteen months of tense relations between the Finns and the Russians. When Hitler launched his campaign against the Soviet Union in June 1941, he declared that the Finns were fighting side by side with the *Wehrmacht*. Although the Finnish government at all times stressed that Finland was waging a separate war on its own terms, the *Continuation War* of 1941–4 did not meet with the same sympathy in the west as had the Winter War. A politically controversial decision was taken when, after about a month of fighting, Finnish troops crossed the border into the Soviet Union itself. Had Finland contented itself with occupying the territories it had lost in the Winter War it would have been much easier to justify the war internationally. The initial success of the war was gradually reversed and, in September 1944, the Finns opted for a separate peace with the Soviet Union. The terms were severe. Finland had to cede large territories along its eastern border; it had to pay war reparations; it was compelled to force the German troops out of Finland (which led to a separate war in northern Finland); it had to lease the Porkkala area outside Helsinki to the Russians as a military base; and it had to accept an allied, Soviet-dominated Control Commission to oversee the implementation of the armistice. Finland had averted a Soviet military occupation: politically, however, it was now included in the Soviet sphere of interest.

The two wars Finland fought against Russia during WWII had widely differing political implications in the west. The Winter War was the 'heroic war' that created a strong wave of international sympathy. The Continuation War reversed this image: Finland was seen as an ally of Hitler's Germany and as part of the Soviet sphere of influence after the war.

The decades that followed the 1944 armistice were characterised by a balancing act in which Finland constantly had to reconcile two seemingly contradictory goals: on one hand, to maintain the country's democratic political order and its ties with the west, Scandinavia in particular; on the other hand, to convince the Soviet Union that good Finnish–Soviet relations constituted the number-one priority for Finnish foreign policy. The political dynamics of this period will be dealt with at some length in Chapter Two. Here, only some central elements will be mentioned.

The late 1940s are often characterised as the 'Years of Danger' in Finnish history (Hyvämäki 1954). The large communist movement apparently plotted for a takeover of the kind that had occurred in much of eastern and central Europe. As Finland was not occupied, conditions in Finland were not as conducive to a communist takeover as in the Soviet satellites. While the acute risk of a communist coup had subsided by 1950, the controversy over the proper way to handle Finland's relations with Russia continued well into the 1950s. With the rise of Urho Kekkonen to the presidency in 1956, this controversy was gradually replaced by consensus. Kekkonen had initially been regarded as too lenient towards the Russians by his political opponents, the social democrats and conservatives in particular. As president, he used his far-reaching constitutional powers to make all parties toe his foreign-policy line. His long presidency (1956–81) was marked by international criticism of 'Finlandization', that is, undue acquiescence *vis-à-vis* Soviet interference in the country's internal affairs. On the other hand, Kekkonen was able to secure Finland's vital interests in the west, including a free-trade treaty with the European Common Market in 1974. Kekkonen's successor, Mauno Koivisto, proceeded to limit the president's role in domestic politics. When the Soviet Union collapsed in 1991, he resolutely declared the treaties that had provided the eastern power with influence over Finland obsolete.

Against considerable odds, Finland managed to maintain its democratic western system and its ties with the west throughout the Cold War. The influence that the Soviet Union had over Finland along with the exaggerated role of the president in domestic politics, however, cast a shadow over Finnish democracy during this period.

The post-Cold-War years entailed a rapid march towards being at the heart of west European integration. An application for membership in the European Union was made in 1992; in 1994, 57 per cent in a referendum voted 'yes' to Finnish membership. While the opinion patterns were largely similar to those in Norway and Sweden, Finnish opinions were somewhat more in favour of EU membership for two reasons. Finland was in the middle of an economic depression; a collapse in its trade with Russia was a major cause. Moreover, security-policy concerns weighed more heavily than in neighbouring Scandinavia. As an EU member, Finland has sought to integrate itself with the core of the Union. The Finnish decision to opt for EMU membership, unlike its Nordic neighbours, is the most visible sign of this policy. Finland has also sought a high level of integration with NATO, although domestic opinion has remained negative towards full NATO membership. In domestic politics, a reduction of the president's constitutional powers in favour of pure parliamentarism has taken place (for details, *see* Chapter Four).

The Soviet shadow over Finland gone, Finland has secured a position in the west European core. The country weathered both the depression of the early 1990s and the financial crisis from 2008 onwards and is today one of the financially more stable EU countries.

The institutional setting

Finland is a unitary state and a parliamentary democracy. The former has been the case throughout Finnish independence: regional agencies are branches of central government administration, and the absence of elected assemblies at the regional level[10] is a defining feature of the Finnish system. On the other hand, local (municipal) governments possess considerable powers, although welfare legislation decided by parliament has tended to limit the leeway of municipal governments by imposing strict standards for welfare-provision at the local level. Today, there are 320 municipalities. Municipal amalgamations have reduced this number by more than a hundred in just the past decade; immediately after the Second World War, the number of municipalities was as high as 558.

---

10. The autonomous province of Aaland in the south-western archipelago has an elected regional assembly and a cabinet chosen by the assembly for administering matters covered by Aaland's autonomous powers. Moreover, an experiment was carried out in the north-eastern region of Kainuu in 2004–12 in which fairly extensive powers were transferred to a popularly elected regional assembly.

Finland's status as a *parliamentary* democracy is a fairly recent creation. Until the constitutional reforms of the 1990s that culminated in the Constitution of 2000, the Finnish president had such extensive powers that it was accurate to classify the Finnish form of government as semi-presidential. Of course, the parliamentary mechanism is always present in semi-presidential systems as well, as the cabinet must have the confidence of the parliamentary majority. However, the 2000 constitutional reform reduced the president's powers in domestic politics so decisively that Finland must now be classified as a parliamentary democracy. Most importantly, it abolished the president's role in the process of cabinet-formation. This crucial part of the parliamentary process is now entirely in the hands of the parties in parliament. The President of the Republic is still elected by popular vote every six years but his role today is mainly ceremonial. The President's remaining powers pertain to foreign policy. Even in this area, they are strongly curtailed by foreign-policy co-operation within the European Union, as matters related to the EU are handled by cabinet, not president. The background of the reform, as well as its evolution and effects, are described in Chapter Four.

The 200-seat Finnish parliament is elected for a four-year term from 14 multi-member constituencies and one single-member district;[11] median district magnitude for the former is around thirteen seats. The calling of early elections is constitutionally complicated (*see* Chapter Four) and therefore an unlikely event. The electoral system that has been used in Finnish parliamentary elections since 1954 combines a proportional list system with mandatory candidate voting. Parties and party alliances nominate candidates for lists that are normally ordered alphabetically. Voters simply write the number of their candidate of choice on the ballot paper (Figure 1.1); there is no possibility of casting a mere party vote.

When calculating the results, candidate votes are first summed so as to determine the vote totals of the various lists at the district level. The number of seats won by each list in each constituency is determined on the basis of these list vote totals by using the d'Hondt divisor. This means that the most popular candidate on each list is assigned the total list vote. After that, the list totals are divided by two and the result is assigned to the second most popular candidate on each list, whereupon the list totals are divided by three to determine the ratio for the third most popular candidates, and so on. The first seat in an electoral district is awarded to the candidate whose list has the highest vote total. Thereafter, the vote ratios of all candidates are compared to determine who gets the second seat. Seats are assigned to candidates in the order of their descending vote ratios until all seats in the district have been filled.

---

11. That of the autonomous province of Aaland. As Aaland in the south-western archipelago of Finland has a provincial political system of its own, including a separate party system, it will be excluded from the empirical analyses in this book. As of the 2015 election, the number of mainland constituencies will be 12, as South Savo will be amalgamated with Kymi and North Savo with North Karelia.

Figure 1.1: A ballot paper in a Finnish parliamentary election

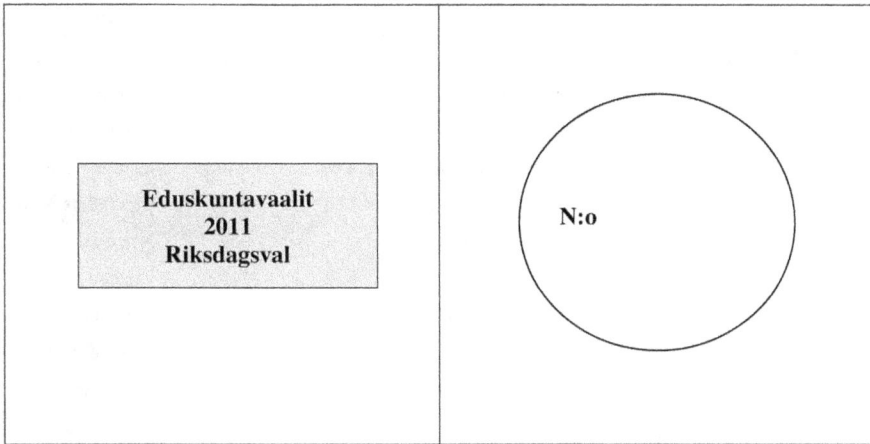

An example from the 2011 election shows how the system works in practice. In South Savo, one of the smallest electoral districts (6 seats), the distribution of votes for the main parties and their top candidates was as shown in Table 1.1.

This example shows that candidates with fairly high personal vote totals may fail to be elected; while at the same time others with more limited personal votes do gain seats. The True Finn Turunen had fewer personal votes than both Taavitsainen (Social Democrat) and Nepponen (Conservative). However, the True Finn list in South Savo mustered enough votes for the party's top candidate to become elected, despite the fairly limited number of personal votes won by this candidate. In this case, there was a relatively even spread of personal votes across the list. Even more often, however, candidates with limited personal votes are elected thanks to one or several individually popular candidates who secure the party list a high vote-total and thus 'pull up' one or several weaker candidates. An important feature of the Finnish electoral system is that, unlike several other preferential list systems, it does not stipulate a minimum requirement concerning personal votes (Raunio 2008: 476–82; *cf.* Müller 2008: 404; Karvonen 2010: 47).

Finnish parliamentarism displays features typical of parliamentary systems with proportional list systems. As cabinets are dependent on the will of the parliamentary majority, party discipline is important in the parliamentary process. Although the d'Hondt method gives large parties a slight advantage compared to some of the alternative proportional list systems, the Finnish system is still highly proportional. Since no minimum vote share has been stipulated by law in order for parties to gain representation, it has been fairly easy for small parties to win parliamentary seats. On the other hand, the preferential element in the Finnish electoral system sets Finland apart most other parliamentary countries. The system with mandatory candidate voting encourages candidates who seek to win seats to actively pursue personal electoral campaigns.

Table 1.1: The distribution of the six seats in South Savo in the 2011 election

Party (total party vote)	Candidates	Personal vote	Vote ratio	Result
Centre Party (22,351)	Jari Leppä	5,567	22351	Elected as Nr 1
	Katri Komi	4,966	11175.5	Elected as Nr 5
	Seija Korhonen	2,556	7450.3	Not elected
Social Democrats (19,988)	Jouni Backman	5,478	19988	Elected as Nr 2
	Pauliina Viitamies	4,476	9994	Elected as Nr 6
	Satu Taavitsainen	2,921	6662.7	Not elected
True Finns (17,107)	Kaj Turunen	2,632	17107	Elected as Nr 3
	Jukka Pöyry	2,342	8553.5	Not elected
Conservatives (15,532)	Lenita Toivakka	5,778	15532	Elected as Nr 4
	Olli Nepponen	2,910	7766	Not elected

The party setting

The historical evolution of the Finnish party system as a result of structural cleavages and social and political conflicts will be described in Chapter Two. The present section focuses on parties in contemporary Finland, essentially in the past decade.

In a west-European comparison, the following features that are in many ways strongly intertwined appear characteristic of the Finnish party system:

1. *The high degree of party-system fragmentation and the large number of parties that gain parliamentary representation.* The largest party does not normally win more than just over a quarter of the seats in parliament.
2. *The absence of a party that is decisively larger than its main competitors.* No party has been able to establish itself even as primus inter pares among the largest parties. Quite the contrary: the position as the largest party has shifted over the years. In recent decades, the Social Democrats, the Conservatives and the Centre Party have pursued a close contest for this position. Up until the mid 1970s, the predecessor of the Left Alliance also belonged to the category of the largest parties. The 2011 'earthquake election' created a new pattern whereby all the three largest parties were challenged by the landslide won by the populist True Finns; at the same time, the Conservatives, for the first time in history, emerged as the strongest party in parliament. For the Centre Party, this was the poorest electoral showing since 1972. As a result of the 2011 elections, the Finnish party system is even more fragmented than previously, with four rather than three parties of a relatively equal size.
3. *The increased weakness of the parties on the left.* A unique election in 1966 resulted in a parliamentary majority for the left. Since then, the electoral and parliamentary strength of the left has been in steady decline. In 2007, the

combined strength of the two left-wing parties (the Social Democrats and the Left Alliance) sank below one-third for the first time; the 2011 election continued this declining trend. As early as the 1980s, however, the left was down to around 40 per cent of the seats in parliament. A left-wing government has not been a numerically viable option for a very long time.

4. *The strength of the Centre Party that is historically an agrarian party.* The Finnish Centre Party, until 1965 the Agrarian Union, is a rare case of the survival of basically agrarian politics in a post-industrial society. Aided by the lateness of the urbanisation process in Finland (*see* Chapter Two) and supported by a strong organisational network, the Centre Party has displayed considerable strength, in contrast to the decline of similar parties in most of western Europe. However, the 2011 election once again showed the party's vulnerability in face of a populist challenge. As in the 1970s and 1980s, when the Centre Party was challenged by the populist Rural Party, the party suffered a painful loss to the True Finns.

5. *The absence of a liberal party.* The Liberal Party lost its position as one of the main contenders in Finnish party politics in the first elections after Finnish independence. It lingered on as a minor parliamentary party until the late 1970s and subsequently disappeared from the parliamentary scene. The prolonged rural dominance in Finnish society did not make for a friendly environment for political liberalism; moreover, liberal opinion was split between Finnish-speakers and Swedish-speakers. The attempt to revive political liberalism in the form of the Young Finn Party in the 1990s was short-lived. Today, the Greens seem to have occupied the position as an urban liberal alternative among Finnish parties.

Most of these features are apparent from Table 1.2, which lists the seats won by the various parties in the Finnish parliament in 1999–2011.

Chapters Three and Five will present the ideological foundations, organisations and patterns of popular support of the various parties in considerable detail. Here, a few basic facts of the contemporary Finnish parties will suffice.

The Centre Party (Suomen keskusta)

The Centre Party (until 1965: The Agrarian Union) has been the dominant party of the Finnish countryside. This should be interpreted in the widest possible sense. In rural Finland (except for the Swedish areas), it is the dominant party. Also in the urban and semi-urban areas of central and northern Finland it is often decisively larger than its competitors. Its attempts to establish itself as one of the main parties in southern Finland and the greater Helsinki area have, by contrast, not been particularly successful. A bourgeois party, the Centre Party is favourable to private enterprise. However, as agricultural and regional subsidies are of vital interest to its core supporters, it is not hostile to an active government role in social, economic and regional policy. As noted above, it has, on several occasions, displayed vulnerability *vis-à-vis* challenges from populist parties.

Table 1.2: Number of parliamentary seats held by the various parties, 1999–2011

Party	1999	2003	2007	2011
Centre Party	48	55	51	35
Conservatives	46	40	50	44
Social Democrats	51	53	45	42
Left Alliance	20	19	17	14
Greens	11	14	15	10
Swedish Party*	12	9	10	10
Christian Democrats	10	7	7	6
True Finns	1	3	5	39
Others	1	–	–	–
Total	200	200	200	200

* Including the MP for the Aaland Isles.

The Conservative Party (Kansallinen kokoomus)

The party's official name translates as 'the National Coalition', but it will be named the Conservative Party throughout this volume. Traditionally the party of the Finnish-speaking business elite and the educated upper classes, the Conservatives have, in recent decades, established themselves as somewhat of a catch-all party for the middle classes in urban southern Finland. The party has become increasingly dominant in the greater Helsinki area. The number-one choice of the business and industrial communities, the party wins votes among large segments of entrepreneurs and professionals throughout Finland. Although market-oriented and favourable to a strong EU and Finnish NATO membership, the party has endeavoured not to appear hostile towards the universal welfare state.

The Social Democratic Party (Suomen Sosialidemokraattinen Puolue)

Reformist social democracy was the result of the split in the social democratic movement in 1922. The core of the social democratic electorate has consisted of industrial workers and urban wage-earners in the southern half of the country; the party's ties with many of the major labour unions have been strong. Social Democrats positioned themselves as the central cabinet party in the 1970s, 1980s and 1990s and managed to make inroads into the middle class as well. The party's ideological baggage has been derived from the Nordic social democratic movement, with a strong emphasis on the welfare state and full employment. In recent years, the Social Democrats have had difficulty reaching out to younger cohorts of voters and in recruiting young party activists to replace the party gerontocracy.

The Left Alliance (Vasemmistoliitto)

Historically speaking, the Left Alliance also has its roots in the social democratic rift of 1922. All of its predecessors[12] were dominated by the Finnish Communist Party, which did not officially contest elections but used front organisations for this purpose. Founded in 1990, after the definitive collapse of Finnish communism, the Left Alliance has strived to position itself as a reformed socialist party to the left of the Social Democrats. A far cry from the strength of its predecessors some half century ago, the party must content itself with the support of diminishing parts of the working class as well as some remnants of intellectual radicalism. In terms of policy platforms, the Left Alliance does not differ from the Social Democrats very much.

The Greens (Vihreä liitto)

The environmental movement managed to gain two seats in the parliamentary election of 1983. Four years later, the movement organised itself as a party, officially called the Green League. After that, the ideological profile of the Greens has been moderate in an international comparison. The party has run candidates in all elections and actively sought influence by parliamentary means; it has not been implicated in extra-legal or extra-parliamentary activity. As early as 1995, the Greens became a cabinet party for the first time. They continued in cabinet after the 1999 election as well but left it prematurely in 2002. They became a cabinet party again in 2007 and have remained in cabinet ever since. A pronouncedly urban movement, the Greens have attracted support among young and well educated segments of the Finnish electorate. Although founded on the ecological perspective, the party has increasingly presented itself as the urban liberal alternative, with a highly tolerant attitude towards immigrants and sexual minorities.

The Swedish Party (Svenska folkpartiet i Finland)

The Swedish People's Party in Finland, as it is officially called, is the dominant party alternative among Swedish-speaking Finns. Approximately 70 per cent of the Swedish-speaking population regularly votes for the candidates of this party. The vote share of the Swedish Party has declined in parallel with the long-term decrease of the share of Swedes in the population of Finland. As the Swedish-speaking population is heterogeneous in terms of socio-economic characteristics, lifestyles and values, the Swedish Party must pursue a moderate line on most issues. In economic policy and as concerns Finland's external relations, it is closer to the right than the left. In issues related to immigration and multiculturalism it is, by contrast, clearly more radical. Eager to safeguard the interests of the Swedish language in Finland, the Swedish Party is one of the most frequent cabinet parties.

---

12. The Left Party will be used as a generic label for the historical predecessors of the Left Alliance.

Christian Democrats (Kristillisdemokraatit)

Unlike in most Catholic countries or religiously heterogeneous societies, Christian parties have never been prominent in religiously homogenous Scandinavia. The Finnish party, called the Christian League (*Kristillinen liitto*) until 2001, has been represented in parliament since 1970 but has never managed to win more than 5 per cent of the vote. A centrist party in most respects, it distinguishes itself from most other parties in moral questions, such as abortion, same-sex marriage and legislation on alcohol.

True Finns (Perussuomalaiset)

The populist True Finns[13] won a spectacular electoral victory in 2011, leaping from 4 to 19 per cent of the vote and from 5 to no fewer than 39 seats in parliament. This was the third coming of Finnish populism. The predecessor of the True Finns, the Rural Party, won a couple of impressive electoral victories in the early 1970s, only to succumb to internal conflicts in parliament. It repeated its electoral success in 1983 and even became a cabinet party in 1983 and 1987. However, cabinet responsibilities weakened its populist image and the party disappeared from the parliamentary scene after the 1995 election. Timo Soini, then a fairly young Rural Party member, founded the True Finns on the ruins of the Rural Party in 1995. With him as a rhetorically gifted leader, the party started to regain ground in Finnish politics. As in earlier decades, Finnish populism seems to thrive on the losses of the Centre Party; the 2011 election was no exception. In terms of ideology and policy, the True Finns display nostalgia for the period when Finland was already a well-to-do welfare state but not yet in the grip of globalisation. They want a strong, government-financed welfare state, a weaker and less ubiquitous European Union and restrictive immigration policies. Although xenophobic voters are likely to support this party, anti-immigration issues are less central to the True Finns than for many other populist parties in western Europe. An important question is whether the party will be able to maintain internal unity despite the highly heterogeneous group of individuals that represent it in parliament and local government.

---

13. The translation of this party name into English is somewhat problematic. 'True Finns' has a more exclusively nationalist ring to it than *Perussuomalaiset* that means 'Ordinary Finns' or, literally, 'Basic Finns'. In the summer of 2011, after its historical breakthrough in the parliamentary election, the party resolved that it should simply be called 'The Finns' in English. This has been criticised severely by the other Finnish parties. As 'True Finns' has become an internationally known party label, it will be used throughout this book.

Chapter Two

Three Pillars Transformed

Parties are institutionalised conflicts. Wherever opposing interests and values create lasting divisions in the population, parties can be established to articulate these tensions and bring people together to defend their viewpoints and needs. The particular mixture of parties in a given country almost always reflects generic divisions that are to be found in numerous other societies. To these general features, the specificities of each case must be added to account for why a country has its particular set of political parties and voter constellations.

In a classic and brilliant contribution (1967: 47), Lipset and Rokkan demonstrated how four *deep-seated cleavages* interacted with *critical junctures* in European history to produce fundamental issues in politics, around which parties were organised throughout western Europe. To be sure, two of the cleavages mentioned by Rokkan and Lipset play limited roles in the history of party systems and voter alignments in Finland. 'Centre–Periphery' and 'State–Church' deal with the conflicts over national versus supranational religious organisation and secular versus church control over mass education, respectively. While powerful determinants of party formation in religiously mixed and Catholic countries in western Europe, these issues were of limited importance in the religiously homogeneous Nordic countries (Karvonen 1996: 121–2). All the more crucial to the Finnish party structure are the two remaining cleavages in the Lipset-Rokkan model. 'Land–Industry' became a central dividing line throughout western Europe as the industrial revolution swept across the continent. It entailed conflicts related to the extent of public control versus freedom of industrial enterprise. Most importantly for the Finnish case, it brought about a defence of the interests of agricultural producers. The protection or openness of agricultural markets was to be a central bone of contention for the better part of the twentieth century. Finally, the 'Owner–Worker' cleavage was also a product of the rise of industrial production. However, it acquired a special significance in the aftermath of the Russian revolution. Besides the fundamental tension between capital and labour, working-class movements had to face a choice between integration into the national polity and commitment to the international revolutionary movement. More than for most other west-European countries, this final division came to mark Finnish politics through most of the twentieth century.

Structural cleavages are powerful determinants of party systems throughout Europe and Finland is no exception. While it would be foolish to overlook their importance, it would be equally insufficient to limit the analysis of parties and voter alignments in Finland, or anywhere else, to such factors. Finnish politics, including the formation of political parties, has always reflected the country's *geopolitical location*. With her roots deep in west-European culture and Scandinavian social structures, Finland shares a common border of nearly 800 miles with Russia. Ever since Finland came under the influence of western Christianity in the twelfth century, pressures from the neighbouring big power in the east have been an overshadowing concern for Finnish security and sovereign existence. Early on, political parties came to differ on how best to protect Finnish interests *vis-à-vis* Russia. Through most of the twentieth century, relations between political parties reflected the state of Finnish–Russian relations; there were periods of both fundamental disagreement and rigorous consensus in this respect. Finnish parties repeatedly had to face rapid and unexpected transformations that they had little control over, as changes in this regard were largely determined by events and forces outside Finland (Pesonen 1995; Mylly 1987).

Finally, the *intensity of political conflicts* must be considered if one wishes to understand the dynamics of Finnish politics and the extent of change in the fundamentals of political life in Finland. From its independence in 1917 up until the 1960s, except for the war years 1939–44, Finland was a politically divided society. The degree of ideological polarisation was high and the divisions separating the various political parties deep. In the apt expression of Finnish political scientist Rauli Mickelsson (2007), this was the period of 'political camps' in Finland. The contrast with developments from the 1970s on is striking: in an astonishingly short period, consensus replaced conflict as the overarching principle of Finnish political culture. This change has, of course, had a profound effect on the conditions of government-formation, party campaigns and voter alignments in the Finnish political system.

The structural foundations of Finnish parties

How social structure shaped the party system

The basic features of the Finnish party system were complete by the 1922 parliamentary election. That election featured five parties that, despite name changes and other transmutations, have mustered the lion's share of the popular vote ever since. Table 2.1 shows the vote shares of these parties compared with the share of votes for other parties.

The five original party families in the Finnish party system have met with increasing competition from other parties. The Liberal Party that existed until the 1980s, and made up part of the 'other' column, has now definitely left the political scene. The demise of a Liberal-Party formation is, historically speaking, the most significant long-term change in the Finnish party system (Soikkanen 1987: 58–95). Instead, one of the largest Green parties in Europe (7–9 per cent of the vote in recent elections) has been part of the scene since the 1980s. The 2011 election, of course, brought about a spectacular change in the form of a landslide victory for the populist True Finns (from 4 per cent in 2007 to 19 per cent in 2011). It remains to be seen whether this is the start of a long-term presence for populists in Finnish politics or if their success turns out to be as volatile as that of their

Table 2.1: Vote shares (per cent of valid vote) of five 'constituent' parties in Finnish party system, compared with vote shares of other parties, in 1922, 1962, 2007 and 2011

Year	Left Party	Social Democrats	Agrarian/ Centre Party	Swedish People's Party	Conservatives	Other
1922	14.8	25.1	20.3	12.4	18.1	9.3
1962	22.0	19.5	23.0	6.1	15.0	14.4
2007	8.8	21.4	23.1	4.6	22.3	19.8
2011	8.1	19.1	15.8	4.3	20.4	32.3

Left Party: in 1922 Socialist Worker's Party; in 1962 Finnish People's Democratic League; in 2007 Left Alliance.

ideological predecessors in the 1970s and 1980s. In addition, there is a small Christian Democratic party (4–5 per cent of the vote) that has established itself as a fairly stable feature in modern Finnish politics.

Despite the toughened competition, more than two out of three votes are still cast for the parties that were around already in the early 1920s. These five constituent parties have their roots in the structural and cleavages and foreign-policy conflicts that marked Finnish society in the 1920s and in the decades prior to this period. The present section describes the way social structure shaped the party landscape. It is followed by an account of the change that these structures have undergone during the nine decades of Finnish independence.

Finland was a rural society in the 1920s. Almost 70 per cent of the gainfully employed population worked in the primary sector, agriculture and forestry in particular. An overwhelming majority of the population lived in rural areas; the percentage of the population residing in cities and towns was under 20 in 1920 (Valkonen 1985: 210). Moreover, Finland was even more sparsely populated than it is today. In the early 1920s, it had a population slightly less than three million in an area roughly equal to the territory of modern Germany. By continental standards, it had no major cities. The inhabitants of the capital, Helsinki, by far the largest city in the country, numbered no more than roughly 160,000. All of this means that any party would have to reach out to the rural population and cater to its needs in order to gain major support in Finnish politics in the 1920s. Finland was a small, rural and fairly backward society in the northern periphery of Europe.

Finland may have been an undeveloped country in an economic sense. As for its political institutions Finland had, by contrast, taken a giant step, thanks to the 1906 Representative Reform (*see* Chapter One). In fact, save for the extreme left, the constituent parties in the Finnish party system were in many ways products of this reform (Mylly 1987: 17–21). Basically overnight, the reform replaced the last representative assembly in northern Europe, based on the four estates, with the first parliament elected through general suffrage for both women and men *in the whole of* Europe. Naturally, this change compelled the various political quarters to organise in a way that would enable them to compete in an entirely new institutional setting. Parties that had previously been an affair for the numerically limited upper echelons of society had, in order to survive the transition to mass democracy, to reach out to the common people, most of who resided in rural areas.

In this predominantly agrarian society, the structural conditions of the primary sector naturally became highly important for the emerging political organisation. The nineteenth century, particularly its latter half, had witnessed a major transformation of the economic and social structures of the Finnish countryside. The situation in the early twentieth century stood in clear contrast to the conditions prevailing a hundred years earlier. When Finland was separated from Sweden and became an autonomous Grand Duchy within the Russian empire, the agricultural landscape was dominated by a broad class of independent small farmers. Feudalism, as social order, had never been established in the Swedish kingdom and even manorial farming was a comparatively limited phenomenon. A hundred years later, however, independent small farmers no longer formed the majority of the population in the Finnish countryside. To be sure, they were still an important group that made up a little over a third of the agrarian population. Numerically, however, they had been surpassed by crofters and landless agricultural workers (Alapuro 1985: 44–9).

The change was not due to any political scheme by the Russian sovereign, let alone a legal change in the position of the peasantry. The Czar honoured his pledge to allow the Finns to maintain their rights and freedoms from the Swedish period, including the independent position of the peasantry. Instead, a fundamental change in the agrarian economy, coupled with major demographic shifts, lay behind the change. The second half of the nineteenth century had seen a definite shift from subsistence farming based on a variety of crops to a market-driven pattern of production where especially timber from peasant-owned forests became a central source of agrarian income. Moreover, dairy farming had grown rapidly at the expense of grain production. The natural conditions for the former were much better than for the latter, and the export markets for dairy produce grew rapidly, due to the urbanisation and industrialisation of western Europe. Parallel to this change, the rural population increased fast, thanks to improved living conditions. As an increasing percentage of the population reached adult age, small farms could no longer support all the members of growing families. At the same time, larger farms involved in timber sales and other market-driven processes needed more manpower. The surplus population thus came to form an expanding class of crofters and landless farm hands. This change was particularly pronounced in southern and south-western Finland, whereas independent small farming largely retained its position in the south-east and along the upper west coast. In the north and north-east, most of the farms were minuscule and heads of household typically combined forestry work with independent subsistence farming to make ends meet (Alapuro 1988: 40–7; Alapuro 1985: 44–60).

The 'crofter question' – the increasingly difficult position of crofters and agricultural workers – became the thorniest social problem in the final decades of the autonomy period. Both larger landowners and, to a certain extent, small independent farmers were fearful of the change that would have been required for a decisive improvement of the conditions of the rural proletariat. The former largely rallied behind the Conservative Party, the National Coalition. Founded in 1918 as an heir of the Old Finn Party, the Conservative Party became the main representative of Finnish-speaking well-to-do citizens, rural as well as urban. As for independent small and medium-sized farmers, the Agrarian Union founded in 1906 became their party *par excellence* (Arter 1999a: 159–60). The Social Democratic Party (1903) mustered most of the support of the rural proletariat. These political patterns are clearly reflected in the electoral geography of Finland in the decades after the introduction of universal suffrage. In those parts of southern and south-western Finland where larger farms were common – and, consequently, where there were numerous crofters and landless farm workers – the Conservatives and the Social Democrats had a strong following. The Agrarians were the main party in which independent small farmers were predominant: in the south-east and along the upper west coast (save for the Swedish-speaking areas).

Industrialisation started late in Finland. In 1870, merely 5 per cent of the workforce was employed in industry; in the 1920s, this figure was still under 15 per cent. The absolute size of the industrial workforce grew fairly rapidly but this was mainly due to general population growth. Up until the Second World War, the primary sector continued to be a more important source of employment for Finnish workers than the secondary sector. The structure of Finnish industry reflected the importance of timber, the country's primary natural resource. Around one-third of the industrial workforce was employed in sawmills, paper mills and furniture factories.

Reliance on timber as an important basis for Finnish industry added one more characteristic feature to the process of industrialisation in Finland. Although industrialisation in Finland – just like everywhere else – led to a process of urbanisation, this effect was comparatively weak in Finland. A large proportion of the major industries were established in the countryside, close to the raw-material sources, hydro power and waterways necessary for industrial production. Large portions of the workforce were recruited from the landless agrarian proletariat. Many of these workers were able to continue living in a rural environment even after gaining industrial employment. Most of Finnish industry was located in the southern part of the country, frequently in those areas where the proportion of crofters and landless farm workers was highest. Consequently, there was never a particularly sharp division between urban and rural workers in the Finnish working class. Quite the contrary, Finnish workers in primary as well as secondary production were subject to market forces in much the same way. The Finnish *Arbeiterfrage* concerned rural and urban worker alike (Alapuro 1988: 48–9).

The growing industrial working class was mobilised politically by the Social Democratic Party. As Finland was industrialised at a late stage, however, the role of the agrarian proletariat remained important in the working-class movement all the way up to the Second World War. The party was dependent on the electoral support of the agrarian workers, which is why it was important that the working-class movement was not divided along the lines of industrial *versus* agricultural production (Becker 2003: 132).

Industrialisation gave rise to a small class of industrial owners and managers and a somewhat larger segment of functionaries. These groups overwhelmingly supported the bourgeois parties. However, no party was able to establish itself as the self-evident representative of the industrial and commercial bourgeoisie. The reason was language. In the 1920s industrial ownership and management were still in the hands of Swedish-speakers, to a much greater extent than the share of Swedes in the Finnish population at large might lead one to expect. The party preferences of the industrial bourgeoisie were, to a significant degree, therefore, decided on the basis of language. The main contenders were the Conservative Party and the Swedish People's Party, that is, the heirs of, respectively, the Finnish and Swedish parties of the pre-democratic era.

Language was, in fact, the only cultural feature of major importance to Finnish politics. The religious structure of Finnish society was highly homogeneous with an overwhelming majority of the population belonging to the Lutheran Established Church. After the separation from Sweden, the higher social levels of the population remained almost entirely Swedish-speaking for another century. However, there was also a large group of Swedish-speaking common people along the west and south coasts. When the language question became topical in the latter half of the nineteenth century, it was mainly a matter for the upper classes. The two parties established along linguistic lines remained loosely organised and confined to the educated classes. With the sudden transition to universal suffrage in 1906, however, the question came into a radically different light. The Swedish-speaking elite was compelled to reach out to the Swedish common people in order to mobilise all available forces in defence of the Swedish language (Mylly 1987 14–20). The result was the Swedish People's Party (*Svenska folkpartiet*, founded in 1906), which proved highly successful in mobilising the Swedish-speaking population. More than two-thirds of Swedish voters rallied behind the party. The Social Democrats created a bilingual organisation and adopted a moderate line in the language question; they were the main contender for the Swedish vote. The Social Democratic Party gained a certain following in Swedish-speaking areas, particularly in communities dominated by large-scale industry. The two main bourgeois parties, the Conservatives and the Agrarians, opted for a clearly anti-Swedish position. Their electoral following was therefore confined to Finnish-speakers (Sundberg 1985: 51–70; Sundberg 2005: 10–14).

In sum, when the main features of the Finnish party system had emerged, Finland was still a markedly rural society. The socialist movement had to pay equal attention to agrarian and industrial workers. The bourgeois parties were divided by the interests of larger farmers *versus* those of the independent small peasantry as well as by the linguistic strife between Finns and Swedes. Table 2.2 summarises the structural foundations of four constituent parties in the Finnish party system.

A rapid and thorough transformation

To say that the structural foundations of Finnish politics look radically different today would be a truism and an understatement all at once. All west European societies have undergone fundamental changes since the First World War; why

Table 2.2: Original structural foundations of four constituent parties in Finnish party system

Party	Cleavages	Main bases of support
Social Democrats	• Landowners *vs.* landless rural proletariat • Employers *vs.* workers	• Crofters, agricultural and forest workers • Industrial workers
Agrarians*	• Urban *vs.* rural areas • Primary *vs.* secondary production • Language	• Independent farmers: Finnish-speaking, small and medium-sized farms
Swedish People's Party	• Language • Socialist *vs.* non-socialist	• Swedish-speakers, excl. socialists
Conservatives	• Socialist *vs.* non-socialist • Language	• Finnish-speaking upper strata, incl. large farmers

* *Today, the Centre Party.*

would Finland be any different? The answer is that the degree of change in Finland is so remarkable that the country stands out as a case apart. Moreover, the structural transformation of Finnish society took place late in time and so rapidly that Finland is a case in a west-European comparison in this respect, too (Pesonen and Riihinen 2002: 37–42).

A comparison with other west-European states is useful for highlighting these specific Finnish features. Ten countries culturally and politically closest to Finland were selected for this comparison: Austria, Belgium, Denmark, France, Germany (between 1950 and 1990: West Germany), The Netherlands, Norway, Sweden, Switzerland and United Kingdom. Table 2.3 shows the shares of the economically active population in three sectors: primary, secondary and tertiary. The primary sector comprises agriculture, forestry and fishing; the secondary sector industry, manufacturing, extractive industry and construction; while commerce, finance, services, transport, communications and other similar occupations form the tertiary sector. The figures portray the situation every ten years from 1920 to 2000; in addition, the percentages for 2004 are included. The year 1940 is excluded from the table, due to the special wartime conditions.

Even given considerable variation among the ten countries used as a point of comparison, it is safe to say that Finland is a case apart in a west European context. Finland is extreme in terms of both the importance of the primary sector during most of the period, the lateness of socio-economic transformation and the rapidity of the change once it got under way. Not a single one of the countries in the comparison group can match the Finnish development; in fact none of them comes anywhere near Finland in these respects. The share of the workforce employed in the primary sector fell by roughly 64 percentage points in Finland between 1920 and 2004. The corresponding figure for the comparison group was around 27 per cent. Tertiary employment rose by more

Table 2.3: Economically active population by sector (percentages) 1920–2004:
Finland compared to ten other west-European countries

Finland

Sector			
Year	Primary	Secondary	Tertiary
1920	68.8	12.8	18.3
1930	64.6	14.7	20.7
1950	45.9	27.7	26.3
1960	35.5	31.5	33.1
1970	20.3	34.3	45.5
1980	12.6	33.4	54.1
1990	8.5	28.3	63.2
2000	5.7	26.9	67.4
2004	4.9	25.5	69.7

Averages for ten other countries in western Europe

Sector			
Year*	Primary	Secondary	Tertiary
1920	29.7	37.1	33.2
1930	28.3	37.8	33.9
1950	20.7	41.5	37.8
1960	14.5	43.7	41.8
1970	9.1	41.7	49.2
1980	6.3	35.7	58.0
1990	4.8	30.2	65.0
2000	3.5	26.8	69.7
2004**	2.9	25.7	71.4

* *Year of observation varies somewhat from country to country.*
** *Data not available for The Netherlands.*
Source: International Historical Statistics, Europe 1750–2005: 147–70.

than 51 per cent in Finland during the same period, as compared with an average growth by some 38 per cent in the ten other countries. In Finland, industry was never the largest sector in terms of employment, while this was the case in the comparison group in both the 1950s and 1960s. With a minor simplification, one may argue that Finland went from a pre-industrial directly to a post-industrial economic structure. The lion's share of this structural transformation took place between the Second World War and 1980. Elsewhere in western Europe, the corresponding process had started much earlier and proceeded much more smoothly over an extended period of time.

To sum up, Finnish parties have had to cope with a dramatic structural transformation of their social bases. In not more than four decades, Finland went from being a poor agricultural country to a wealthy post-industrial society. Much of this book deals with the pressures that this change has created for parties, voters and parliamentary politics.

Parties and geopolitics: How Finland's relations with Russia shaped the party system and inter-party relations

[…] given our geographical location, the three main security challenges for Finland today are Russia, Russia and Russia.[1]

Speaking at the Center for Strategic and International Studies in Washington DC in September 2007, Finnish Minister of Defence, Jyri Häkämies used these words to characterise Finland's national-security situation. The characterisation would, however, be equally valid for the external determinants of party-formation and political alignments in Finland. Time and again, parties have differed over the correct way to deal with the neighbouring big power in the east. Deeply entrenched disagreements have alternated with a high level of consensus in the area of Finnish *Ostpolitik.* As will be shown below, parties have, on several occasions, been founded due to disagreements about Finland's relations with Russia or because of changes in Finnish–Russian relations. Sometimes, such changes have led to the demise of a party. By the same token, the relative balance of power between parties has frequently been affected by foreign policy.

From autonomy to independence

Even before the introduction of universal suffrage, the Finnish Party had split over the correct way to meet the mounting Russian threat against the autonomous position of the Finnish Grand Duchy. The majority of the party that came to be called Old Finns advocated a policy of acquiescence *vis-à-vis* Russian demands directed against the privileges of the Finns. The opposition, to be known as the Young Finns, demanded that attempts at 'Russification' be resisted with reference to Finnish laws, and the pledges to uphold them, that the Czar had made when Finland was ceded to Russia in 1809. The Young Finns organised themselves as a parliamentary group in 1894 and gradually broke away from the Finnish Party. *This was the first effect of Finland's eastern relations on party-formation.* Meanwhile, the Swedish Party took a similar stand towards the Russian demands to that of the Young Finns. In many ways, these two parties came to join forces within the constitutionalist front that opposed attempts at Russification (Mylly 1987: 17). However, many Finns wanted to go further in defence of Finland's rights against Russia. In the first years of the twentieth century, the Party of Active Resistance was established as a

---

1. http://www.defmin.fi/%3F663_m%3D3335%261%3Den%26s%3D270

clandestine organisation. Its goal was to prepare for military resistance against the Russian threat and to undermine loyalty to the Czar among the Finnish population. However, activism never became a basis for a lasting party-formation: although a decisive factor behind Finland's transition to independence, activism remained an undercurrent rather than a manifest organisation in parliamentary politics.

During WWI, the Activists organised a clandestine collaboration with imperial Germany. Some 2,000 young men from Finland were transported to Germany, where they received military training. The aim was to help liberate Finland from Russian rule as soon as the opportunity to do so arose. With the revolution in Russia in 1917, the time seemed ripe for Finnish independence. Meanwhile, however, the Social Democrats had reconsidered their position *vis-à-vis* Russia. Prior to the revolution, the Social Democrats had been staunch defenders of Finland's rights and even campaigned for Finnish independence (Rintala 1962: 9). With the revolution in Russia they saw a chance to have their social and economic policies enacted with Russian support. Having seized the parliamentary majority from the socialists, the bourgeois parties declared the country independent on 6 December 1917. This brought about a political stalemate that eventually gave rise to the Civil War of 1918, in which the socialist Red Guards were defeated by the bourgeois White Guards, backed by German intervention (Upton 1980).

The communists vs. the rest: 1918–44

After 1918, there was a pro-Soviet Finnish party – but not primarily in Finland. Red Guard members who had fled to Russia founded the Finnish Communist Party in Moscow in 1918. This party, illegal in Finland from its inception, operated in Finland through front parties such as the Socialist Worker's Party, founded in 1922. *By 1922, therefore, Finland's eastern relations had given rise to the fifth party in the Finnish five-party system.* All other parties, including the reorganised Social Democratic Party, were staunchly anti-Soviet. The communists controlled large parts of the labour unions and organised a series of strikes in the second half of the 1920s (Meinander 1983: 79–89). From the heated conflicts in the labour market a right-wing extremist movement arose, culminating in the Lapua Movement (1929–1932). The pressures from the extreme right wing finally led in 1930 to a ban on all forms of communist activity, including those labour unions and other associations that were dominated by the communists. Up until the armistice with the Soviet Union in 1944, the reformist Social Democratic Party was the only left-wing party in Finland. The communists having been legislated out of politics, the variation in party attitudes *vis-à-vis* the Soviet Union concerned the degree of rancour with which it was condemned (Karvonen 2000).

The post-war struggle over power, 1945–61

In the settlement between the allied powers towards the end of the Second World War, Finland was defined as part the Soviet sphere of interest. One of the points required by the Soviet Union in the 1944 Armistice Treaty was the re-legalisation of the organisations banned by the anti-communist legislation of 1930. The result was the establishment of the Finnish People's Democratic League, with the Communist Party as the dominant element. The party in many ways came to represent the Soviet point of view in internal Finnish politics (Pesonen 1995: 12). *Once again, Finland's relations with Russia affected the Finnish party system in an important manner.* In Finland, as elsewhere in the Soviet sphere of interest in Europe, the late 1940s were a critical period. In those countries that were to become Soviet satellites, the presence of the Red Army decisively affected the political balance of power in the favour of the communists. In these countries, social democrats were compelled to join forces with communists and, in a matter of a few years, a one-party dictatorship was established. Finland, by contrast, was never occupied by Soviet forces and the Social Democrats as well as the bourgeois parties could operate freely. The Finnish Social Democrats had no intention of allowing the communists to dominate the scene. Quite the contrary: they took up a fierce struggle against communist influence in parliamentary politics and in the labour unions (Rentola 1997: 67–107; Salminen 1979: 108–9). Although Finland was to have one of the numerically strongest communist parties in western Europe throughout the Cold-War period, the immediate danger of a communist takeover had subsided by the early 1950s (Majander 2004: 11–38).

Although the Finnish communists failed to steer the course of events in the same direction as in eastern Europe, Finland's relations with the Soviet Union continued to be a central factor in Finnish domestic politics. In 1948, the Soviet Union proposed that the two countries conclude a similar treaty on 'Friendship, Co-operation and Mutual Assistance' as Moscow had imposed on its east European satellites. Although the Finnish government managed to rewrite the proposal so as to avoid the Soviet *carte blanche* that the east-European treaties constituted, the treaty between Finland and the Soviet Union contained the possibility of a military co-operation between the two countries in given circumstances. The overarching concern for Finnish security policy throughout the Cold War years, therefore, became to avoid a situation in which this co-operation would actually come about (Vloyantes 1975: 50–64). Much was on the shoulders of the Finnish leaders, as the correct course *vis-à-vis* the neighbouring superpower became a matter of national survival.

Urho Kekkonen's powerful presence marked Finnish politics through most of the Cold-War period. The prime minister of five cabinets from 1950 until 1956, he was elected president in 1956 with the narrowest possible margin. He was to hold this office longer than any other president in Finnish history, all the way up to 1981. During the better part of his presidency, he was the unquestioned political leader of the country. The foreign policy associated with him was hardly ever criticised after he had consolidated his presidential power. During his first term as president (1956–62), however, he faced a strong domestic opposition that was all but absent in the remainder of his presidency (Häikiö 1993; Lehtinen 2002).

The story of Finnish politics during the extended Kekkonen presidency should be divided into these two phases. The first phase was characterised by a strong domestic opposition against Kekkonen, paired with an openly critical attitude towards the way he handled Finland's relations with Moscow. During the second phase, he had overcome this domestic opposition and established himself as the unchallenged power-centre of Finnish politics. Meanwhile, international criticism started to mount that Finland had become unacceptably subservient to the Soviet Union; accusations about 'Finlandization' marked the period during which Kekkonen was the unchallenged political leader in Finland (Laqueur 1980; Hakovirta 1975).

Before his election as president, Kekkonen was a leading figure in the Agrarian Union. In ideological terms, his political views were non-socialist. After the war with the Soviet Union, however, he rapidly became known as one of the bourgeois politicians who demanded a new policy of close and friendly relations with Moscow. This was, of course, noticed by the Kremlin, who supported Kekkonen both openly and through diplomatic and intelligence channels. The Social Democrats and the Conservatives, who formed the core of the struggle against the burgeoning Finnish communist movement, took an increasingly critical attitude towards Kekkonen. They claimed that Kekkonen was, in fact, playing into the hands of the communists. Above all, they criticised Kekkonen for using Finland's eastern relations in the domestic power struggle (Lehtinen 2002).

Well ahead of the 1962 presidential elections, the Social Democrats and the Conservatives joined forces to declare that Olavi Honka, Chancellor of Justice, would be their candidate for the presidency. In addition, three smaller parties joined the 'Honka front'. This multi-party campaign presented a real challenge to a continued Kekkonen presidency. But this was not to be an ordinary presidential election. On 30 October 1961, while Kekkonen was on a state visit to the US, the Soviet Union sent a diplomatic note to the Finnish foreign ministry. With reference to a heightened tension around the Baltic Sea due to German militarisation, the note proposed that consultations about military co-operation between Finland and the Soviet Union take place in accordance with Article 2 of the 1948 treaty. This was the worst-case scenario of Finnish foreign policy and it aroused widespread fear in Finland and elsewhere in northern Europe. Honka announced that he would refrain from running in the presidential election. Kekkonen himself flew to Novosibirsk in Siberia to meet with Soviet premier Nikita Khrushchev. At this meeting, Kekkonen convinced Khrushchev that military consultations were not necessary. Honka's decision to step down removed the chief obstacle in Kekkonen's path to a continued presidency. In terms of domestic politics, the 1961 'Note Crisis' also signalled the end of the powerful anti-Kekkonen axis between the Social Democrats and the Conservatives (Vloyantes 1975: 109–25; Anckar 1971: 173–208).

Historians still disagree widely concerning Kekkonen's role in the Note Crisis. Moreover, the relative importance of domestic political motives, as compared with real concerns about Soviet pressure against Finland throughout Kekkonen's prolonged period in power, is still subject to heated controversy (Suomi 1992: 475–569; Rautkallio 1992). Whatever Kekkonen's role and whatever motives may have guided him, the domestic outcome was that any serious political opposition to him vanished and his personal power grew dramatically.

The politics of Finlandization, 1962–82

The two decades of Kekkonen presidency that followed upon the Note Crisis were marked by several intertwined features, all of them problematic from a democratic point of view. The president's power over domestic politics reached unprecedented levels and he often intervened in details of parliamentary and administrative processes that lay outside the president's constitutional powers. The use of foreign policy arguments – that is, hints at implications for Soviet relations – became part and parcel of the domestic power struggle. Moreover, public criticism of conditions in the Soviet Union, or of Soviet actions abroad, all but disappeared. Such criticism was only voiced by marginal groups and minor parties, while all major parties toed the line determined by Kekkonen (Tuikka 2013: 202–11; Tiihonen 1990: 237–42).

With a minor simplification, two opposing interpretations of these political constellations can be found in the Finnish debate (Karvonen 2003). Those who defend the Kekkonen legacy emphasise the external origins of the Finnish political development. According to this view, Finland's position between east and west was extremely precarious. Finland was dependent on the goodwill of an expansive and suspicious superpower. Any ill-conceived manoeuvre in Finnish politics might have been disastrous from the point of view of the country's independence and national security. Therefore, it was necessary to have a strong and determined leader with a personal reservoir of trust in the Kremlin. Whatever Kekkonen did, including his actions *vis-à-vis* domestic political actors, was motivated by a concern for the national interest. Although not unproblematic from a democratic point of view, resolute domestic action on the part of the president, combined with a cautious line towards the Soviet Union in the Finnish public debate, was necessary in order to safeguard the country's independence and social order.

The contrary view stresses the domestic background of Kekkonen's actions. In this view, the core question was where the centre of power in Finnish domestic politics was to lie. If Kekkonen wanted to be the centre of political power, he had to prevent political coalitions directed against him. The 1961 Honka Front had been such a coalition. Its core was an alliance between the Social Democrats and the Conservatives, the two main anti-communist and anti-Kekkonen parties. It became imperative to Kekkonen to guarantee that this alliance would not re-emerge. The fact that the alliance broke apart in 1961 in the face of a mounting threat from the Soviet Union was a decisive victory for Kekkonen. Having gained re-election in 1962, Kekkonen set out to assure that the threat from a social-democratic-conservative alliance was eliminated once and for all. In this endeavour, the constitutional powers of the president in the government-formation process were a powerful weapon. According to the 1919 constitution then in force, the president selected the members of the cabinet, including the prime minister. Most previous presidents had been careful to consider the results of parliamentary elections and the will of the parliamentary majority when deciding on the composition of cabinets. Kekkonen, by contrast, increasingly neglected these considerations and hand-picked prime ministers and other cabinet members more or less at will. The Social Democrats were kept outside cabinet politics for eight years (1958–66). Still more conspicuously, Kekkonen sent the Conservatives into an even longer exile from executive power. Despite varying electoral fortunes and fervent attempts to appear acceptable from the point of view of Finnish–Soviet relations, the Conservative Party remained outside cabinet politics for all of the 21 years from 1966 to1987 (Arter 1987: 186–95; Nousiainen 2006: 278–89).

This policy of divide and rule strongly favoured Kekkonen's own party, the Agrarian Union/Centre Party. The party was represented in almost all cabinets; and in half of them[2] it held the post of prime minister. However, Kekkonen gradually allowed the Social Democrats to assume a stronger role. Kekkonen's relations with several Centre Party notables had grown increasingly complicated and, from the 1970s on, the Social Democrats positioned themselves as the dominant government party (Lehtinen 2002: 569–636). Moreover, Kekkonen pursued a policy of co-optation *vis-à-vis* the Finnish communists. Communist and socialist politicians were frequently appointed as ministers in coalitions that also included ministers from bourgeois parties. Kekkonen and his policies created difficult pressures within the communist camp. On the one hand, the communists could hardly criticise a president who was the favourite of the Kremlin. On the other hand, the economic policies pursued by cabinets appointed by Kekkonen were in line with those in any western capitalist country. Accusations that communist and socialist ministers were being used to 'administer the capitalist state' mounted in the communist movement. Of far-reaching importance was the conclusion of a free-trade treaty with the EEC in 1973. Kekkonen knew that west European markets were vital for Finnish export industry and his role in the process that led to the conclusion of the treaty was central. To many communists, this was the final proof of the fact that they were being held hostage in Kekkonen's power politics. In the course of the 1970s, a definite split between the 'Stalinist' and 'reformist' wings of the Communist Party took place. This was the start of the final decline of Finnish communism (Mäkelä 1987: 180–4). With the benefit of hindsight, one might say that by integrating the communists almost into the mainstream of Finnish politics Kekkonen hugged them to death.

Domestic politics and foreign policy became completely impossible to separate during Kekkonen's prolonged presidency (Vihavainen 1991: 108–19). Having defeated the anti-Kekkonen coalition of Social Democrats and Conservatives he presided over an order in which opposition to the president was synonymous with antagonism towards Finland's friendly relations with the Soviet Union. The president's wide constitutional powers, particularly as concerns the appointment of governments, were a key factor in disciplining the domestic political scene. Parties and individual politicians who wanted to pursue a career at the highest levels of Finnish politics knew that this was hardly possible if the president disapproved (Nousiainen 2006: 279).

---

2. There were no less than sixteen cabinets in Finland between 1962 and 1982. Twelve were composed of party representatives; of these, six had a prime minister from the Agrarian Union/ Centre Party. The four remaining cabinets were caretaker cabinets, another typical feature of the Kekkonen reign.

Finns will probably continue to disagree over the legacy of the Kekkonen years for generations to come (H. Meinander 2008: 272–80). Some will maintain that the centralisation of power was a necessary tool for safeguarding Finland as a western society and that Kekkonen's fundamental motives were patriotic (Suomi 1994: 567–72). Others will stress the domestic background of his actions; in this view, Kekkonen's goal was to become the dominant factor in internal Finnish politics (Lehtinen 2002: 356–81, 661–4; Rautkallio 1992: 267–75). According to Kekkonen's critics, Finland's relations with the neighbouring superpower were a means to this end. These analysts will also point to the fact that Koivisto's more low-key style provoked no protests from Moscow, although the Soviet Union was still a potent superpower (Majander 2013: 221–34).

Irrespective of which view one embraces, it cannot be denied that the end result from the point of view of Finnish parties was the same. Power *was* centralized around the president; criticism of the president *was* tantamount to opposition to the predominant foreign-policy line. For parties and for individual politicians seeking a career at the highest levels of Finnish politics, this fact became as decisive as the will of the people as manifested in elections.

Towards normalisation, 1982–91

In 1981, around his eighty-first birthday, Kekkonen's health deteriorated decisively. Following his resignation in October, presidential elections were held in January 1982. The winner was Mauno Koivisto, a Social Democrat who had been prime minister when Kekkonen was compelled to resign. He was scarcely on the Kremlin's list of favourites. He was, however, all the more popular among the voters: 167 of the 300 members of the Electoral College cast their ballots for him in the first round of voting and he was elected president without a runoff. As the indirect electoral system, then in use, basically contained unlimited possibilities for deals behind the scenes, voters took no chances. Electoral candidates who were assumed to be unwavering in their loyalty towards Koivisto were elected with large vote totals. Social Democratic candidates mustered around 45 per cent of the popular vote, compared to around 25 per cent in a parliamentary election. The mobilisation of the people behind Koivisto's candidature was a resounding protest against the way the country had been run in the past (Häikiö 1993: 356–8).

As president, Koivisto was careful to underline that his term in office would not entail a change in Finland's foreign policy. To be sure, the floral style of Finnish-Soviet communiqués characteristic of the Kekkonen years was gradually replaced by a somewhat more matter-of-fact prose but the change was more due to the internal transformation of the Soviet Union than any attempt at reorientation on the part of the Finnish government. In domestic politics, Koivisto set out to alter the president-centred practice that had established itself during Kekkonen's reign (Nousiainen 2000: 343–4).

The use of foreign-policy arguments as weapons in domestic politics declined rapidly in the Koivisto years. Still, *Finland's relations with the Soviet Union were to affect the party system one more time.* The prolonged internal strife in the Finnish Communist Party led to a formal organisational split in 1986, as the Stalinist minority was expelled from the party and went on to form a party of its own. Neither communist party was to survive much longer. By 1990, Gorbachev's reforms had convinced the majority of the Finnish communists and socialists that Soviet-style communism had come to the end of its road. They went on to form the Left Alliance, a reformed leftist party purged of the vestiges of communism – and indeed, in many respects, of socialism as well (Mickelsson 2007: 261–5).

Despite the changes during *glasnost* and *perestroika*, the collapse of the Soviet Union in 1991 came as a surprise to most Finnish politicians. A factor that had conditioned internal Finnish politics for decades was suddenly gone. Finland's relations with the Russian Federation are a far cry from the fateful air that surrounded the country's dealings with Moscow during the Cold War. After 1991, Finland swiftly and resolutely moved towards full integration in the western community of states. Its relations with its eastern neighbour have basically ceased to affect inter-party affairs.

From camps to consensus

In the first four decades of its existence as an independent state, Finland experienced a civil war, a heated linguistic strife, a strong right-wing extremist movement, two periods of war against the Soviet Union and a painful settlement after World War II. It is no wonder that the level of conflict in domestic politics was high. Multiple and deep divisions separated the various political and organisational 'camps'. There was the division between the communist movement and, basically, all other political forces in Finland. There was the Social Democratic and Conservative antagonism to Kekkonen and his foreign and domestic policies. There was the agrarian suspicion against urban and industrial areas. There was the antagonism between the labour movement and the employers' organisations. Not least, there was the deep division between social democratic and communist-controlled unions in the labour movement.

All of this is clearly visible in both parliamentary politics and labour-market relations in the first post-war decades. Stable governments were extremely difficult to form; during a prolonged period, the average duration of a Finnish cabinet was less than a year. At the same time, numerous industrial disputes characterised the labour-relations field. Finland was among those countries in western Europe in which labour-market disputes were most widespread and the number of workdays lost due to such disputes highest.

The shift from conflict to consensus took place through three interrelated processes, partly parallel, partly consecutive. In each of these fields, the change was astonishingly rapid, given the previous level of conflict. First, the pattern of labour-market contracts changed as of 1968. That year, the first comprehensive Incomes Policy Agreement was concluded between the central organisations of labour and employers and the government. This was to be the first of a dozen such agreements in the 1970s and 1980s (Kyntäjä 1993: 128–9). The core of these agreements concerned industrial wages. However, thanks to the active role of the government, important legislative reforms supported the agreements. Many social-policy reforms came about thanks to incomes-policy agreements. Thus, one might say that the government agreed to share an important part of the economic burden that would otherwise have fallen on the employers had the agreements been about wages only. On the other hand, the incomes-policy system compelled the parliament to pass legislative reforms that the parties might otherwise not have been able to agree on.

Several factors help explain this change in wage-agreement policies. Between 1969 and 1974, the labour-union movement overcame its organisational split. Prior to this, separate organisations led by communists and social democrats operated in the labour-relations field, thus complicating negotiations and maintaining a high level of unrest and conflict. To be sure, the competition between the parties continued in the unions, but now there was at least a common organisational structure for the labour-union movement. For the employers, the incomes-policy agreements were a way to enhance continuity and predictability in the labour market. Many of them also believed that comprehensive agreements would favour the reformist social democratic element among the unions. Finally, it was in line with Kekkonen's long-term goals to bring about economic stability in Finland. He was therefore a strong supporter of the incomes-policy-agreement system; in fact, one of the main deals came about through his direct intervention (Hallberg *et al.* 2009: 251–8).

A second area in which Finland went from conflict to consensus was industrial relations. As long as the labour-union movement remained organisationally split and parliamentary politics divisive and unstable, the Finnish labour market was characterised by frequent and often large work stoppages. With the establishment of a pattern of comprehensive incomes-policy agreements and the growing political consensus, the high level of industrial disputes was also replaced with a more conciliatory style of conflict resolution. Some data may be used to illustrate this change. The average annual number of workdays lost due to industrial disputes was (in thousands of days) 1,322 in the 1950s. In the 1970s the corresponding figure was still 1,051, but in the 1980s as low as 316. During the first nine years of the 2000s it was down to 152.[3] These simple figures bear witness to a shift from a pattern of industrial relations in which manifest conflict was the overarching principle to the consensual culture typical of most of northern Europe.

Finally, a marked change in cabinet stability took place as of around 1980. Up until then, cabinets frequently resigned after about a year. Outright cabinet crises were common and many cabinets did not represent a parliamentary majority. Caretaker cabinets were frequently resorted to, due to problems in forming political coalitions. All of this changed after the 1970s, as is evident from Table 2.4.

Starting at the beginning of the 1980s, Finland embarked on a prolonged period of majority parliamentarism. Since that time, every single cabinet has had the backing of the parliamentary majority. Both minority cabinets and caretaker governments seemingly vanished for good around 1980. Moreover, with arguable

---

3.   *International Historical Statistics*: 186–7; http://laborsta.ilo.org

Table 2.4: Types of cabinets in Finland, 1950–2009

	1950s	1960s	1970s	1980s	1990s	2000s
Total number of cabinets	12	7	9	4	2	4
Majority cabinets	6	4	4	4	2	4
Minority cabinets	3	2	2	–	–	–
Caretaker cabinets	3	1	3	–	–	–

Note: If a cabinet was in office during two different decades, it was assigned to the decade during which it sat longest.
Source: http://www.valtioneuvosto.fi

exceptions (*see* Chapter Four), the rule since then has been that Finnish cabinets remain in power throughout the inter-election period.

Increased cabinet stability was part and parcel of the pervasive shift to consensus in Finnish politics and society starting in the late 1960s. Representatives of political parties, labour unions, government bureaucracies and the business and commercial communities gradually agreed that the previous conflictual approach in the labour market and in parliamentary affairs produced suboptimal results from everyone's point of view. It was necessary to agree on concerted action in order to meet the demands of large-scale development and change in these fields. The shift towards consensus reached a symbolic climax at a conference at Hotel Korpilampi outside Helsinki in 1977. A meeting convened by Social Democratic Prime Minister Kalevi Sorsa, assembled the leading figures of business and labour-market organisations, along with high representatives for government and political parties, to discuss the future of the Finnish economy. The participants expressed a strong commitment to contribute to strengthening the competitiveness of Finnish enterprises in an economic situation marked by the effects of the oil crisis. The 'spirit of Korpilampi' signified a new national unity on the fundamentals of economic policy in Finland (Becker 2003: 148–9).

Conclusion

Contemporary Finland is a technologically and economically advanced society that tends to fare well in international comparisons on a number of important indicators.[4] Democracy is stable and deeply rooted and corruption is low. The educational system produces students and is held in high esteem both nationally and internationally. Finns trust each other as well as government institutions to a very high degree. The universal welfare system continues to produce a high level of social security; despite all talk of 'welfare under pressure', the principle of universal coverage has not been altered.

---

4. One example is the 2010 Newsweek assessment, according to which Finland was 'the best country in the world'.

What perhaps few foreign observers realise is that this modern Finland is a fairly recent creation. As this chapter has demonstrated, Finland has undergone a transformation that is not only thorough but occurred with unprecedented rapidity and at a late point in time. The social structures and external and internal forces that conditioned party constellations and voter alignments a generation or two ago, have either disappeared or look entirely different today. What happens to parties, party strategies and voting behaviour when the fundamentals of social life change as rapidly as they have done in Finland? This is the basic query addressed in the remaining chapters of this book.

Chapter Three

Parties Under Pressure

When society changes, parties face challenges. The greater the contrast between those divisions that once gave rise to the established party-formations and the dominant contemporary conditions in society, the more uncertain is popular allegiance to parties. Thus, well documented features witnessed in the political life of most western democracies: attenuated party identification; waning party membership; declining turnout; and increased electoral volatility (*see* Chapter One). Indeed, many observers would agree that parties are under pressure.

Parties are, however, far from defenceless in the face of these challenges. For one, parties may *adapt their programmes and messages* to changing conditions in society. If the needs and wishes of citizens change, then parties should adjust accordingly. Save for dogmatic groupings on the fringes of the party system, most parties probably readily accept the idea that parties are there for the needs of the people and not *vice versa*. If these needs change, then it is in the nature of democracy that parties should pay heed by revising their programmes, campaigns and policy proposals. Moreover, parties may develop their *organisations* and seek new *financial bases*. They can use their influence over the *state* and the public sector to consolidate their position. Parties can develop new *campaign methods* and renew their patterns of *recruitment* for elective office and party personnel.

Like all organisations, parties strive to maintain and improve their position. This chapter shows how Finnish parties have fought to cope with the pressures brought on by rapid social and political transformation. To a considerable extent, this will be done against a comparative European background. As Finland is an extreme case when it comes to the timing and rapidity of social change, it is of course an interesting question whether parties in Finland display special features when striving to cope with changes.

The structure of competition: Old *vs.* new parties

The parties that already existed or were established at the time when mass democracy was introduced had an advantage from being present at the creation. As long as there were major restrictions on suffrage and political competition, parties could not be formed freely to meet the demands created by social divisions. Once this was possible, parties were formed in rapid succession and they occupied the political space available to them. When electorates had been mobilised behind these parties it was much more difficult for newcomers to establish themselves on the party-political scene (Mair 1997: 13–6).

With the thorough social transformation that western democracies have undergone, opportunities for new political organisations have been created. Dissatisfaction with the traditional party alternatives, together with the emergence of new issues that do not match the traditional political cleavages, has opened up some of the political space that was previously more or less monopolised by older parties. Recent decades witnessed a greater degree of party-system change than earlier periods. Some traditional parties have split into several new parties; others have vanished altogether. Some of the latter have been succeeded by parties founded on their ruins. In still other cases, parties entirely new to the political scene have managed to establish themselves as viable electoral alternatives.

Gallagher *et al.* (2011) have compiled data on the electoral support of new parties in 16 west-European democracies during a half century. Parties that began to contest elections in 1960 or later are defined as new.

Table 3.1 conveys a fairly straightforward impression. With the exception of Malta and (partially) of the United Kingdom, there has been an almost linear growth in the vote-share of new parties in western Europe. This growth

Table 3.1: Mean aggregate support for new political parties in 16 west-European democracies, 1960–2009

Country	1960s	1970s	1980s	1990s	2000–2009
Austria	1.7	0.1	4.1	11.5	17.8
Belgium	2.8	11.4	12.9	23.7	23.38
Denmark	8.7	26.9	30.7	24.9	27.4
Finland	1.6	8.2	13.7	22.3	20.5
France	16.3	29.1	27.1	41.7	58.2
Germany	4.3	0.5	7.5	13.9	15.2
Iceland	2.4	4.7	19.3	21.6	53.6
Ireland	0.3	1.4	7.9	10.0	7.6
Italy	9.5	3.3	7.9	66.8	100.0
Luxembourg	3.1	12.0	11.5	22.4	23.3
Malta	13.1	0	0.1	1.5	1.0
The Netherlands	2.3	26.6	44.5	45.9	60.1
Norway	3.9	13.6	15.1	19.7	30.8
Sweden	1.1	1.6	4.5	14.5	15.0
Switzerland	0.4	5.3	12.2	14.9	11.0
UK	0	0.8	11.6	2.3	2.7
Mean	4.4	9.1	14.4	22.4	29.3

Note: Entries are decennial averages of vote shares won by new parties. New parties are defined as those that began to contest elections in 1960 or later.
Source: Gallagher *et al.* 2011: 308.

has been particularly marked since the 1980s. While the direction of change is nearly uniform, its extent varies a great deal. In some cases a minor party has been added to the party system. In some others, notably Italy, the change has been so pervasive that one can speak of an entirely new party system. In most countries, however, the established parties have not been wiped out by the newcomers. Nevertheless, parties throughout western Europe have faced tightened competition in recent decades.

Finland by no means stands out in this broader European comparison. True, the share of the votes won by new parties displays a clear growth over time in Finland. Still, the Finnish figures come close to European averages. These data would seem to indicate that the extreme pace of social transformation has not created dramatically different conditions for new parties from elsewhere in Europe. However, had the 2011 election results been included for Finland, the picture would have been somewhat different. With the spectacular advance of the True Finns, the vote share of new parties rose to 40 per cent. Continuity and change in the various party families in Finland will be described briefly in the following.

Most *established parties* have been able to avoid major organisational breakdowns, but several of them have experienced temporary splits and internal opposition to the party elite.

A reunified social democracy. In 1959, the Social Democratic Party split over the correct way to handle Finland's relations with the Soviet Union and the party's relations with President Kekkonen. A minority of the party's parliamentarians went on to form the Social Democratic League of Workers and Smallholders. However, by 1973 the new party had lost most of its support and was reincorporated into the SDP. Since then, the organisational structure of the party has remained intact (Mickelsson 2007: 211–12).

A vigorous Centre Party challenged by populists. The Finnish Centre Party has a strong organisational structure that has remained intact since 1960 (*ibid.* 207–10). However, the first organised populist party was formed in 1959, as a splinter from the then Agrarian Union. Since then, the Centre Party has been challenged electorally several times by populist parties but managed to retain its organisational unity. This goes for the challenge from the Rural Party in the 1970s and 1980s (Arter 1999a: 164–5) as well as its successor the True Finns in 2011 (*see below* and Chapter Five). Whether the Centre Party's extensive organisational network will once again help it overcome the populist electoral challenge remains to be seen; according to the latest opinion polls, its period of opposition has elevated it to the position of the most popular party in Finland.[1]

A successful conservative party. In 1973, the Conservative Party lost an MP when the Constitutional People's Party was formed in opposition to the extension of President Kekkonen's mandate without election (Mickelsson 2007: 205–7). The Constitutional Party never had more than two MPs and was dissolved in 1991. Overall, the conservatives have not faced major internal crises and their electoral following has risen from around 15 per cent in 1960 to around 20 per cent today.

---

1.   http://svenska.yle.fi/artikel/2014/01/29/partikartan-oforandrad

A Swedish party facing problematic demographics. The Swedish Party also lost an MP to the Constitutional Party in 1973. No splits have occurred since the disappearance of the Constitutional Party. The main worry of the Swedish Party has been the decline of the proportion of Swedish-speakers in the total population. On the other hand, Swedish-speaking voters have remained highly loyal to their party (Sundberg 2005: 5–16).

One[2] party family that existed already in the 1920s has undergone a *major transformation* in recent decades:

A far left that collapsed and reappeared. The communist-dominated Finnish People's Democratic League was one of the largest parties from 1945 until the 1970s. Mounting tension between the more nationalist majority and a 'Stalinist' minority brought about a definitive split in 1986 (Mäkelä 1987: 180–5; Mickelsson 2007: 262). That year, the latter group went on to form a party of its own, with ten of the total of 27 FPDL MPs as its parliamentary base. The new party was named Democratic Alternative. It lost six of its MPs in the 1987 election and was dissolved simultaneously with the FPDL in 1990. That year, a new party called the Left Alliance was established. It has endeavoured to rid itself from the vestiges of its communist past. It holds fourteen of the 200 seats in the parliament elected in 2011.

The following parties that hold seats in the 2011 parliament can be considered *new*:

The three peaks of Finnish populism. Finnish populism first established itself as a parliamentary force in 1959, when legendary Veikko Vennamo broke with the Agrarian Union and founded the Small Farmers' Party. The party failed to gain representation in the 1962 elections but, four years later, Vennamo entered parliament again. In 1966, when the Agrarian Union had changed its name to the Centre Party, Vennamo renamed his party the Rural Party. Four years after that, Finnish populism won its first major electoral victory when the Rural Party mustered more than 10 per cent of the vote and gained 18 parliamentary seats. Merely two years later, however, the party had split over internal differences and the 1975 election left the Rural Party with no more than two seats. However, with Vennamo's son Pekka as leader, the party again scored a victory in 1983 and increased its share to 17 seats. Unlike his father, whom Kekkonen did not allow to participate in cabinets, Pekka Vennamo did not remain in opposition. The Rural Party was a cabinet party in 1983–1990 and its popularity gradually waned. It reached the end of its road in 1995, when the True Finns were founded on the ruins of the Rural Party. After a rather slow start – one MP in 1995, two in 1999, three in 2003 and five in 2007 – the True Finns caused a political earthquake by winning no less than thirty-nine seats in 2011 (Arter 2012a: 813–14; Wiberg 2011: 20–1; Toivonen 2011: 82–92). Arter (2012a: 821) in fact argues that in the transformation culminating in 2011, the True Finn Party 'appears to have become a significantly different party to its predecessor'.

The humble progress of the Christian Party. Religion has never been a major bone of contention in Finnish (or Scandinavian) politics (Karvonen 1996: 121–2). Since gaining a first parliamentary seat in 1970, the Christian Democrats (until 2001: the

---

2.   Or two, if one wishes to include the disappearance of the liberal party alternative.

Christian League) have never managed to gain more than ten seats or 5.3 per cent of the vote. The 2011 result – 4 per cent of the vote and six seats – approximates its average electoral support for the past forty years (Paloheimo and Raunio 2008: 18). The party held a cabinet post in 1991–4 and a post in the 2011 Katainen cabinet as well.

A pragmatist Green Party. Like most ecological parties, the Finnish Greens (officially: the Green League) have their historical roots in various environmentalist and alternative movements. Unlike many other ecological movements, the Finnish Greens have long stood out as a pragmatic centrist or liberal party rather than a dogmatic or radical single-issue movement. The success of the Greens in parliamentary elections has frequently been somewhat weaker than their popularity in opinion polls. Since gaining their first MPs in 1983, they have established themselves as a medium-sized party, peaking at 8.5 per cent and 15 MPs in 2007 (Mickelsson 2007: 280–4; Paloheimo and Raunio 2008: 18). They have been a cabinet party on several occasions, including in the 2011 Katainen government.

In sum, established Finnish parties have met with competition from newcomers in a similar fashion to parties elsewhere in western Europe. In a comparative perspective, it is nevertheless difficult to argue that the support of new parties clearly reflects the exceptional pace and magnitude of social change in the Finnish case. This conclusion may need to be modified if the success of the True Finns in 2011 breeds increasing turbulence in Finnish politics in future elections.

Mass appeal: Programmes and propaganda

A recurring theme in the literature about parties and elections concerns the attenuated role of ideology and programmatic convergence among political parties. Catchphrases such as 'the end of ideology' (Bell 1960) or 'the catch-all party' (Kirchheimer 1966) appeared as early as the 1960s to describe a social development in which class divisions had become blurred and the erstwhile structural foundations of political parties weakened. Three decades later, in a highly acclaimed book, Francis Fukuyama not only spoke about the end of ideology but 'the end of history'. The demise of the Cold War had ended the universal contest between ideologies for good:

> We who live in stable, long-standing democracies face an unusual situation. In our grandparents' time, many reasonable people could foresee a radiant socialist future in which private property and capitalism had been abolished, and in which politics itself was somehow overcome. Today, by contrast, we have trouble imagining a world that is radically better than our own, or a future that is not essentially democratic and capitalist [...] we cannot picture to ourselves a future that is *essentially* different from the present one, and at the same time better (Fukuyama 1998: 46; italics in original).

If it is true that an overall reduction of ideological differences has taken place, this should be visible in analyses in which a sufficient number of cases is studied over extended periods of time. Thanks to a large-scale enterprise by a group of European scholars, analyses of this kind are possible. The Manifesto Research Group (MRG) has, among other things, carried out a comprehensive study of party manifestos (electoral platforms) from 1945 until 2003. In a careful content analysis, the texts of these manifestos were assigned to 56 different categories. The number of countries included in the study has been expanded over time; the stable democracies of the west have been included throughout the period (Budge *et al.* 2001; Klingemann *et al.* 2008).

One of the instruments developed by MRG is a left-right scale ranging from -100 to +100. In the former case, a party programme is devoted completely to left-wing issues; in the latter case, the programme exclusively contains right-wing items. As the manifesto data are unique in their coverage of countries, parties and time periods, and as the left-right dimension is, arguably, the most universally applicable aspect of party politics (Bobbio 1996), this should make the MRG left-right scale a highly appropriate tool in the present context. Below, it will be applied to 15 stable west-European democracies, including Finland.

The basic question to which an answer is sought with the MRG data is whether the distances between parties on the left-right scale have diminished over time. The maximal theoretical distance between two parties is 200, that is, from -100 to +100. As there are more than two parties in almost all countries, and as the periods covered comprise several elections, the *standard deviation* of party positions on the left-right scale is used as the measure of ideological distance. If parties are placed far from each other, the standard deviation is large; if they are adjacent to each other on the scale the standard deviation is small. Consequently, *if a programmatic convergence has taken place over time, we expect the standard deviation of party positions on the left-right scale to have declined.*

The content of electoral manifestos naturally reflects the particular circumstances surrounding each election. The themes that are topical at a given election may be all but absent at the next one. When looking for more fundamental changes, the comparison must be based on large bodies of data, in which the idiosyncrasies of individual elections cannot be expected to weigh too heavily in the scales. For the purposes of this chapter, the period covered by the MRG data was divided into six sub-periods. The standard deviation of party positions on the left-right scale was calculated for each sub-period as a whole. Figure 3.1 shows the development for 15 stable democracies in western Europe.

There is certainly no common west-European pattern when it comes to either the level or the development of left-right polarisation. There is a group of countries, including Finland, in which polarisation peaked a long time ago and where the most recent data point to a lower level of polarisation (*see* top third of Figure 3.1). The group in the middle displays a roller-coaster pattern, with a slight trend towards heightened polarisation at the end. Finally, the bottom group displays little variation throughout the period. Generally speaking, the level of polarisation has been higher among the Nordic countries than elsewhere in western Europe; the Nordic peaks mark the highest levels of polarisation to be found among the 15 cases. The chart does not lend particularly strong support

Figure 3.1: Left-right variation in west-European party manifestos, 1945–2003

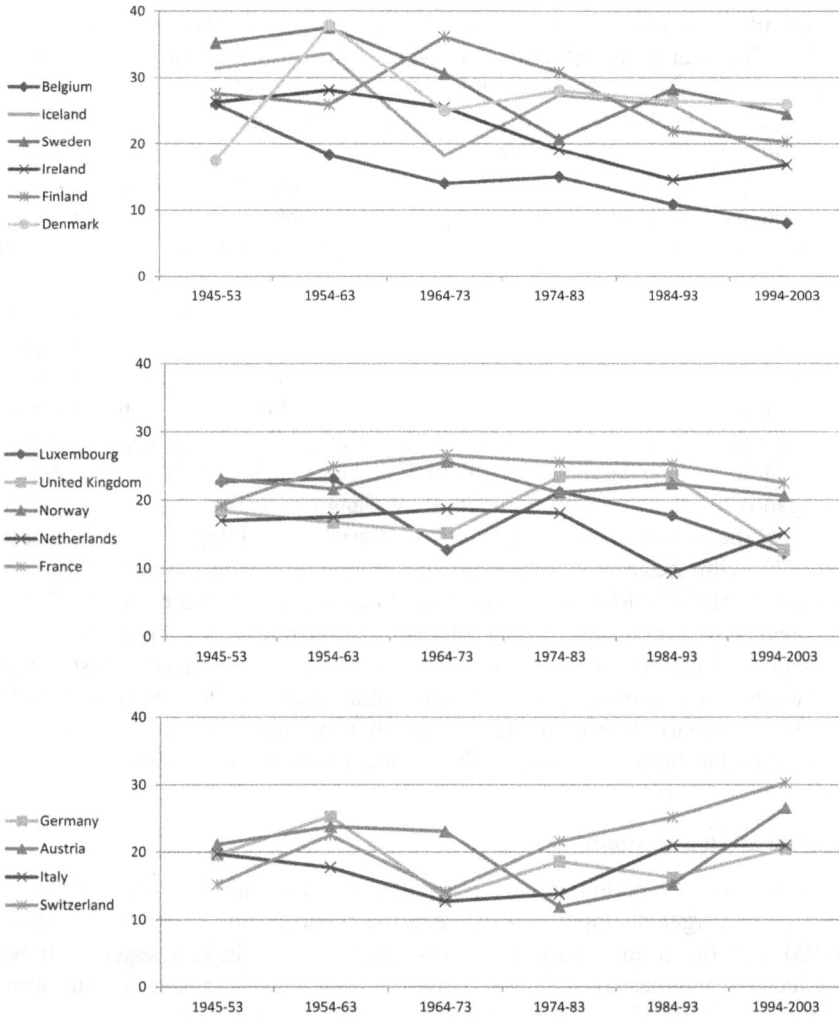

Legend: Entries represent standard deviation of party positions on a scale from +100 (maximum right) to -100 (maximum left)
Data source: Manifesto Research Group, *see* Budge *et al.* 2001 and Klingemann *et al.* 2008.

to the hypothesis about an ideological convergence. Most of the cases either fail to support the notion or run counter to it. The only case in which data come out in more or less unequivocal support of it is Belgium. However, if we relax the assumption and look for cases where polarisation peaked a long time ago and the recent decades witness declining trends, then Denmark, Finland, Iceland, Ireland and Sweden can also be said to support the hypothesis.

The decline of polarisation in Finland since the mid 1960s is more than 15 percentage points, which represents one of the clearest changes among the cases studied. It would seem to indicate that the parties have, indeed, come closer to each other on this fundamental ideological dimension. The evidence offered by the MRG data is, in fact, corroborated by Finnish studies that use other forms of comparable data. Karvonen and Rappe (1991) studied editorials in party newspapers in connection with four parliamentary election campaigns between 1954 and 1987. They examined the group-orientation of political parties and their use of propaganda techniques. In a study published in 1996, Rappe presented a similar analysis of electoral programmes and party posters in connection with five elections between 1954 and 1991. Carlson's analysis (2000) of election posters and slogans from 1958–62 and 1987–91 is still another relevant study.

The main conclusion from these studies is that the programmes and propaganda of Finnish parties were much more oriented towards their traditional bases of support (*classe gardée*) at the beginning of the periods studied than during more recent years. Parties have shifted their appeal from clearly defined population segments to the electorate at large or to the voter as an individual. This change appears more or less linear over time. Parallel to this, there has been a decline in the use of offensive propaganda techniques; harsh and aggressive language was all but absent towards the end of the period. However, the study by Karvonen and Rappe indicates that the mid 1970s witnessed a temporary return of a more propagandistic prose (1991: 253). Still the overall development seems clear: Finnish parties have been transformed from aggressive proponents of class interests to moderate catch-all parties.

Overall, therefore, it seems that Finnish parties have indeed adjusted their programmes and messages to a considerable degree. The 1960s and 1970s witnessed a polarisation of politics. From then on, the reduction of ideological polarisation has been more marked than in most other west European countries.

Organisation and membership

In a classical formulation about the origin and organisation of political parties, Maurice Duverger distinguished between mass parties and cadre parties (1951: 84–95). For the former, party members constituted their very essence. It was by educating the mass of their members that these parties created an elite group capable of shouldering political responsibilities. Without a mass membership, these parties were like 'teachers without students' (Duverger 1951: 84). Socialist parties were the prime example of mass parties.

Cadre parties, by contrast, were assemblies of notables who joined forces in order to contest, finance and win elections. Their personal influence and skills were the party's core resource. Membership and organisation were secondary: gaining power by winning elections was the overarching goal. Moderate and conservative parties were prime examples (Duverger 1951: 85).

For a considerable period, Finnish parties conformed to this pattern. Originally, only the Social Democratic Party had an organisation based on mass-membership. After the Second World War, however, two other parties created nationwide organisational structures modelled on the mass party. When communism was re-legalised in 1944, the Finnish People's Democratic League rapidly organised itself throughout the country (Sundberg and Gylling 1992: 273–4). From the 1950s on, the Agrarian Union (as of 1965, the Centre Party) created the strongest and most comprehensive organisational structure of all Finnish parties (Sundberg 1996: 45–7).

By the 1970s, basically all parties had followed suit, and their organisational structures largely resembled the description of a mass party. A major impetus behind the increased organisational similarity of Finnish parties was the introduction of public subsidies for political parties in 1966. This decision was highly controversial and led to demands that the concept of 'party' be given a clear legal definition and that parties receiving public subsidies be obliged to account for their use of taxpayers' money (Anckar 1974: 73–102). A political compromise was reached through the introduction of a Party Law in 1969 that defined political parties in legal terms, provided for their registration and made them accountable for their use of public funding. Only registered parties that have seats in parliament are eligible for public subsidies. To be registered, an association must fulfil the following requirements:

1. Its aims must be 'essentially political'.
2. It must present the signatures of at least 5,000 eligible voters.
3. Its statutes must guarantee the observation of democratic principles in its internal decision-making and its activities.
4. It must present a party programme that contains the principles and goals of its political activity.

The introduction of public subsidies and, as its immediate consequence, the Party Law, had considerable effects on the internal organisation of Finnish parties. Although the law did not provide a detailed description of the 'democratic principles' required in point 3, these were interpreted to mean an organisation based on individual mass-membership. As a consequence, Finnish parties rapidly became basically uniform in their organisational structure (Sundberg 1996: 13–40).

The basic unit of Finnish parties is the local branch; individual party members belong to local party branches. In larger communities, branch activity is co-ordinated by municipal party organisations, particularly when it comes to municipal politics. The next level is the district organisation, normally coincident with electoral districts. The national-level organisation includes the party congress, the party council, the executive committee, the central party bureaucracy and a varying number of special committees. The congress is the supreme decision-making body; it convenes annually or every 2–3 years, depending on the party. It appoints the party council, which normally meets once or twice a year. Day-to-day political decisions are taken by the executive committee, chaired by the party leader (Sundberg and Gylling 1992: 292; Sundberg 2008: 62–74).

Most parties have separate auxiliary organisations, for example, women's and youth organisations. When a party is represented in parliament, the parliamentary party-group can be considered a part of the party organisation, as can the group of cabinet ministers for those parties that are in government (Sundberg and Gylling 1992: 292; Sundberg 2008: 62–74).

Comparative data on party membership are notoriously difficult to gather, due to varying membership practices and definitions and the propensity of parties to over-report their membership figures. Thanks to a long-standing and persistent effort on the part of a cross-national group of scholars, however, longitudinal data are available for most of the stable western democracies. Table 3.2 shows how party membership has developed in western Europe during the past three decades.

Throughout western Europe, political parties have suffered severe membership losses. Among the 13 cases surveyed, not a single one comes anywhere near to being an exception to this rule. In general terms, the smaller

Table 3.2: Party membership in western Europe during the past three decades

Country (year)	Electorate (millions of voters)	Total Party membership (1000)	Membership as % of electorate (M/E)	% change in number of members between first and last year
Austria				
1980	5.2	1477	28.5	
1990	5.6	1335	23.7	
1999	5.8	1031	17.7	−28.6
2008	6.1	1055	17.3	
Belgium				
1980	6.9	617	9.0	
1989	7.0	644	9.2	
1999	7.3	480	6.6	−31.0
2008	7.7	426	5.5	
Denmark				
1980	3.8	276	7.3	
1989	3.9	232	5.9	
1998	4.0	205	5.1	−39.7
2008	4.0	166	4.1	
Finland				
1980	*3.9*	*607*	*15.7*	
1989	*4.0*	*543*	*13.5*	
1998	*4.2*	*401*	*9.7*	*−42.7*
2006	*4.3*	*347*	*8.1*	

Table 3.2 (continued)

Country (year)	Electorate (millions of voters)	Total Party membership (1000)	Membership as % of electorate (M/E)	% change in number of members between first and last year
France				
1978	34.4	1737	5.0	
1988	37.0	1100	3.0	−53.2
1999	39.2	615	1.6	
2007	43.9	814	1.9	
Germany				
1980 (West)	43.2	1955	4.5	
1989 (West)	48.1	1873	3.9	−27.2
1999	60.8	1780	2.9	
2007	61.9	1424	2.3	
Ireland				
1980	2.3	114	5.0	
1990	2.5	120	4.9	−44.7
1998	2.7	86	3.1	
2008	3.1	63	2.0	
Italy				
1980	42.2	4074	9.7	
1989	45.6	4150	9.1	−35.6
1998	48.7	1974	4.1	
2007	47.1	2623	5.6	
The Netherlands				
1980	10.0	431	4.3	
1989	11.1	355	3.2	−29.6
2000	11.8	294	2.5	
2009	12.3	304	2.5	
Norway				
1980	3.0	461	15.4	
1990	3.2	419	13.1	−62.6
1997	3.3	242	7.3	
2008	3.4	172	5.0	

Table 3.2 (continued)

Country (year)	Electorate (millions of voters)	Total Party membership (1000)	Membership as % of electorate (M/E)	% change in number of members between first and last year
Sweden				
1980	6.0	508	8.4	
1989	6.3	506	8.0	−47.5
1998	6.6	366	5.5	
2008	6.8	267	3.9	
Switzerland				
1977	3.9	412	10.7	
1991	4.5	360	8.0	−43.2
1997	4.6	293	6.4	
2007	4.9	234	4.8	
United Kingdom				
1980	41.1	1693	4.1	
1989	43.2	1137	2.6	−68.4
1998	43.8	840	1.9	
2008	44.2	535	1.2	

Source: van Biezen *et al.* 2012: 43–6.

countries of Europe have had higher percentages of party membership than the largest countries. Interestingly enough, the rates of change do not seem to be systematically related to the general level of party membership. Both countries that have had high levels of membership, and those where membership has always been comparatively low, display similar patterns of change; Norway and the United Kingdom are cases in point. Austria is something of an outlier, with a membership rate of still around 17 per cent. However, even in the Austrian case, the decline has been nearly 30 per cent.

Finland belongs to those countries where party membership has been relatively high. Overall, Finnish parties have lost substantial portions of their members over the past three decades. Still, in quantitative comparative terms, Finland is a typical rather than an exceptional case. The decline in party membership for Finland is 42.7 per cent, almost exactly the average decline (42.6) for the 13 cases. Finnish parties have suffered membership losses that are highly troublesome but they share this fate with parties throughout western Europe.

When parties lose nearly half of their members, the change has far-reaching effects throughout their organisations. In a small country such as Finland, many local party branches have always been so small that considerable membership losses threatens their very existence. A decline, not in just membership figures but in the number of local organisations, has made itself felt in many parties. The trend is, however, not uniform: some parties have fared better than others. This is evident from Tables 3.3 and 3.4, which show the development in the number of the parties' basic organisations and individual members, respectively.

The established parties expanded their organisational networks in the decades following the war. The organisational work carried out by the Agrarian Union (Centre Party) was particularly impressive. All parties profited organisationally by the introduction of public subsidies from the late 1960s on. As of the 1990s, all established parties have witnessed a decline in the number of local organisations. This has been most marked for the Left Party, while the Swedish Party has retained most of its local branches. The organisation of the True Finns is still a far cry from the heyday of the Rural Party in the 1970s but has been expanded during recent years. The Greens have almost doubled the number of local branches in a little over a decade but the numbers are still low when compared to the larger parties.

Membership statistics for Finnish parties since WWII tell a story of growth, stabilisation and rapid decline. The membership of established parties began to grow after the war and was boosted by the introduction of public party subsidies. For most of these parties, membership peaked in the 1970s or 1980s. From there on, an accelerated process of decline has been visible. For the Left Alliance

Table 3.3: The number of basic (local) organisations of Finnish parties since 1945

Year	Centre Party	Left Party	Social Democrats	Conservatives	Swedish Party	Christian Party	Populists	Greens
1945	453	976	1,115	186	No data	n/a	n/a	n/a
1950	1,230	1,435	1,542	467	82	n/a	n/a	n/a
1960	2,614	1,924	1,457	720	99	No data	No data	n/a
1970	2,876	1,731	1,360	848	86	No data	1600	n/a
1980	2,886	1,748	1,499	1,208	102	370	1000	n/a
1990	2,837	1,624	1,417	1,141	152	No data	1200	32
2000	2,616	609	1,103	1,011	157	No data	No data	114
2005	2,502	596	1,037	1,006	152	No data	170	167
2012	2,500	640	1,000	1,000	150	198	250	210

Centre Party = until 1960, the Agrarian Union; Left Party = until 1990, the Finnish People's Democratic League, from 2000, the Left Alliance; Christian Party = until 2000, the Christian League, thereafter the Christian Democrats; Populists = until 1990, the Rural Party, thereafter the True Finns.
Sources: 1945–2005, Mickelsson 2007: 405; for 2012, data gathered from parties' official websites or provided by party functionaries.

Table 3.4: Party membership in Finland since 1945

Year	Centre Party	Left Party	Social Democrats	Conservatives	Swedish Party	Christian Party	Populists	Greens
1945	29,506	54,041	63,745	60,000	35,000	n/a	n/a	n/a
1950	143,096	58,417	67,268	72,500	35,000	n/a	n/a	n/a
1960	253,339	59,000	42,926	78,270	50,593	No data	9,000	n/a
1970	288,093	51,529	60,707	81,116	49,197	3,376	27,000	n/a
1980	304,679	47,000	100,161	76,815	42,423	20,280	15,000	n/a
1990	276,859	34,000	81,896	68,091	42,042	16,770	No data	875
2000	216,506	12,108	61,089	40,000	29,444	14,000	No data	1,480
2005	191,657	9,687	54,171	40,000	24,700	13,000	2,000	2,429
2011	163,000	9,100	50,000	41,000	28,000	13,000	5,000	4,600

Centre Party = until 1960, the Agrarian Union; Left Party = until 1990, the Finnish People's Democratic League, from 2000, the Left Alliance; Christian Party = until 2000, the Christian League, thereafter the Christian Democrats; Populists = until 1990, the Rural Party, thereafter the True Finns.
Sources: 1945–2005, Mickelsson 2007; for 2011, *Kauppalehti* 13 June 2011 (figures rounded off).

(and its predecessor), the decline has been dramatic indeed; the party is down to merely 15 per cent of the membership it had in the 1960s. The remaining 'old' parties have lost approximately half of their membership when compared with their highest figures. Of the new parties, the Christian Democrats and the True Finns have considerably fewer members than in the 1980s and 1970s, respectively. In the case of the True Finns, however, a fairly rapid growth of party membership is taking place today. As for the Greens, their membership figures have grown steadily over the years but are still on a fairly low level.

In sum, Finnish parties have suffered considerable losses in terms of the number of local organisations and individual members in the past three decades. For the Left Alliance, the decline is so dramatic that one might argue that this party family has lost its erstwhile character of mass party. As for the other established parties, the losses are clear as well. Overall, however, they retain their general character as mass parties. The new parties display a somewhat different developmental pattern but none of them has a membership that would yet qualify them as genuine mass parties.

Overall, the social changes that have taken place in Finland are certainly reflected in the form of weakened party organisations and declining membership statistics. In a west-European comparison, however, Finland still stands out as a typical rather than a deviant case.

Finance

In a widely cited article in 1995, Katz and Mair formulated the 'cartel party' thesis. They spoke of 'colluding parties [which] become agents of the state and employ the resources of the state (the party state) to ensure their own collective survival'

(Katz and Mair 1995: 5). An instrument of paramount importance in this process, whereby the ties between party and state were strengthened at the expense of the ties between party and civil society, 'was the regulation of state subventions. [They] now constitute one of the major financial resources with which the parties can conduct their activities both in parliament and in the wider society' (Katz and Mair 1995: 15).

Finland very much conforms to this description of the cartelisation of the party system. We have already seen how the introduction of public party subsidies and a special Party Law streamlined the organisations of Finnish parties. From an economic point of view, public subsidies rapidly made parties highly dependent on taxpayers' money. A study conducted in the late 1970s (Karvonen and Berglund 1980), showed that it took no more than a decade to create this dependence on the state. By 1977, party subsidies accounted for two-thirds or more of the finances of all parties in parliament (Karvonen and Berglund 1980: 99). A 2008 study by Tomi Venho showed that this pattern had persisted into the 2000s (Venho 2008: 51–5). In fact, political parties are financially even more dependent on the state than the mere share of the official party subsidies would seem to indicate. Party subsidies have never been popular among the voters, which is why spectacular hikes in the amounts paid out have been somewhat of a political liability. Basically, the growth of public party subsidies has followed changes in the general cost of living. Today, €18 million per year are divided among the parties in parliament, according to the number of seats that each party has; each MP is 'worth' 90,000 euros. However, parties have found additional and faster ways to expand their public subventions. The 'office subsidies' paid to parliamentary parties to cover various administrative functions related to parliamentary work are not as conspicuous as party subsidies proper. The growth of office subsidies has, therefore, been more rapid; today, they amount to nearly €4 million per year. Moreover, another €18 million is channelled by the parties in support of their press and communicative functions. This money was formerly called parliamentary press support and decided upon separately. As it was criticised by the European Commission as a potential case of government subsidies to economic activity, in 2008, parliament decided to make it part of the party-subsidy budget. Although this money is still to be spent for press and communicative functions, it is today, perceived to be part and parcel of the public money directly controlled by the parties (Tarasti 2010: 148–9). All in all, Finnish parties as organisations have been almost completely dependent on the state for decades.

One of the main arguments behind the introduction of public party subsidies was to reduce the risk of undesirable economic ties between parties and, often unidentified, economic and social interests (Anckar 1974: 82–8). If parties are mainly funded by public money then the risk of moneyed interests gaining undue influence over politics should be reduced. For several decades, the general impression was that this argument was valid. The public remained fairly sceptical of party subsidies but political finance at large was not perceived to be a particularly problematic field.

The 2000s brought about a change in this regard and the problem was related to campaign finance. A combination of factors lay behind the development of the perception that political finance was getting out of hand. The basic systemic factor was the Finnish electoral formula. The system of compulsory preferential (candidate) voting creates strong incentives for presumptive representatives to run individual campaigns; the possibilities of enhancing one's chances of election are considerable in the Finnish system. Individual campaigning means individual finance. For many years, a large proportion of candidates, including most of the candidates who have actually been elected, have relied more on the money they can raise through their personal support-groups than on funds provided by the party organisation. Second, campaigns have become vastly more expensive than a decade or two ago. New channels of communication and campaigning have been added to the traditional ones, while candidates must continue to utilise the latter as actively as always. Between the 2003 and 2007 elections, the average campaign budget of the 200 elected MPs rose from €26,000 to €38,500 (Arter 2009: 26). Third, the number of elections is larger than in many comparable countries. Sweden, for instance, has general (national, regional and local) elections simultaneously every four years, plus European elections every five years. Finland has separate four-year cycles for parliamentary and local elections, European elections every five years and presidential elections every six years. There is an election campaign going on almost every year. Finnish campaigns are decentralised, they have become increasingly expensive and their frequent occurrence puts a severe strain on both party organisations and the government agencies that are supposed to monitor political finance.

An awareness of growing problems related to campaign finance was manifested in a law that went into effect in 2000. This legislation required that all elected MPs and their substitutes submit a report on their campaign budgets to the Ministry of Justice. These were to account for the use of the candidates' own money as well as funds received from other sources. Failure to submit reports or incomplete reporting would not, however, lead to legal sanctions. The idea was that such behaviour would create negative publicity, which, in turn, would constitute a form of political penalty (Tarasti 2010: 11).

For several years, it seemed that the law did not have noticeable consequences for Finnish politics. In 2008, however, things suddenly started to happen. Timo Kalli, the leader of the Centre Party parliamentary group, told media that he had not submitted a report on his campaign expenses, as a failure to do so would not lead to sanctions. This astonishingly blunt statement led to heightened – and long overdue – media interest in the reports filed by MPs as well as in other matters pertaining to campaign finance. Meanwhile, a Council of Europe unit called the Group of States against Corruption (GRECO) had decided to conduct a special survey on political finance in Finland. External interest in internal Finnish affairs is always taken quite seriously in Finland; this time was no exception. GRECO presented a report with ten recommendations, many of which implied fairly strong criticism of the rules and practices concerning political finance in Finland (Tarasti 2010: 12–13).

GRECO's criticism was serious enough but what the media subsequently dug up was far worse. It turned out that candidates – particularly those representing the Centre Party and the Conservatives – had been receiving considerable support from corporations, foundations and individual businessmen. A particular source of wealth was connected to businesses with an interest in land-development schemes, an area in which political decisions often have far-reaching economic consequences. An organisation called 'The Finland of Developing Regions' (*Kehittyvien maakuntien Suomi*), led by five well-known businessmen, was found to be a particularly prominent actor. The organisation, apparently formed at a meeting in a Centre Party office, donated large amounts of money primarily to Centre Party candidates (Arter 2009, 30–2). Among other political sponsors, were not just private companies and individuals, but also foundations dependent on government subsidies and companies of which the state was a majority owner. Overall, the impression was that there was a great deal of 'sleaze' in Finnish political finance. In a nation that had repeatedly been rated as the least corrupt country in the world[3] this was no small matter.

The pressure had mounted on the government to regulate campaign finance in a more credible way. Within less than two years, two important pieces of legislation were introduced. The toothless 2000 law on candidates' campaign finance was replaced by new legislation that went into effect on 1 May 2009. A little more than a year later, important amendments concerning party financing were made in the Party Law.

The regulation of political finance is a complicated issue and countries such as the US, with a long history of legal regulation, have ample experience of the fact that it is impossible to create watertight rules. Money and political influence tend to find ways to meet, despite all attempts to prevent it. Still, it is safe to say that the reforms open a new chapter in the legal regulation of political finance in Finland. They concern all elections – local, parliamentary, European as well as presidential. They make candidates and parties accountable for all forms of support, including contributions of a non-monetary nature. They oblige parties and candidates to name all contributors who have donated more than a given amount (€1,500 to a candidate in a parliamentary election). Repeated contributions from a single source are added together and considered a single contribution. The amount that a single contributor can donate is limited to €6,000 per candidate in a parliamentary election. Anonymous contributions are forbidden, as are donations from foreign sources. Most importantly, responsibility for examining political finance has been transferred from the Ministry of Justice to the National Audit Office. The role of this agency is much more active than that of the Ministry of Justice had been. The latter had simply functioned as a sort of archive for the reports filed in by the MPs. The National Audit Office has the right to require that MPs and parties complete and specify their reports. Failure to deliver reports or repeatedly incorrect or insufficient reporting will lead to legal sanctions (Komiteanmietintö 2009: 1; Komiteanmietintö 2009: 3).

---

3.   *See* http://www.transparency.org/research/gcb/gcb_2010

The new legislation has already had visible effects. Candidates and parties report their finances much more speedily than before. Media scrutiny is much more intrusive (Kantola 2012: 84–5) and both political and economic actors seem aware of this. Companies are reported to have reviewed their internal policies concerning political contributions; and these have tended to become more restrictive. A prolonged pattern of growth was reversed in the 2011 parliamentary elections – where economic irregularities by the 'established parties' constituted one of the themes exploited by the populist True Finns (Pernaa 2012: 32–40). At this election, the mean individual campaign budget of an elected MP was some €3,000 lower than four years earlier.

Overall, party finance in Finland has long conformed to the pattern of party-system cartelisation. The economic role of individual members has declined and parties are highly dependent on public party subsidies – a form of support that they themselves introduced and of which they are in control. The rapid growth in campaign costs in recent decades created an impression that sources other than government money were again becoming more important. The scandals related to campaign finance in recent years have led to changes that may, once again, increase the role of public subsidies in the economy of political parties at large.

Parties and candidates in the electoral arena

Institutional incentives

The basic features of the Finnish electoral system were presented in Chapter One. The system has been in use since the mid-1950s and has only undergone minor revisions related to electoral districting. For the better part of the post-war era, therefore, the strategic incentives inherent in the system have remained basically unaltered. Three features of the Finnish system are particularly important from a strategic point of view:

1. The system is *proportional*. This means that even quite small parties stand a chance of gaining seats, although this is much easier in the larger districts than in the smaller ones. Furthermore, there is no legal threshold for entry into parliament. Parties with no more than 1 or 2 per cent of the total vote may gain representation if they do well in one or several of the larger constituencies.

2. It is a *list system*. This means that the number of seats that a party will win in an electoral district is calculated on the basis of the total list votes it musters. Therefore, candidates on party lists share an interest in maximising the party-list total. The more votes the list gets, the more seats the party will gain; the more seats for the party, the better the relative chances of each individual candidate being elected. This discourages candidates from attacking co-partisans too fiercely because negative campaigning among candidates on the same party list may lead to a lower total vote for the list.

3. It includes *compulsory preferential voting*. Voters must pick a candidate for whom they cast their ballot. There is no possibility of casting a party vote as such. The order in which the candidates are elected from a list is entirely determined by the number of personal votes that the candidates

receive. Consequently, the system provides strong incentives for individual campaigning. Successful candidate campaigns may boost the candidates' chances of election considerably. The Finnish system not only differs from closed-list systems, in which the candidate list-order determined by the party is decisive. Even among preferential voting systems, the Finnish system is one of those in which the incentives for individual campaigning are strongest. Table 3.5 compares preferential voting systems. It represents a revised form of an index proposed by Shugart (2001: 183); the values range from 0 to 2, where 2 stands for a system with maximally strong incentives for candidate campaigning.

All in all, the Finnish electoral system contains an interesting mix of collective and individual incentives. Attention must therefore be paid both to party campaigns and to the efforts of candidates.

Selecting candidates

Candidate-selection has been called 'the secret garden of politics' (Gallagher and Marsh 1988). True, the processes by which candidates are recruited, screened and chosen often take place far from the public eye, which has complicated the empirical study of candidate-nominations, especially in a comparative perspective. Still, research to date has produced sufficient empirical knowledge to establish certain general patterns. So, for instance, Lundell has concluded that 'Nordic parties apply

Table 3.5: Incentives for individual campaigns in preferential voting systems

Country	Index value
Ireland	1.57
Malta	1.57
Finland	1.43
Belgium 1999–> [a]	0.80
Austria 1994–>	0.80
Switzerland	0.80
Denmark	0.80
The Netherlands	0.60
Belgium–>1995	0.60
Austria–>1990	0.60
Luxembourg	0.60
Sweden 1998–>	0.60

[a] A year indicates that the position of individual candidates has changed in the system.
Sources: Andeweg and Irwin 2005; Lundell 2005; Shugart 2001; Electoral Systems and the Personal Vote (http://thedata.harvard.edu/dvn/dv/jwjohnson/faces/study/StudyPage.xhtml?globalId=hdl:1902.1/17901).

decentralised selection methods, whereas candidate selection in southern Europe is centralised' (2004: 39). In other words, candidate-selection in Scandinavia is largely left to local party meetings or selection committees; whereas party leaders or national party committees have a much stronger say in southern Europe.

Finland represents the Nordic pattern: candidate-nomination is a process managed by the district and local organisations of the parties. The district organisation that in most cases coincides with an electoral district determines the number of candidates that the party will field in the district in a given election. Most of the candidates for nomination are proposed by the local party branches; but 30 party members in the same district or 15 members of the same local branch can join forces to propose candidates without a formal decision by a party organisation. In practice, at least nine out of ten candidates are proposed by local party branches. One-fourth, or more of local party branches, normally propose candidates (Paloheimo 2007: 316). The decision on who gets nominated is made in a vote among party members in the district. A 1988 change in the electoral law gives the district organisation a right to deviate from the result of this ballot but it may not alter more than one-fourth of the candidate list. District organisations use this right in order to balance the ticket, so that it contains an optimal mix in terms of the gender, locality and social group of the candidates (Paloheimo 2007: 316).

Up until the late 1960s, there was little legal regulation of candidate-nomination procedures; systematic evidence about the selection of candidates from earlier periods is scarce. It is, however, safe to say that the central party organisations had a stronger say before than after 1969. That year, the widespread practice of running the same candidate in several districts was prohibited by the Law on the Election of Parliamentary Representatives.[4] The parties had previously used prominent politicians to attract voters to their lists in several districts, although each candidate could of course gain a seat in one district only. The decision to field candidates in this fashion was of a nature that required the involvement of central party actors. Consequently, when this practice was banned, the central party machinery lost an important channel of influence. A 1975 amendment to the law regulated candidate-nominations more generally. It obliged parties to either have explicit rules on candidate-nomination or, in the absence of such rules, to conduct a secret and equal nomination ballot among party members in the district. An additional amendment in1998 made the ballot compulsory whenever there were more proposed candidates than the party was going to nominate in a district. Over time, parties have increasingly begun to practice nomination ballots, whether or not required by law (Paloheimo 2007: 312–15).

What do we know about the individuals who are nominated as candidates for parliament? To begin with, over the long term they have become *more numerous*. In the first elections arranged in independent Finland (1919) there were 668 candidates. In the 2000s, the figure has been over two thousand. As the number of seats to be filled has been 200 from the beginning, competition among candidates is on an entirely different level today from that of the first elections.

---

4. *See* http://www.finlex.fi/sv/laki/alkup/1969/19690391

In 1919, almost a third of all candidates were elected; today, less than 10 per cent win seats. However, the ratio between candidates and eligible voters has remained basically unaltered: there is one candidate approximately per two thousand voters and this has been the case from the very beginning (Paloheimo 2007: 312). The rise in the number of candidates, therefore, primarily reflects population growth.

The proportion of *women* among candidates has grown considerably. Throughout the era of universal suffrage, Finland has been among those countries in which the share of women holding elective office is highest (Ruostetsaari 2000: 57–60; Mateo Diaz 2005; Karvonen *et al*. 1995: 345). Still, immediately after the Second World War, women continued to make up but a small fraction of elected representatives. Table 3.6 shows the growth in the numbers of women among candidates as well as among those elected.

The proportion of women among candidates has more than tripled in the post-war era and the same goes for elected MPs. The rise to prominence of the True Finns in 2011 halted the growth of women candidates but did not stop the linear rise of the proportion of women among elected MPs. One-third of the True Finn candidates in 2011 were women. The other extreme is represented by the Greens. They fielded 52 per cent women candidates, which matches the share of women in the population at large.[5]

As in all post-industrial countries, the *age structure* of the Finnish population has undergone rapid and marked changes. The age distribution among candidates for parliament has changed, too, but, as Table 3.7 shows, this change is not as marked as among the population at large.

In the past three decades, the proportion of the youngest third of the Finnish voting-age population has declined from nearly half to a third; while the proportion of voters aged sixty years or more has grown from a little over one-fifth to nearly a third. The middle-aged group has changed the least. As for candidates, this middle group aged 40–59 years has consistently been over-represented. However, the 2011 election saw a fairly clear change in this regard, as the share of both the youngest and the oldest age cohorts increased. The True Finns ran a fairly high number of older candidates, with 24 per cent of their candidates aged sixty years or more. Again, the Greens represent the other extreme; the youngest age cohort was clearly over-represented (47 per cent) among Green candidates. As for elected

Table 3.6: Proportion of women (%) among candidates for parliament and elected MPs, in selected years

	1948	1954	1966	1975	1987	1995	2003	2011
Candidates	12.1	15.2	16.0	24.2	36.0	39.1	39.8	39.0
MPs	12.0	15.0	16.5	23.0	31.5	33.5	37.5	42.5

Source: Electoral statistics.

5.   http://www.stat.fi/til/evaa/2011/evaa_2011_2011-04-29_kat_001_en.html

Table 3.7: Age distribution (%) among candidates for parliament, voting-age population and among elected MPs, in selected years

	Age groups		
	18–39	40–59	60+
Candidates			
1983	38.3	53.0	8.7
1995	33.7	59.1	7.2
2003	29.6	57.6	12.8
2011	34.6	48.0	17.4
Voting-age population			
1983	47.4	30.0	22.6
1995	39.2	36.1	24.7
2003	35.6	38.0	26.4
2011	33.2	34.5	32.3
Elected MPs			
1983	33.5	57.5	9.0
1995	15.5	83.0	1.5
2003	19.5	68.5	12.0
2011	24.5	61.5	14.0

tSources: Paloheimo 2007: 325; http://www.stat.fi/til/evaa/2011/evaa_2011_2011-04-29_kat_001_ en.html (Statistics Finland); data provided by Heikki Paloheimo.

MPs, the middle-aged group has also been overrepresented throughout the period, although the degree of this overrepresentation has varied from election to election.

Parliamentary candidates have consistently had a higher level of *education and income* than the voting-age population at large; for elected MPs, these differences are still more pronounced. Throughout the 1990s and 2000s, a college-level education has been about three times more common among candidates than in the entire population. As for economic status, the average income-level of candidates has been about 1.7 times that of the average among eligible voters; elected MPs earn about twice as much as candidates at large. The differences do not seem to be growing. In fact, with the rising level of education among the population at large they may even shrink in the future (Paloheimo 2007: 326–7, 350; http://www.stat.fi/til/evaa/2011/evaa_2011_2011-04-29_kat_001_en.html). As for parties, Green and Conservative candidates in 2011 had the highest level of education; True Finn candidates the lowest. As might be expected, Conservative candidates had the highest average income, whereas it was lowest among Left Alliance, True Finn and Christian Democrat candidates.

All in all, Finnish candidates and MPs were not particularly representative of the population at large a generation or two ago. They were overwhelmingly male, they were middle-aged to a much higher degree than the voters and they were better educated and earned more. When parties pick candidates today, many of these discrepancies persist but changes can also be noted. The proportion of women has grown dramatically. Younger and older candidates seem to be gaining at the expense of the middle group. The educational gap may also be diminishing, albeit slowly. Candidates and elected MPs will probably continue to form a social elite of sorts in the future, but the differences between them and the people may very well become less clear.

The conditions for competition between parties

The most politically important quantitative change in the structure of party competition concerns the relative strength of the largest parties in the Finnish party system. Through most of the post-war period, there have been three parties that are clearly larger than others in terms of vote and seat shares. In the 1950s and 1960s, these parties were the Social Democrats, the Agrarian/ Centre Party and the Left Party. However, as of the 1980s the decline of the Left Party has been rapid, while the Conservatives have emerged as one of the largest parties. Until the 2011 election, the Centre Party, the Social Democrats and the Conservatives competed for the position as the largest party. The long-term trend is for these parties to become increasingly equal in size, which is evident from Figure 3.2.

The decline of the socialist party family is the single most marked long-term change in the Finnish party system. The populists display somewhat of a roller-coaster pattern and their electoral strength is more or less a mirror image of the fluctuations in the vote shares of the Centre Party. The support of the Greens

Figure 3.2: Size of party families in Finnish parliament since the 1950s, decennial averages of vote shares (%)

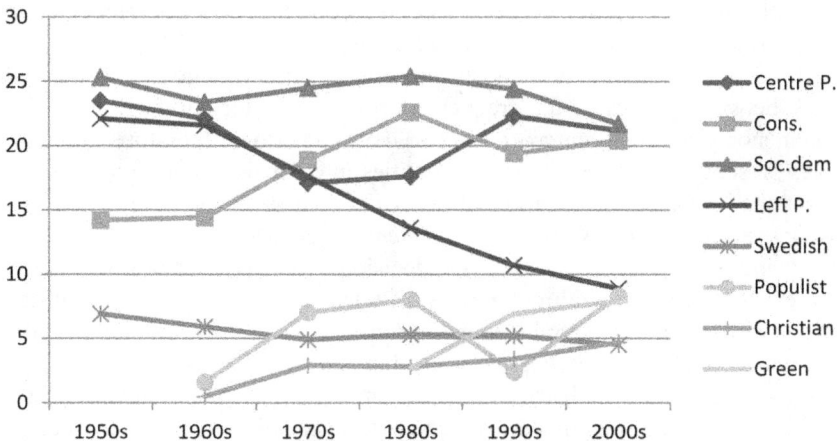

Note: Includes those party families that won seats in the 2011 elections.

displays an upward trend, as does, albeit slightly, that of the Christian Democrats. The Swedish Party has lost a couple of percentage points over the past six decades.

The changes in strength among the largest parties have had profound effects on the arithmetic of parliamentary politics in Finland. This development will be examined in detail in Chapter Four. Here, it is sufficient to note a few fundamental traits. In order to form majority cabinets in Finland, coalitions between several parties are necessary. As three of the parties have been much larger than the others, any majority cabinet must include at least two of the three largest parties. Moreover, the pattern of alternation between left-wing and bourgeois governments found in many countries is not practicable in Finland. At the beginning of the post-war period, the Left Party and the Social Democrats were bitter political rivals. Since the 1970s, the socialist camp has shrunk so drastically that a coalition between the two left-wing parties is insufficient to provide a basis for a viable majority government.

All of this has implications for how the parties forge their electoral strategies. Naturally, as everywhere else, vote maximisation is the key. The larger a party, the better are its chances of being included in the government; in fact, the crucial task of the cabinet *formateur* goes to the leader of the party that has the highest number of seats in the newly elected parliament. On the other hand, if parties aspire to be included in the next cabinet they have to present themselves in a way that does not alienate any of the other possible cabinet parties. As will be shown in Chapter Four, Finnish parties have become highly flexible in their coalition strategies. There are few, if any, combinations of parties that are entirely out of the question.

This coalitional flexibility is clearly visible in the way parties run their electoral campaigns. True, they do criticise each other. All the while, they normally refrain from attacking each other too fiercely or presenting demands that rule them out from particular coalitions. Party campaigns therefore tend to become vague and focus on generalities. Often it is extremely difficult for voters to tell the main parties apart on the basis of their campaign slogans and programme presentations. Populist parties – the Rural Party in the 1970s and 1980s and the True Finns today – form an exception to this rule thanks to their colourful campaigns and more outright attacks against 'established parties'.

An additional feature of Finnish electoral politics that goes to temper the rivalry between parties is the frequent occurrence of electoral alliances. This phenomenon known as *apparentement* in the international literature means that parties present themselves as separate entities in campaigns but their vote totals are summed when the allocation of seats is calculated (Colomer 2004: 547). From a strategic point of view, *apparentement* only makes sense in multi-member constituencies. In the Finnish case, the decision about whether or not to engage in an electoral alliance with other party lists is made by the party district-level organisation. The party central leadership can, of course, make recommendations about with whom district parties should or should not form alliances but the formal authority rests with the district organisation (Paloheimo and Sundberg 2009: 211–12). This means that the occurrence of electoral alliances varies from district to district. Over time, electoral alliances have become increasingly common. They are particularly important to the smallest parties, whose only chance to win seats is, often, to participate in electoral alliances. Until recent years, electoral alliances were practised only by non-socialist parties. In recent elections, however, even the Left Alliance and the Social Democrats have begun to make electoral alliances to a certain extent.

Parties take great pains to explain that electoral alliances are 'technical', not ideological in nature. Nevertheless, the increase in their numbers is indicative of the attenuation of ideological rivalries among the parties. These alliances, in their turn, make aggressive party campaigning less likely. A party that attacks another party at the national level while at the same time being part of an electoral alliance with it, in one or several electoral districts, does not appear particularly credible.

Competition between candidates

Until the early 1960s, parties were clearly the main actors in electoral campaigns. Most campaign finance was channelled through the parties and party messages and advertising formed the backbone of the electoral campaign. From then on, the individualisation inherent in the Finnish electoral system has become increasingly evident. Today, individual candidates are much more salient than half a century ago and the money they raise is more significant than that channelled by the parties centrally (Sundberg 1995: 56–9; Mattila and Sundberg 2012: 232–4).

As candidates are nominated officially by the district organisations of parties, all candidates have the formal endorsement of their party. Moreover, parties do support candidate campaigns organisationally and financially as well. However, for all candidates who make a serious effort to be elected, their personal support-groups – which are not part of the party organisation – are much more important. It is these support-groups that raise most of the money spent by the candidates and it is they who decide on individual campaign strategy and organise and run the day-to-day campaign operations. In a study on the 1999 electoral campaign in the Pirkanmaa district, Ruostetsaari and Mattila report that the average size of support-groups was 22 members; for elected candidates it was more than 70 (Ruostetsaari and Mattila 2002: 98).

As was stressed above, the list system used in Finland tempers overt intra-party rivalry among candidates; it is in the interest of all candidates that their list attracts as many votes as possible. Still, candidates on the same party list are, objectively speaking, each other's competitors. Whoever wins the highest number of personal votes will be elected first from his or her list and this makes the election of other candidates more uncertain. Parties and candidates normally know fairly well how many seats a list can win in a constituency. The appearance of a new candidate with a strong popular following therefore endangers the position of other leading candidates – frequently including incumbent representatives. When the fate of incumbent MPs in elections since 1962 is examined, several rather stable patterns can be noted. Of the 200 MPs, approximately 170 run for re-election. Of these, roughly 40 fail to gain re-election. The better part of these – 55–60 per cent – lose to an intra-party competitor, while the rest fail to gain seats due to losses to other party lists.[6]

Whether a candidate is an incumbent or a 'challenger', it is of vital importance to cultivate one's image among the voters. A candidate known by many voters – either personally or through the media – stands a better chance of election than less well known candidates. Incumbent MPs must visit their electoral districts frequently and strive for positive publicity through the media.[7] Challengers must make themselves known to the public – that is, if they are not well known before they decide to become candidates. The importance of personal reputation and publicity has, in fact, created a long-standing phenomenon that is often mentioned critically when Finnish politics is discussed. That is, the role of *celebrity candidates*, individuals with little or no previous political experience whose public profile as entertainers, athletes or media personalities gives them a publicity advantage.

Parties increasingly like to field celebrity candidates on their lists, simply because these individuals immediately increase the general attention paid to the lists (Arter 2009: 22). It is sometimes suggested that Finnish elections have become 'Americanised' due to the role of celebrity candidates and that the quality of Finnish politics is threatened by this phenomenon (Petersson *et al.* 1999: 137–8). Although a few such candidates do manage to win seats at most elections, the phenomenon is much less important politically than suggested by the media attention that it attracts. Celebrities remain quantitatively marginal in parliament at large. Moreover, they either develop into serious politicians or decide to leave the scene after one parliamentary period.

In fact, a much more pertinent criticism of the electoral system – rather than that it turns celebrities into politicians – is that it lures politicians to become celebrities. The need to cultivate one's public image easily convinces MPs that any publicity is welcome. Their willingness to participate in TV shows and other forms of entertainment, often not even remotely related to political issues, is considerable.

Two-level campaigning

Several factors have, increasingly, compelled parties to opt for cautious, middle-of-the road strategies in their collective electoral campaigns. The intensity of the traditional cleavages defining the electorates of the various parties has declined. Voters increasingly resemble each other in terms of socio-economic status and fundamental values. Electoral volatility has risen. Parties must be careful not to alienate potential coalition partners in a parliamentary culture where, basically, no combination of parties is entirely out of the question.

---

6. *Sources:* for 1962–2003, Paloheimo 2007: 334; for 2007–11, http://www.tilastokeskus.fi/til/evaa/tau_en.html and http://www.eduskunta.fi/thwfakta/hetekau/hex/hxent.htm

7. The kind of constituency work that generates casework and designated constituency offices for representatives such as in Ireland and in the US is, however, not common in Finland (Arter 2011).

Parties face the demanding task of attracting votes from as many quarters as possible, while, at the same time, not alienating their core constituencies. In this endeavour, it seems that they increasingly resort to what might be called two-level campaigning. Party campaigns tend to remain vague and address generalities. Individual campaigns, by contrast, frequently focus on specific issues on which candidates take clear and even controversial stands. It is not uncommon that the campaign of a, say, Left Alliance candidate appears much more left-wing-oriented than that of the party itself; and the same may go for Green, Conservative or Centre Party candidates. Candidates can design their messages to attract targeted audiences in their districts and these messages need not be reflected in the national party campaigns.

The systematic study of individual campaigns is a demanding task and longitudinal data of the kind that would corroborate this impression are, unfortunately, not available. For recent elections, however, the data provided by candidate selectors presents interesting analytical avenues. In connection with electoral campaigns, major media in Finland create online candidate selectors, in which candidates are asked to answer a large number of political questions, in order for citizens to be able to find candidates matching their preferences as closely as possible. Analysis of the 200 elected MPs in online candidate selectors (Paloheimo *et al.* 2005; Reunanen and Suhonen 2009) presents interesting results. Although the present party system does not seem entirely outdated, there are numerous unexpected overlaps and inconsistencies between the parties, in terms of where their candidates stand on various issues. In fact, if there were no organised parties before an election and parties were created based on candidate opinions once the new parliament constitutes itself, the party structure might look quite different from the existing one (Paloheimo *et al.* 2005; Reunanen and Suhonen 2009).

The two-level mode of campaigning gives the parties a chance to have their cake and eat it. The vague catch-all strategy of parties does not endanger their bargaining position in the face of upcoming negotiations on cabinet-formation. Targeted individual campaigns may attract voters who would not be satisfied with the glittering generalities of a party campaign.

Parties in parliament: Turnover among legislators

The role of parties in parliament is to provide a basis for government, to support or oppose it and to pass legislation mainly based on bills submitted by government. This is the core of parliamentary politics. In most parliamentary systems, policy initiative rests with the cabinet in normal times. Only when cabinets are weak and transient may the parliament itself take the centre-stage in policy-making. This goes for Finland as well, which is why the role of parties in the parliamentary process will be discussed in Chapter Four, in which the focus is on the role of and relations between parliament and government.

The present section will provide data on continuity and change in parliamentary party groups on one point only. Focus will be on turnover: what is the extent of change in who represents the various parties from election to election?

The implications of high versus low turnover are potentially far-reaching for parties and parliamentary politics: 'Changes in personnel, even when party control of the legislature does not change, can lead to dramatic shifts in policy position' (Matland and Studlar 2004: 88). If most representatives have held their positions over extended periods of time, their behaviour and collective party positions on policy have had time to adjust to each other. Extensive and rapid changes in parliamentary personnel may, on the other hand, create pressure towards altered policy stands and present challenges to established power structures within the parliamentary groups of political parties.

Matland and Studlar have presented data on legislative turnover in 25 stable democracies during a twenty-year period in the late twentieth century. Portugal, Greece, Canada and Spain were found to be countries with high turnover levels. The other extreme was represented by the UK, (West) Germany and the US. Finland, along with its Scandinavian neighbours, displayed turnover rates near the mean for all countries studied (Matland and Studlar 2004: 94). Figure 3.3 shows the patterns of turnover in the Finnish parliament since 1962.

If turnover is operationalised as the opposite of the incumbent re-election rate, then turnover in Finland in the last half-century displays four peaks: 1970, 1983, 1995 and 2011. As can be expected, these elections are characterised by fairly large changes in the relative size of parliamentary parties. Three of these instances – 1970, 1983 and 2011 – represent electoral peaks for Finnish populism. The 1995 election produced the best election outcome for Finnish social democracy since the Second World War. Finland had just gone through the worst economic depression since the early 1930s while the Social Democrats had been in parliamentary opposition.

Figure 3.3: Turnover in the Finnish parliament since 1962 (number of elected MPs)

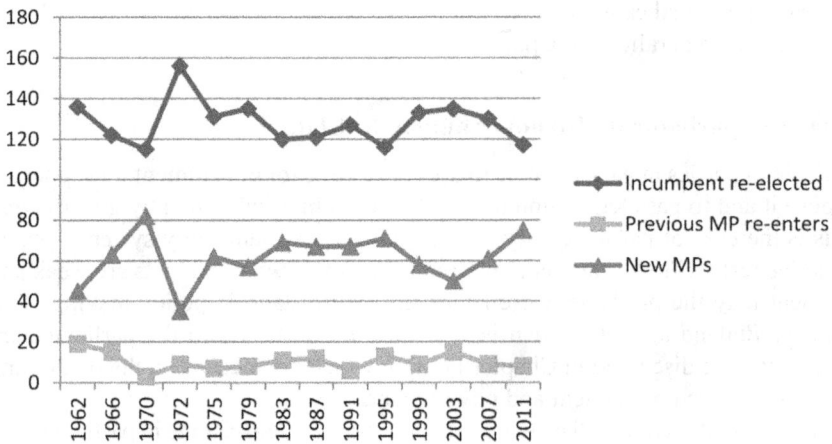

Sources: Paloheimo 2007: 351; http://www.eduskunta.fi

The figure also shows that turnover is related to the entrance of freshmen MPs to parliament. There are always some previous MPs who re-enter parliament after a break but their share has consistently remained under 10 per cent and can, therefore, not account for major shifts in turnover.

Overall, there is no clear trend over time in legislative turnover in Finland. The pattern is one of fluctuation rather than growth or decline. The peaks represent cases of party-political protest. When voters protest by rallying behind a party to a greater degree than normal, this produces a higher turnover among members of parliament. When large numbers of new MPs are elected, these also carry with them a message of political discontent from their voters. A parliamentary period preceded by an election that produces a high level of turnover, therefore, frequently marks a period of more colourful parliamentary debate than normal.

Conclusion

The rapid and thorough transformation of Finnish society depicted in Chapter Two has had clearly visible effects on Finnish parties. They have adjusted their ideologies and campaign messages; they have met with increasing competition from new parties; they have suffered considerable losses in terms of party membership and local organisations; they have become financially dependent on the state and they have struggled, with varying success, to find alternative sources of economic support; they have adjusted their candidate-recruitment to growing demands of gender equality; they have, while softening much of their campaign rhetoric towards other parties worked to target specific voters, often through clearly more pointed individual candidate campaigns; and they have been faced with repeated waves of heightened legislative turnover as a result of protest voting by parts of the electorate.

These features seem to match the expectations created by the late and thorough transformation of Finnish society. It should be remembered, however, that Finland shares many, if not most, of these features with other stable parliamentary democracies. This is particularly true of the formation of new parties and the decline of party membership; on these points, Finland stands out as an average rather than extreme case. It is on the ideological side, in the way parties present themselves in their programmes and campaigns, that the change in Finland seems particularly marked. The decline of ideological polarisation and the contemporary cautiousness of most party campaigns represent a remarkable change in Finnish party behaviour compared to the early post-war decades – but also in comparison with most other west-European democracies.

Finally, this chapter has highlighted a phenomenon that is hardly unique but still a characteristic feature of Finnish politics: the recurrent waves of populist protest in electoral and parliamentary politics. Populism seems to come and go; today, Finland is experiencing the third marked period of populist protest. It does not seem far-fetched to see this pattern as a reaction against many of the features in Finnish party politics surveyed in this chapter.

Chapter Four

The Politics of Oversized Coalitions

In comparative studies of west European politics, Finland is frequently portrayed as a country with unstable cabinets:

> At the more 'stable' end of the spectrum we find Luxembourg, Britain, Austria, and Ireland. At the more 'unstable' end of the spectrum, with the shortest average cabinet durations, we find Italy, France, Finland, and Belgium. Countries with stable cabinets have governments that last, on average, about three years. Those with unstable cabinets have governments that tend to last about a year or even less (Gallagher *et al.* 2001: 366).

> [...] there is considerable cross-national variation in the number of cabinets. While Luxembourg has been a place of cabinet stability (with only 16 cabinets since the Second World War), Finland has had more than twice as many [...] (Müller *et al.* 2008: 8).

The above sources, along with many others, are, of course, quite accurate. Averages based on longitudinal analyses since WWII clearly indicate that governments in Finland have been short-lived in a west-European comparison. Often, however, averages conceal significant variation. As was shown above (*see* Chapter Two), important changes took place in Finnish parliamentary politics as of the early 1980s. From that time on, and in a stark contrast to the first three post-war decades, Finnish politics has been marked by two important features:

1. Cabinets have been stable: in the typical case, Finnish cabinets remain in office throughout the four-year parliamentary period.
2. All cabinets have the backing of a clear parliamentary majority: in fact, Finnish cabinets tend to be *oversized* (or *surplus*) majority coalitions, backed by clearly more than a mere arithmetical majority of the parties in parliament.

This chapter examines the causes and consequences of this major change in Finnish parliamentary politics. What were the most important forces behind the transition to the present form of coalition politics? How has it affected the parties and the relations between them? What strategies are available to parties, given the prevalence of oversized coalitions? How is policy determined and in what ways can parties act to further their political goals and the interests of their constituents? What is the role of the political opposition? How well do parties manage to control and direct the government bureaucracy, given the heterogeneous political makeup of cabinet coalitions? These are some of the queries addressed in this chapter.

Cabinets since WWII: an overview

Cabinets have indeed been a frequent phenomenon in Finland since the Second World War. Since the first post-war election in 1945, Finland has had no fewer than 43 cabinets.[1] Table 4.1 contains basic information about them.

Table 4.1: Cabinets in Finland, 1945–2011

Prime minister	Date of appointment	Duration in months	Party composition	Type of government
Paasikivi	April 1945	11	Lib, Swe, Agr, Soc Dem, Left P	Grand coalition
Pekkala	March 1946	28	Left P, Swe, Agr, Soc Dem	Majority coalition
Fagerholm I	July 1948	19	Soc Dem	Single-party minority
Kekkonen I	March 1950	10	Agr, Lib, Swe	Minority coalition
Kekkonen II	January 1951	8	Agr, Lib, Swe, Soc Dem	Majority coalition
Kekkonen III	September 1951	22	Agr, Swe, Soc Dem	Majority coalition
Kekkonen IV	July 1953	4	Agr, Swe	Minority coalition
Tuomioja	November 1953	5	–	Non-partisan
Törngren	May 1954	5	Swe, Agr, Soc Dem	Majority coalition
Kekkonen V	October 1954	16	Agr, Soc Dem	Majority coalition
Fagerholm II	March 1956	15	Soc Dem, Lib, Swe, Agr	Majority coalition
Sukselainen I	May 1957	6	Agr, Lib, Swe	Minority coalition
	As of July 1957		Agr, Lib	
	As of September 1957		Agr, Lib, Soc Dem fraction	
von Fieandt	November 1957	5	–	Non-partisan
Kuuskoski	April 1958	4	–	Non-partisan
Fagerholm III	August 1958	4	Soc Dem, Cons, Lib, Swe, Agr	Majority coalition
Sukselainen II	January 1959	30	Agr	Single-party minority
Miettunen I	July 1961	9	Agr	Single-party minority
Karjalainen I	April 1962	20	Agr, Cons, Lib, Swe	Majority coalition
Lehto	December 1963	9	–	Non-partisan

---

1. A new cabinet is considered to have been formed if at least one of the following criteria is fulfilled: a) there was a parliamentary election b) a new prime minister was appointed c) a cabinet's majority/minority status was altered. Minor reshuffles, including changes in party composition that did not alter a cabinet's majority/minority status, do not signify a 'new cabinet' (based on Nousiainen 2006: 355–7).

Table 4.1 (continued)

Prime minister	Date of appointment	Duration in months	Party composition	Type of government
Virolainen	September 1964	20	Agr, Cons, Lib, Swe	Majority coalition
Paasio I	May 1966	22	Soc Dem, Cent, Soc Dem fraction, Left P	Majority coalition
Koivisto I	March 1968	26	Soc Dem, Swe, Cent, Soc Dem fraction, Left P	Majority coalition
Aura I	May 1970	2	–	Non-partisan
Karjalainen II	July 1970	15	Cent, Lib, Swe, Left P	Majority coalition
	As of March 1971		Cent, Lib, Swe, Soc Dem	
Aura II	October 1971	4	–	Non-partisan
Paasio II	February 1972	6	Soc Dem	Single-party minority
Sorsa I	September 1972	33	Soc Dem, Lib, Swe, Cent	Majority coalition
Liinamaa	June 1975	6	–	Non-partisan
Miettunen II	November 1975	10	Cent, Lib, Swe, Soc Dem, Left P	Majority coalition
Miettunen III	September 1976	7	Cent, Lib, Swe	Minority coalition
Sorsa II	May 1977	24	Soc Dem, Lib, Cent, Swe, Left P	Majority coalition
	As of March 1978		Soc Dem, Lib, Cent, Left P	
Koivisto II	May 1979	33	Soc Dem, Swe, Cent, Left P	Majority coalition
Sorsa III	February 1982	14	Soc Dem. Swe, Cent, Left P	Majority coalition
	As of December 1982		Soc Dem, Lib, Swe, Cent	
Sorsa IV	May 1983	48	Soc Dem, Swe, Cent, Rural	Majority coalition
Holkeri	April 1987	48	Cons, Swe, Rural, Soc Dem	Majority coalition
	As of August 1990		Cons, Swe, Soc Dem	
Aho	April 1991	48	Cent, Cons, Swe, Chr Dem	Majority coalition
	As of April 1994		Cent, Cons, Swe	
Lipponen I	April 1995	48	Soc Dem, Cons, Swe, Green, Left P	Majority coalition

Table 4.1 (continued)

Prime minister	Date of appointment	Duration in months	Party composition	Type of government
Lipponen II	April 1999	48	Soc Dem, Cons, Swe, Green, Left P	Majority coalition
	As of May 2002		Soc Dem, Cons, Swe, Left P	
Jäätteenmäki	April 2003	2	Cent, Swe, Soc Dem	Majority coalition
Vanhanen I	June 2003	45	Cent, Swe, Soc Dem	Majority coalition
Vanhanen II	April 2007	38	Cent, Cons, Swe, Green	Majority coalition
Kiviniemi	June 2010	11	Cent, Cons, Swe, Green	Majority coalition
Katainen	June 2011	In office at the time of writing	Cons, Soc Dem, Left P, Green, Swe, Chr Dem	Majority coalition
As of April 2014			Cons, Soc Dem, Green, Swe, Chr Dem	

Key to party names:
Lib = Liberals; the Liberal Party alternative has been called, depending on the period, Progress Party, People's Party or Liberal People's Party; Swe = Swedish People's Party; Agr = Agrarian Union. Soc Dem = Social Democratic Party; Left P = Finnish People's Democratic League (1945–1990), Left Alliance since 1990; Cons = National Coalition Party; Soc Dem fraction = Internal fraction within the Social Democratic Party 1945–58, separate party 1959–1973; Cent = Centre Party; Rural = Finnish Rural Party (populists); Green = Green League; Chr Dem = Christian Democratic Party. *Sources:* Nousiainen 2006: 356–7; http://www.government.fi/tietoa-valtioneuvostosta/hallitukset/vuodesta-1917/tulokset/en.jsp?report_id=V2

Majority coalitions have always been the most common kind of Finnish cabinets but the pattern since the late 1970s is, nevertheless, strikingly different from earlier periods. As of 1977, Finland has had nothing but majority coalition cabinets. There have been minor cabinet reshuffles but these have concerned minor parties leaving cabinets; in no case has a reshuffle altered the majority status of a cabinet. Up until the late 1970s, by contrast, minority governments and non-partisan cabinets alternated with majority coalitions.

Cabinet duration has increased markedly. The mean duration of a Finnish cabinet 1945–2011 was slightly less than 19 months (median = 14.5 months). If the period is divided into two halves, with 1980 as the demarcation line, a different picture emerges. Between 1945 and 1979, the mean duration of a Finnish cabinet was 13 months (median = 10 months). Between 1980 and 2011, it was 35 months (median = 45 months). These figures can be compared with Saalfeld's (2008: 328) data on cabinet duration in western Europe 1945–99. According to him, the median cabinet duration in 17 west-European countries was 568 days, that is, approximately 19 months. Between 1945 and 1979, cabinet duration in Finland was clearly below this median value, whereas the corresponding figure for 1980–2011 was markedly higher.

While cabinet duration is a fair indicator of political stability, in fact, it underestimates the degree of coalition stability in Finland since the early 1980s. The more short-lived cabinets since that time do not signify a general crisis in coalition politics. In 1982, Mauno Koivisto resigned as prime minister after having been elected president. He was succeeded by Kalevi Sorsa, who was prime minister during the fourteen months that remained until the following election. Anneli Jäätteenmäki's resignation in 2003 did involve a heated political controversy but this was not concerned with the relations between the coalition parties but with her own actions during the preceding election campaign. She was replaced by Matti Vanhanen as party leader and prime minister, and the party composition, as well as the overall portfolio distribution of the cabinet, remained unchanged. Finally, Vanhanen himself decided to step down as party leader and prime minister in June, 2010. He was replaced by the new Centre party leader, Mari Kiviniemi, who was prime minister during the remaining 11 months before the 2011 election. Again, there was no political controversy between the coalition parties behind this change; nor did it entail any change in cabinet composition.[2] By contrast, the short-lived cabinets up until the late 1970s, were usually a sign of serious political instability. Cabinets resigned routinely due to internal controversies (Jansson 1992: 143–61). All in all, Finnish coalition politics during the past decades has displayed a remarkable degree of stability, compared to the chronic instability of the earlier post-war period.

The 1980s entailed still another important change in cabinet politics. From 1966 until the end of his presidency, Kekkonen kept the Conservatives outside the cabinet. To attain majority status, cabinets during this prolonged period therefore necessarily had to include both the Social Democrats and the Centre (previously Agrarian) Party. When Koivisto, as president, appointed the first Social Democratic–Conservative coalition in 1987, this signalled a new pattern in Finnish parliamentary coalitions. Since then, majority cabinets have always been based on co-operation between two of the three largest parties (Social Democrats, Conservatives and the Centre Party), with one or several minor parties added to the coalition (Myllymäki 2010: 329). The peculiar feature of these coalitions is that any of the three largest parties can join forces with any of the two other large parties. Consequently, there have been 'Red–Green' (Social Democrats plus Centre Party), 'Red–Blue' (Social Democrats plus Conservatives) as well as 'bourgeois' (Centre Party plus Conservatives) coalitions. As to the participation of the minor parties, the pattern is similarly unorthodox from an ideological point of view. To be sure, the Swedish People's Party stands out as a more or less permanent feature of Finnish cabinets. However, even such highly surprising combinations of parties as Lipponen's 'Rainbow Coalition' in 1999–2003 (Social Democrats, Conservatives, the Swedish People's Party, Greens

2. Kiviniemi, until then Minister of Administrative and Local Affairs, was succeeded by Centre Party MP Tapani Tölli in that capacity.

and the Left Party) and Katainen's 'six-pack' appointed in June 2011 (Conservatives, Social Democrats, the Left Alliance, the Greens, the Swedish Party and the Christian Democrats) have been among Finnish cabinet coalitions.

The Finnish propensity for oversized coalitions is evident when cabinet types acros west-European countries are compared. A database created by Guy-Erik Isaksson contains information about all cabinets appointed, subsequent to parliamentary elections, in 16 west-European countries during the period 1945–2009.[3] In Table 4.2, all post-election cabinets are classified either as one-party majority cabinets, one-party minority cabinets, minority coalitions, minimal-winning coalitions or oversized coalitions. Oversized coalitions are defined as cabinets that include more parties than necessary for securing a bare majority of the seats in parliament (Jungar 2000: 28–30).

Table 4.2: Post-election cabinets in 15 west-European countries plus Finland, according to type, 1945–2009 (% of cabinet-types)

Country	One-party majority	One-party minority	Minority coalition	Minimal-winning coalition	Oversized coalition	N
Austria	20	5	0	70	5	20
Belgium	5	5	0	60	30	20
Denmark	0	48	44	8	0	25
France	0	6	24	24	47	17
Germany	0	0	0	81	19	16
Greece	85	0	0	8	8	13
Iceland	0	5	0	84	11	19
Ireland	22	22	11	39	6	18
Italy	0	29	21	21	29	14
Luxembourg	0	0	8	92	0	12
The Netherlands	0	0	0	53	47	19
Norway	24	29	24	24	0	17
Portugal	25	42	0	33	0	12
Spain	40	60	0	0	0	10
Sweden	5	63	5	26	0	19
Average	*15*	*21*	*9*	*42*	*13*	*TOT. 251*
Finland 1945–2007	0	12	0	6	82	17
Finland 1945–1979	0	20	0	10	70	10
Finland 1983–2007	0	0	0	0	100	7

Note: Includes first post-election cabinets only. Percentages have been rounded off and may not add up to 100.
Source: Data provided by Guy-Erik Isaksson, Åbo Akademi

---

3. My thanks are due to Professor Guy-Erik Isaksson of Åbo Akademi for generously providing these data.

When post-election cabinets in western Europe are compared, Finland indeed stands out as the stronghold of surplus majority parliamentarism. Eight out of ten cabinets that took office after an election in Finland since WWII had the backing of clearly more than a mere majority in parliament. Throughout the post-war period, the typical post-election cabinet has been of this type. Up until the mid-1970s, however, these cabinets were frequently replaced by minority or caretaker cabinets in the period between elections. For the past three decades, by contrast, only oversized majority cabinets have occurred. Even compared to those other countries where surplus cabinets have been common, France and The Netherlands, Finland stands in a class of its own.

Stable oversized cabinets: Why?

Finland during the past three decades stands in contrast to Finland during earlier periods, thanks to cabinet stability. In a west-European comparison, it is the prevalence of surplus cabinets that makes Finland a case apart. Consequently, this section needs to answer two questions: Why stable? Why oversized?

The question about the causes of cabinet stability was in several respects highlighted in Chapter Two. It is easy to see that government stability goes hand in hand with a consensual approach in economic, labour-market and social affairs. If the organised interests in these fields can agree on broad and far-reaching solutions, cabinets must be stable enough to be able to carry out the legislative and budgetary reforms that are included in these agreements (Myllymäki 2010: 51). Corporatist consensualism thus ushered in a new era of stability and co-operation in parliamentary politics as well. Cabinet stability was the political equivalent of a spirit of co-operation that had already existed in labour-market affairs for about a decade.

The stabilisation of politics coincides with Mauno Koivisto's assumption of office as president after Urho Kekkonen's prolonged reign. This forms an important part of the causal background of increased cabinet stability in Finland. Kekkonen's leadership style did not encourage coalition parties to work out their differences and hammer out collective long-term policy commitments. As cabinet decisions were frequently bypassed by presidential interventions, and as the fate of individual ministers was decisively affected by the president's decisions, a spirit of aloofness and a lack of collective responsibility characterised cabinet politics (Tiihonen 1990: 235–40). Koivisto, by contrast, systematically encouraged cabinets to assume a central role. He restricted his policy role to Finland's external relations, thus leaving domestic politics to be dealt with in the parliamentary sphere (Majander 2013: 221–2). The parliamentarisation of Finnish politics, which culminated in the 2000 Constitution, was launched by Koivisto as president. He remained loyal to the cabinets he had appointed and stressed the primacy of cabinet and parliament in the political process. This stance both presupposed and enhanced cabinet stability. In order for cabinets to assume a central role in politics, they had to have a sufficient longevity to be able to carry out major policies. Knowing that they had the president's undivided support cabinet leaders and ministers were motivated to resolve internal differences and pursue long-term policy goals.

Why, then, are Finnish cabinets oversized? Why have more than eight out of ten cabinets, that have been appointed subsequent to a parliamentary election in Finland since 1945, contained more parties than necessary to secure a bare majority in parliament? Why has only this kind of cabinet occurred in the past three decades? According to Jungar (2002: 58), surplus-majority governments can be explained with reference either to necessity or opportunity. Necessity may pertain to the requirements on special legislative majorities, the highly undisciplined nature of parties or exceptional political circumstances. Surplus-majority government can also be seen as an opportunity for potential coalition parties, meaning that 'the expected utility of government is higher than the expected utility of opposition' (Jungar 2002: 58).

With the exception of the extreme left in the 1980s, Finnish parties can hardly be regarded as particularly fractionalised and undisciplined during the era of surplus-majority cabinets. Nor can one point to exceptional circumstances that would have called for governments of national unity or the like. However, the Finnish propensity for oversized coalitions is at least partly explained by a constitutional feature that was abolished two decades ago. All the way up to the early 1990s, a third (67 MPs) of the parliament could defer any legislative bill beyond the next election. This institutional feature constituted a potentially powerful weapon in the hands of the parliamentary minority. To be sure, only a minority of bills were the object of attempts to defer; between 1917 and 1986, for instance, deferral votes were annually carried out on roughly 6 per cent of the bills debated in parliament (Helander 1990: 38). However, the potential inherent in this constitutional device was probably more important than its actual use. A government with a bare majority in parliament ran the risk of constantly facing minorities strong enough to sabotage its policies by deferring them beyond the next election (Mattila 1997; Jungar 2000: 107).

The possibility of minorities deferring legislation had originally been introduced as a protective measure, to counter the adverse effects of majority democracy. In practice, it largely functioned as an incentive to create large parliamentary majorities, in order to assure the enactment of government policies. This could, of course, be achieved through *ad hoc* deals on individual policies. Without a firm majority of its own, however, a cabinet could not count on getting its policies enacted over the long run. Of the 16 majority cabinets that took office in Finland subsequent to parliamentary elections in 1945–2011, seven had the backing of at least two-thirds of the MPs. The remaining nine majority cabinets were based on 55–66 per cent of the parliamentary seats. Naturally, such numerically strong cabinets were much less vulnerable to attempts to defer legislation than cabinets that held a bare majority in parliament. Oversized cabinets can therefore be regarded as a safety measure in a particular institutional environment.

Paradoxically, Finland has continued to have oversized cabinets despite the abolition of the deferral mechanism in 1992–95. In 1992, the possibility that a third of the MPs could vote to defer legislation beyond the next election was abolished, except for laws that pertained to basic social security. Three years later, the mechanism was scrapped altogether (Jansson 2000: 26–7). Still, even after these reforms, Finnish cabinets have had the backing of 58–72 per cent of the MPs. Why do cabinets continue to be oversized, despite the disappearance of a basic constitutional feature that called for such cabinets?

Writing in the mid 1990s, Mikko Mattila (1997: 342–3) proposed that Finland may, in fact, be heading for less inclusive cabinets, although this was not yet clearly visible. Coalitional patterns take time to develop and they may also require considerable time to change. However, the validity of this hypothesis is called into question as no change has occurred during the nearly two decades since then. An alternative explanation is that oversized cabinets have come to be seen as part of the pattern of consensualism, which has been the overarching norm for more than three decades. As Jungar (2002: 78) writes, 'the surplus size of the government is no longer a response to an instrumental need to mobilise a broad majority, but rather an expression of a political culture in which compromise and cooperation are virtues'. Therefore, a move toward minimum-winning coalitions might be regarded as a rather radical break with a time-honoured practice.

There is, however, still another explanation that is possibly even more pertinent. The long years of oversized majority parliamentarism seem to have given rise to a political logic that is no less relevant than it used to be. The basic pattern of modern Finnish parliamentarism has been that two of the three major parties (Conservatives, Centre Party and Social Democrats) are in government while the third one forms the core of the opposition. However, the major parties rarely receive more than 20–25 per cent of the seats each. They therefore frequently need to include one of the smaller parties to gain a majority in parliament. Normally, however, the major cabinet parties choose to include more small parties than arithmetically necessary.[4] By doing this they avoid making any of their minor cabinet partners pivotal in the parliamentary game. By including one or two small parties that are not necessary for attaining a parliamentary majority, major parties effectively discipline their smaller cabinet partners. A small party that refuses to toe the line runs the risk of being declared expendable by its larger cabinet partners.

Minor cabinet parties must, from time to time, make painful choices between policy compromises and the prospect of being left out in the cold, therefore. Examples of this are not hard to find in recent Finnish politics. The two minor parties in the 2007–11 cabinet, the Swedish People's Party and the Greens, were compelled to concessions in their core areas. The Swedes decided to stay in government despite several measures that seemed highly problematic from the point of view of the Swedish minority and the position of Swedish as one of two national languages. In a similar vein, the Greens did not resign although the cabinet took a decision to expand the role of nuclear power in Finnish energy production, despite the fact that this caused an outcry among numerous Green supporters.

---

4. During the three decades of stable majority cabinets, only the one that was in office in 2003–7 included just one minor party (Swedish People's Party). As the two major parties combined (Centre Party and Social Democrats) held 108 of the 200 parliamentary seats, the Swedish Party was not pivotal. Four other cabinets have witnessed the departure of a minor party without losing their majority status, which very much proves the point in this section.

The 'earthquake election' of April 2011 relegated the Centre Party to a position as merely the fourth largest party in parliament. The two other traditional major parties held their ground somewhat better but they, too, suffered from the historic victory of the True Finns. Consequently, the cabinet-formation process after the election became a test of the basic coalitional pattern in Finnish politics. The negotiations indeed proved difficult and in fact broke down once. Still, the government that emerged in June was 'very Finnish'. Its core consisted of the Conservative and the Social Democratic parties, flanked by no fewer than four small parties. This ideologically highly unorthodox coalition commanded 124 of the 200 seats in parliament. With the exit of the Left Alliance in April 2014, the parliamentary backing of the Katainen cabinet was reduced to 111 – still a clear majority.

Like most political phenomena, oversized majority parliamentarism is explicable in terms of several factors: institutions, political tradition and rational calculation among parties. As the main institutional impetus behind oversized cabinets is long gone, it is quite possible that majority cabinets with a narrower parliamentary base may become more frequent. Still, as was shown above, a certain political equilibrium continues to support oversized cabinets in Finland. In terms of internal power relations among cabinet parties, oversized cabinets are not necessarily less 'rational' than minimum-winning cabinets. Giving a minor party one or two cabinet posts is certainly a concession on the part of the larger parties. On the other hand, if this secures a solid majority in parliament and decisively reduces the 'blackmail' potential of minor parties, it is, understandably, a potentially palatable alternative for major cabinet parties. A second motive behind the inclusion of small parties is that they can function as mediators in conflicts between the two main cabinet parties. Should only two parties form the government, the risk that internal disagreements escalate into serious intra-coalition conflicts would probably be much higher. Finally, major parties may sometimes deem it strategically wiser to co-opt a minor party, rather than giving it free rein in opposition; a case of 'keep your friends close and your enemies closer'.

The life and times of Finnish cabinets

Cabinets are formed, they govern and they are terminated. This is the basic 'life cycle' of the executive in parliamentary systems (Müller *et al.* 2008: 10). Each of these main phases presupposes or contains several elements. Someone must be chosen as government *formateur*. Agreement has to be reached about which parties will be included in the new cabinet. These parties must agree on the main features of government policy, either in the shape of a formal government programme or as a set of main policy guidelines to be followed. The distribution of portfolios between cabinet parties must be determined and the individuals who will hold the various portfolios must be selected. Depending on the constitutional blueprint and previous practice, the formal appointment of the cabinet as a collective, and the ministers as individuals, will then normally follow.

The way the cabinet governs similarly varies according to constitutional features and national practices. Some cabinets are prime-minister-centred; others are more egalitarian, with the prime minister as *primus inter pares* (Sartori 1994: 101–20). Some cabinets work through internal committees, other perform their main duties at general cabinet meetings. In some systems parliament has an active part in decision-making; in others it stays on the side-lines. The variation is almost unlimited.

Cabinets are terminated either due to an election or prematurely. They can be voted out of office through a vote of no confidence by the parliamentary majority, or they can resign due to internal disagreements. Their resignation may be contingent on an actor or institution outside the parliamentary sphere, usually the president, in the case of a republic. In some systems, calling an early election is an active instrument in the hands of the prime minister; in some others it is exceptional or even impossible.

All these phases and aspects of a cabinet's life cycle have been affected by the constitutional transition from a semi-presidential to an almost pure parliamentary system that was completed in Finland when the new constitution was enacted in 2000. It is necessary, therefore, to highlight this constitutional-reform process before presenting the central features of contemporary cabinet politics in Finland.

Constitutional change: From semi-presidential to parliamentary rule

The Finnish constitution that was in force from 1919 to 2000 (Act 94/1919 with subsequent amendments) defined popular sovereignty and parliamentarism as central principles of government. According to Paragraph 2, public power was vested in the people who were represented by the parliament. The cabinet had to have the confidence of the parliament and its members were answerable to parliament in both political and judicial terms (Paragraphs 36 and 43).

The constitution did not, however, provide for unlimited parliamentary sovereignty. Quite the contrary: executive power was divided between an elected president and the cabinet responsible before parliament. Reading the list of presidential powers, in fact, conveys an impression of a strongly president-dominated system. According to the constitution, the President of the Republic

- Appointed and dismissed cabinets and individual ministers;
- Had the right to dissolve the parliament and call for early elections;
- Could convene extraordinary sessions of the parliament;
- Presented government bills to parliament;
- Ratified laws approved by parliament;
- Issued decrees;
- Appointed high judges and senior civil servants;
- Led Finnish foreign policy;
- Was the supreme commander of the armed forces; and
- Granted pardons and citizenship.

This dualism in the Finnish constitution was a result of a political compromise in the young Republic of Finland immediately after WWI. Parties and groups on the centre-left favoured pure parliamentary rule, whereas the right argued for monarchy. The attempt to establish a monarchical order having failed, the right reluctantly settled for a republican form of government. As a result of conservative suspicions against parliamentarism, however, the 1919 Constitution provided for a president with far-reaching powers, independent of the will of the parliament. The aim was to create a counterweight to the potentially radical role of a parliament elected by universal suffrage (Arter 1987: 40–1).

There is often a discrepancy between the blueprint and the actual application of a constitution. In the Finnish case, it took four decades before the full force of the president's constitutional powers manifested itself in politics. Until then – to use Dag Anckar's (2000: 11) apt characterisation – the president's powers were like a buffet table, from which presidents could choose functions and roles to suit their particular tastes (*see also* Laakso 1975: 208–63). With the consolidation of Urho Kekkonen's power from the early 1960s on (*see* Chapter Two), these powers began to be used to their fullest extent. To quote Anckar once more: as a guest at the buffet table, Kekkonen was a *gourmand* (Anckar 2000). Not only did he utilise his constitutional powers maximally; he also adopted an activist stance in matters outside his constitutionally defined domain. Jaakko Nousiainen has summed up Kekkonen's presidential leadership style in a way which deserves to be quoted at some length:

> [...] Kekkonen stretched [the presidential authority] from the core areas to wider and wider circles of influence. He used his presidential regulative powers in a very personal way: he selected prime ministers, pushed parties into coalitions, forced governments to resign, appointed non-partisan presidential cabinets and dissolved parliaments. On the policy-making side certain behavioural rules were established: the president had the right to be informed about important matters, the right to take initiatives, and the right to exercise his veto. The powers also applied to matters belonging to the cabinet's formal jurisdiction. In the 1960s and 1970s the president was the highest regulator and guarantor of consensual national policies. He broke the constitutional isolation by penetrating the administrative structures and making allies in competing parties [...]. In appointing ministers and the supreme officer corps, Kekkonen created an invisible network of dependencies and loyalties. The use of formal presidential power gave rise to contacts behind the scenes and to 'anticipated reactions' among central bureaucracies. This was the only period during which the balance of the dyarchy was seriously shaken. The cabinet's 'autonomy potential' was noticeably reduced and in many ways it became president-dependent (Nousiainen 2000: 343).

In Heikki Paloheimo's words, at the heyday of the Kekkonen presidency 'presidential power in Finland [...] was clearly greater than that of US president' (Paloheimo 2001: 100).

The change in leadership style as of Koivisto was followed by a series of constitutional reforms from the late 1980s on. The president's autonomous right to appoint ministers was curtailed, by ordaining that he would have to hear the opinion the parliamentary party groups before making an appointment. The president's power to dissolve parliament was eliminated, by a clause according to which his decision would be tied to the initiative of the prime minister. The president could no longer use dissolution as an active instrument; he could merely disagree with the prime minister by not following the prime minister's initiative. At the same time, this change eliminated the president's power to dismiss a government by calling for early elections. Moreover, the president's powers of veto were limited and the range of presidential appointments reduced. Finally, the enormously important field of national EU policy was defined as the cabinet's prerogative.

Parallel with these reforms, it became increasingly evident that the constitution was in need of a complete overhaul. The partial reforms that had been gradually introduced over the years created pressures towards a structural rationalisation and a linguistic revision of the entire blueprint of the constitution. At the same time, certain constitutional issues remained unresolved and required further political negotiations and preparatory work. An authoritative constitutional commission was therefore appointed in 1997; it presented its report, including a draft constitution, in 1998. On the basis of this proposal, a bill containing a new constitution was presented to parliament and adopted almost unanimously after the 1999 parliamentary election. The new Finnish constitution went into effect on 1 March 2000.

The 2000 Finnish Constitution incorporates the reforms of the preceding decade. At the same time, it introduces elements of central importance that had not been agreed upon earlier and that signify major changes. Above all, the crucial powers connected to government-formation are now decisively tied to parliament (Myllymäki 2010: 186–8); the president's role is purely formal:

The Parliament elects the Prime Minister, who is thereafter appointed to the office by the President of the Republic. The President appoints the other Ministers in accordance with a proposal made by the Prime Minister.

Before the Prime Minister is elected, the groups represented in the Parliament negotiate on the political programme and composition of the Government (Section 61).[5]

The president's role in legislative processes has similarly been reduced to a minimum. His/her power to change the content of government bills has been all but eliminated. The suspensive veto that previously enabled the president to delay legislation is today toothless, as parliament may immediately override it. The presidential power to issue decrees has been transferred to cabinet. Foreign policy, formerly an exclusive presidential prerogative, is now conducted by the president 'in co-operation with the government' (Section 93). Finally, the president's powers of appointment have been reduced to a very limited group of top civil servants.

All in all, the gradual process that culminated in the 2000 Constitution transformed the Finnish political system from a semi-presidential regime sometimes bordering on pure presidentialism to a basically purely parliamentary form of government. The remaining powers of appointment and the president's role

---

5.   An English translation of the 2000 constitution can be accessed at http://www.finlex.fi/en/laki/kaannokset/1999/en19990731.pdf

in foreign policy[6] continue to be debated and are likely to be eliminated in coming constitutional revisions. Table 4.3 presents a summary of the constitutional-reform process in Finland up until the 2000 Constitution.

Table 4.3: Constitutional division of power at three points in time

Powers	Old constitution 1919–late 1980s	Gradual reform 1990s	New constitution 2000
Government-formation	President	President	Parliament; president's role purely formal
Government-resignation	Parliament or prime minister, or president by dissolving parliament	Parliament or prime minister	Parliament or prime minister
Dissolution of parliament	President	President, upon initiative by prime minister	President, upon initiative by prime minister
Government bills	President may alter	President may alter	President's power basically eliminated
Legislative veto	President may postpone bills beyond next election	President may postpone until next legislative session	Parliament may immediately override veto
Legislative decrees	President and cabinet	President and cabinet	Cabinet
Appointments	President appoints considerable number of senior civil servants; other personnel appointed by cabinet or ministries	Number of appointments by president reduced	President appoints very limited number of top officials
Foreign policy leadership	President	President	President, in co-operation with cabinet
EU policy		Cabinet	Cabinet

Note: The table draws heavily on Paloheimo 2003: 225.

---

6. In 2012, the Constitution was clarified so that any conflicts between cabinet and president in the area of foreign policy should be referred to parliament to resolve. As Finnish cabinets rely on strong parliamentary majorities, in fact, this strengthens the cabinet's foreign policy powers considerably.

The constitutional shift away from semi-presidentialism was a gradual and prolonged process that was made possible by several confluent changes in Finnish society and politics. The rise of a more consensual mode of social and political exchanges was one important precondition. Along with this change, a stronger sense emerged among parties and politicians that the practices under Kekkonen had perverted Finnish parliamentarism (cf. Arter 2006: 89). For each new generation of politicians that entered party organisations and representative bodies, it was increasingly apparent that parties had, to a great extent, let themselves be marginalised by the president in the 1970s. Finally, the transformation in the Soviet Union as of Gorbachev, along with the heightened role of European integration, radically changed the way domestic and international factors interacted in Finnish politics (Paloheimo 2003: 240).

Cabinet-formation

Cabinet-formation is the process that takes place between the resignation of one cabinet and the appointment of the next. In most cases, it is indisputable that one government has been terminated and another has replaced it in office. A closer look at the empirical reality reveals, however, that cabinet turnover is not always clear-cut; it is often a matter of degree. In a report presented by a large research project on cabinets and coalition bargaining, the authors 'count a new cabinet whenever there is a general election, a new PM, or any change in the partisan composition of the cabinet' (De Winter and Dumont 2008: 124). This is, in fact, a highly reasonable operational formula. In a study that compares a large number of cases both in terms of countries and cabinets, a fairly simple and consistent definition is necessary. Still, this inevitably leads to a sample in which politically quite different events are regarded as representatives of the same general category. In fact, it is imaginable that scholars concentrating on the details of a few cases or a single country might have objections to each of the elements in the definition.

Elections in democratic countries are naturally very important as determinants of cabinet-formation. Whether each election produces a 'new' cabinet is debatable. For instance, Sweden during the long social democratic reign, offers examples of how elections came and went while social democratic cabinets continued to rule (Bäck and Larsson 2006: 101–2). The social democratic party leader remained prime minister and most of the other main ministers stayed put as well. These cabinets were, of course, politically considerably less 'new' than the non-socialist coalitions that have replaced them in the more recent past.

Similarly, recent Finnish cabinets demonstrate that the change of prime minister does not need to signal a general cabinet crisis. Anneli Jäätteenmäki resigned in 2003 after only a couple of months in office. Her resignation had certainly been preceded by strong criticism from the Social Democrats, the second main cabinet party (Arter 2006: 223–7; Pesonen 2004). However, the criticism did not concern the prime minister's party (the Centre Party) at large but her personally. Jäätteenmäki was simply replaced by Matti Vanhanen as prime minister and the coalition went on to govern until the next general election, four years later.

Vanhanen's own resignation as PM in 2010 was, officially, due to health reasons. While this was not a mere pretext, there had been considerable inner turmoil in his party prior to his decision. However, again, there was no cabinet crisis at large; the relations between the coalition parties remained stable as did the party and personnel composition of the cabinet.

Finally, the party composition of Finnish cabinets has frequently changed, but the political importance of these changes has varied. As was pointed out above, cabinets normally contain more minor parties than necessary for attaining a majority in parliament. Cabinets can, therefore, afford to lose a minor partner without risking a vote of no confidence in parliament. Such changes in party composition are a far cry politically from earlier crises that led to loss of majority status or/and the resignation of a major cabinet party.

None of this should be interpreted as criticism of the operational definition cited above. Studies of single cases can simply afford the luxury of finer distinctions than is possible in macro-level cross-national research. The point is rather that in Finnish politics since WWII, the various elements of the operational definition of 'new cabinet' have had varying significance. Contemporary cabinet-formation is marked by following features:

1. The role of election results has increased.
2. The role of parliament has been strengthened at the expense of the president.
3. The role of party organisations in choosing individual ministers has been strengthened.
4. Cabinet-formation between elections is no longer a prominent feature.

The first and the fourth point are very much aspects of the same phenomenon, and they form a natural starting point for our empirical account. Before the 1980s, most cabinets were formed between elections rather than as a result of elections. In the 1950s, only 25 per cent of cabinets were clear post-election cabinets. For the 1960s, the corresponding figure was 29 per cent; for the 1970s, 22 per cent;[7] for the 1980s, 75 per cent; for the 1990s, 100 per cent; and for the 2000s, 67 per cent. Again, a clear difference can be discerned between the Kekkonen era and later periods.

The formateur

Both the role and the characteristics of the *formateur* reflect the overall change in Finnish parliamentary politics. As Kekkonen used his constitutional powers regarding government-formation to their fullest extent, and since most cabinets were not the product of an election, the choice of *formateur* very much reflected his preferences. It is in fact not quite accurate to speak of a *formateur* at all. In many cases, Kekkonen's preferences were visible in both the party and personnel composition of the cabinets; thus, it was often he, rather than the new

---

7. Not counting Teuvo Aura's first cabinet in 1970. It was a non-political cabinet formed after the 1970 general election, which was followed by a failure to form a political cabinet.

prime minister, who formed the cabinets (Murto 1994: 96, 332–4; Jansson 1992: 143–61). Especially in the case of Centre Party prime ministers – there were eight of them in the Kekkonen era – he handpicked them at will. The choice of Social Democratic PMs – there were eight of them as well under Kekkonen – was left up to the party organisation to a larger extent (Nousiainen 2006: 279).

Since Mauno Koivisto took office in 1982, every cabinet except one[8] has been formed by the leader of the largest parliamentary party, with him or her as prime minister. Although the formal powers of the president concerning government-formation remained considerable until the new Constitution of 2000, presidents allowed the parties in parliament to handle the formation process. To dispel any remaining uncertainties, in 2002, the parliamentary parties agreed that the task of the *formateur* after an election would go to a person appointed by the party that was largest in terms of parliamentary seats. In practice, this means that the leader of the largest parliamentary party has this role. To be sure, political circumstances may be such that the first *formateur* fails to form a government and a cabinet under someone else's leadership may come about. This has, however, not occurred yet, and the 2002 party agreement may be regarded as a powerful common-law specification of Section 61 of the constitution (Nousiainen 2006: 322; Wiberg 2009: 18).

The focus on party leaders in the selection of cabinet *formateurs* has created still another contrast to the Kekkonen years. As Kekkonen often handpicked prime ministers at will, and as the constitution does not require ministers to be MPs, it was common that persons outside parliament were cabinet leaders (Jansson 1992: 143–61). Holkeri in 1987 was the last non-MP to be selected as prime minister (Murto 2010). It is safe to say that future prime ministers will most likely hold seats in parliament.

Who gets in?

The *formateur*'s task is to assemble a cabinet. Cabinets consist of ministers who represent parties. Thus, when the *formateur*'s work has been completed, we know what parties are in government and who fills the cabinet posts on behalf of the parties.

Despite the great number of cabinets that took office during the Kekkonen era and in spite of the variation in the party composition of these cabinets, one coalition remained conspicuous by its absence for almost thirty years (1958–87). After 1958, Kekkonen refused to appoint cabinets that contained both the Social Democrats and the Conservatives. During this long period, the Conservatives displayed a marked growth in their popular following and scored several electoral victories; but to no avail. Kekkonen's refusal to let the Conservatives participate in government is normally explained with reference to foreign policy; the party was

---

8. The cabinet led by Harri Holkeri (1987–91). It was preceded by a pre-election agreement between the bourgeois parties, without informing the president, to form an all-bourgeois cabinet after the 1987 election. This provoked Koivisto to appoint a Conservative-Social-Democratic cabinet instead (Nousiainen 2006: 287-8, 299, 301).

considered a risk for Finland's relations with the Kremlin (Arter 1999b: 290). An equally plausible explanation is that Kekkonen wished to punish the Conservative-Social-Democratic co-operation that, up until 1961, had been the chief challenge to his dominant political position (*see* Chapter Two).

Koivisto's decision, in 1987, to appoint the Conservative-Social-Democratic coalition not only rehabilitated the Conservatives as a cabinet party and reintroduced the political axis that Kekkonen had shunned for decades. It also launched a pattern that has been dominant in Finnish cabinet politics for more than two decades. With the exception of the Aho cabinet (1991–5), the backbone of Finnish cabinets has consisted of those two parties that are largest in terms of parliamentary seats. As the Centre Party, the Conservatives and the Social Democrats have been of about equal size, they have taken turns as cabinet parties and as the leading opposition party. Today, it is more or less the expectation that the two largest parties join forces in government, no matter which these two parties are. Consequently, Social Democratic-Centre Party coalitions, Conservative-Social-Democratic coalitions and 'bourgeois coalitions' (Conservatives plus Centre Party) are equally thinkable. The coalition elasticity of the major parties is, in other words, quite remarkable (Arter 2006: 262–6).

The change as of 1987 is apparent if one examines the political composition before and after this point in time. Finnish parties can be placed fairly conveniently on a left-right scale, with the Left Party farthest to the left, followed by the Social Democrats, the Greens, Agrarians/Centre Party, Liberals (as long as they existed), Swedish People's Party, Christian Democrats and the Conservatives. Of the 27 post-war coalitions before 1987, only two (7 per cent) were composed of parties other than those adjacent to each other.[9] In other words, the typical cabinet during this period consisted of ideologically 'connected' parties (*cf.* Gallagher *et al.* 2001: 345). The opposition was, therefore, normally either to the left or to the right of the cabinet. As of 1987, five of the coalitions have been of this 'connected' type while four others have not. In these latter cases, the parliamentary opposition has been clearly divided ideologically. In Arter's laconic words, 'the Finnish opposition does not constitute an alternative government' (2006: 264).

The flexible posture of the contemporary major parties may seem strikingly un-ideological. In fact, parties and voters have drifted toward the political middle ground and the level of fundamental conflict is low indeed. At the same time, the various coalition alternatives are not un-political; when two of the major parties find common ground, some of the supporters of the third may find themselves at the losing end. Table 4.4 summarises the political logic of the main types of coalitions.

The major parties may be flexible when it comes to alternative cabinet coalitions but their flexibility is dwarfed by that of the Swedish People's Party.

---

9. Based on the assessment that the Liberals and the Swedish Party occupied the same position on the scale.

Table 4.4: Political logic of main coalition alternatives

Coalition	Common ground	Potential tensions	Potential victims
Conservatives + Centre Party	'Bourgeois coalition', private enterprise, limiting labour union influence	Agricultural and regional subsidies, level of taxation	Labour unions
Conservatives + Social Democrats	'Urban-industrial coalition', pro-EU	Labour-market policies, level of taxation	Regional, agricultural interests
Social Democrats + Centre Party	'Welfare coalition', tax-financed social security	Regional policy, centralisation *vs.* decentralisation	Corporate and high-income taxpayers

This small party, which today musters about 5 per cent of the vote, is something of a fixed feature in Finnish cabinets. It has been in government continuously since 1979 and it belonged to a clear majority of the previous cabinets as well. The party has deemed it important to be in government in order to safeguard the rights of the Swedish-speaking population. It has therefore adopted a flexible posture in issues not related to the Swedish language and is usually considered to be a constructive cabinet partner by the major parties.

The remaining parties have somewhat less cabinet experience. The populist True Finns are the only contemporary party that has remained outside government, and their spectacular victory in the 2011 elections failed to bring about a change in this regard. The Left Alliance participated in cabinets in 1995–2003 and again in 2011–14, despite the fact that the Conservatives were a government party. As for the Christian Democrats, their cabinet participation was long confined to three years in 1991–4 but they, too, got a seat in Katainen's 'six-pack coalition' in 2011. Finally, the Greens had participated in cabinets in 1999–2002 and 2007–11 before entering the Katainen coalition formed in June, 2011.

What about the choice of the personnel for the various cabinet posts? Who becomes a cabinet minister and how is this determined? Here, too, a pattern of change reflecting the overall political and constitutional transformation is visible; at the same time, there are regularities that have persisted despite this change. Kekkonen's activism was not confined to the choice of *formateur*; in many cases he handpicked other ministers as well. This was especially the case with ministers representing the Centre Party. The other side of the coin was that he did not content himself with handpicking. Certain individuals were simply blacklisted as ministers by him and presumptive prime ministers knew that they should not include these names on their lists of cabinet members (*cf.* Myllymäki 2010: 81). Koivisto refrained from interfering in the government-formation process, although his choice of Holkeri as prime minister does represent a deviation from the pattern.

Since the early 1990s, the choice of individual ministers has been wholly in the hands of the cabinet parties.[10]

The choice of ministers within the parties is an intra-party matter not regulated by public statute. The internal processes through which parties choose their ministers are an under-researched field in Finnish politics.[11] Nevertheless, it is apparent that parties have to cater to several needs and interests when choosing their ministers. Especially for the larger parties, which have more numerous cabinet posts, this puzzle may be quite complicated to solve. Although Finnish parties are not markedly factionalised, parties need to consider the interests and importance of their various constituencies and supporter groups. Regional aspects are weighed in and so is, increasingly, the gender balance among ministers. Women's representation in elective offices in Finland has always been among the highest in the world (Inglehart and Norris 2004: 127–48; Karvonen and Selle 1995). In the cabinets appointed in 2003 and 2007, around 60 per cent of the ministers were women; in the 2011 Katainen cabinet, nine out of 19 ministers were women. Two women have so far served as prime ministers (Anneli Jäätteenmäki in 2003 and Mari Kiviniemi in 2010–11).

Minna Puoskari's data on the background and characteristics of ministers during the period 1983–2001 can be used to portray some of the trends behind the selection of ministers. A major change has occurred in the educational background of ministers. In recent decades, no less than 80 per cent of ministers have possessed an academic degree. The aforementioned increase in the share of women is also apparent in the data; this change has been steady and basically linear throughout the period. Concerning age, the trend has pointed downwards; the average age of ministers is today clearly under 50 years. In other words, the importance of seniority in the choice of ministers has declined. While earlier periods witnessed a fair share of ministers with little or no political experience, almost all recent appointments have concerned individuals with experience from parliament, local government or high-level party assignments. The latter factor appears to be of decisive importance; mere parliamentary experience does not seem to suffice. To the extent that non-MPs were selected as ministers, they usually came from top positions in the public sector. Over time, a diminishing share of the ministers has been chosen primarily on the basis of experience in the sector of their respective ministry. Increasingly, therefore, ministers are political professionals who are deemed competent to lead various sectors of the political and administrative field (Puoskari 2002: 341).

At the time of writing, there were 19 ministers in the cabinet. Self-evidently, the two main cabinet parties occupy the lion's share of these posts. The minor parties have to content themselves with a maximum of two posts each. Moreover, some

---

10. There is a tradition that the choice of foreign minister should be discussed with the president, who is the formal leader of Finnish foreign policy. With time, this tradition has lost much of its importance and is today more or less a formality.

11. Although Nousiainen 1992a does contain interesting interviews that shed some light on the period up to the late 1980s.

posts are considered more significant than others. As one of the two main parties in government has the post of prime minister, the other will be given the Ministry of Finance. The Ministry of Foreign Affairs also normally goes to one of the two main parties as do, most of the time, the posts of Minister of Education, Minister of Industry and Commerce and Minister of the Interior. Certain ministries seem to have strong party-political affiliations that have resisted the overall political and constitutional change that Finland has undergone. Some illustrations are in order. Since the beginning of the 1970s, the Centre Party has held the post of Minister of Agriculture and Forestry in *every* cabinet (N=15) in which the party has participated. During the same period, the Ministry of Labour was led either by a Social Democratic or Left-Party minister in all but one of the cabinets in which either of these parties was included. The post of Minister of Health and Social Affairs was held by one of the left-wing parties in ten out of 15 possible cases. The choice of ministers in these fields has given rise to a debate about important sectors' being 'party political fiefdoms'.

Under the 2000 constitution, the final appointment of the cabinet ministers by the president is a pure formality. The president cannot appoint any other prime minister than the one that the majority of the parliament has selected. Nor can he/she appoint cabinet ministers other than those on the list presented by the new prime minister. All of this stands in stark contrast to the blueprint of the old constitution and to former political practice, especially during Kekkonen's presidency. Cabinets are formed today as a result of deliberation in and among parties in parliament.

Agreeing on a programme

As of 1991, '[t]he Government shall without delay submit its programme to the Parliament in the form of a statement' (Section 62 of the constitution). A Government Statement to parliament is always followed by a vote, which means that the parliamentary confidence of the new cabinet is tested as soon it has taken office. Through this clause, Finland, in fact, adopted a form of positive parliamentarism (investiture); by approving a cabinet programme the parliament explicitly demonstrates its support of the cabinet (Mattila and Raunio 2002: 264). It was previously assumed that the cabinet had the confidence of parliament until proven otherwise, which amounted to a form of negative parliamentarism (*cf.* Müller *et al.* 2008: 24).

Work on the cabinet programme proceeds parallel to the negotiations on the party composition of the incoming cabinet and the portfolio distribution within it. It goes without saying that parties will not form a coalition unless they can agree on fundamental policy guidelines. It is in the nature of programme negotiations that their details are shrouded in secrecy. The election campaigns of the participating parties rarely offer intimations as to the coming government programme. As described in Chapter Three, parties are careful not to make campaign pledges that might complicate negotiations with potential cabinet partners.

Governing together

The legal and institutional framework

Formal decisions about government bills to parliament, high-level appointments and similar matters are made at the joint meeting of cabinet and the President of the Republic. The decisions are made by the president on the basis of cabinet proposals presented by the minister to whose remit the issue in question belongs. As was described above, the president's autonomous powers in legislative matters have been effectively eliminated; he/she retains some limited powers concerning appointments. Before presenting matters to the president, the cabinet formulates its standpoint at its plenary meeting, which is the formal arena for decisions about politically and constitutionally important issues. Decisions on legislative bills, cabinet decrees, statements, reports and written communications to parliament, matters that are being prepared in the EU, as well as other questions that are of far-reaching political or economic importance, are made at the plenary meeting. The matters that must be decided at the plenary are enumerated in the Cabinet Statute. In 1988, the number of appointments that were decided at the plenary was reduced (Murto 1994: 263). In 1994 it was decided that only matters that were explicitly mentioned in the cabinet statute would be dealt with at the plenary (Wiberg 2009: 41). These measures reduced the number of items at the plenary agenda considerably.

Cabinets are required by law to have four standing committees for the preparation of important decisions in the corresponding areas. Only cabinet ministers can be members of these committees. They are the Cabinet Committee for Foreign and Security Policy; the Cabinet Committee for the European Union; the Cabinet Fiscal Committee; and the Cabinet Committee for Economic Policy. Other committees may be established if need be.

Other issues may be decided in the ministries that are headed by cabinet ministers. In 2014 there were twelve ministries:

- The Office of the Prime Minister;
- The Ministry of Foreign Affairs;
- The Ministry of Justice;
- The Ministry of the Interior;
- The Ministry of Defence;
- The Ministry of Finance;
- The Ministry of Education and Cultural Affairs;
- The Ministry of Agriculture and Forestry;
- The Ministry of Transport and Communications;
- The Ministry of Employment and the Economy;
- The Ministry of Social and Health Affairs;
- The Ministry of Environmental Affairs.

Coalition government as a political process

Finnish cabinets are collegiate bodies, in which formally equal ministers make collective decisions for which they are collectively responsible. The prime minister presides at the formal plenary meetings as well as at the more informal meetings.

In a broad comparison, the position of the Finnish prime minister is not particularly strong. Finland belongs to the category of systems in which the prime minister is the first among equals rather than the sovereign leader of the cabinet. The choice of ministers is not up to him/her but to the parties that participate in the cabinet (*cf.* Sartori 1994, 103).

Before the era of stable majority parliamentarism, Finnish cabinets, more than today, in fact, governed as collegiate bodies. Ministers assembled to discuss, debate and decide on a wide range of matters collectively. Much of the time, however, they kept a close watch on one another. As the level of political conflict was higher than today and the expectation was that few cabinets would last throughout the parliamentary period, it was equally as important to prevent other parties from gaining too much as it was to implement a jointly agreed set of policies. There were cabinet programmes but these did not matter very much in a world in which cabinets came and went.

With the stabilisation of Finnish parliamentarism, cabinet discipline became attainable and cabinet programmes began to mean more. While it had been difficult earlier to compel individual MPs to toe the cabinet line in parliament, the demands on internal discipline among the cabinet parties rose sharply from the mid 1980s. Since that time, cabinet parties have agreed on a code of conduct that poses strict rules on the parliamentary behaviour of MPs. For instance, the parties that made up the 2007 Vanhanen cabinet agreed on the following set of rules (Wiberg 2008: 172–3):

1. It is the common endeavour of the parliamentary groups of the cabinet parties that government bills and other matters that come up in parliament be dealt with unanimously by the parliamentary groups of the cabinet parties, both at the plenary session of the parliament and in the committees.
2. Matters agreed upon in cabinet can only be changed through joint negotiations and agreements. Should the committee groups not be able to agree on such changes, the matter will be brought up at the meeting of the parliamentary group leaders, at which any changes will be decided.
3. The content of parliamentary committee reports will be determined jointly by the committee members of the cabinet parties. To alter a legislative bill or include a statement leading to a parliamentary resolution in a report requires a unanimous joint decision by the committee groups of the cabinet parties and the parliamentary group leaders.
4. MPs representing cabinet parties shall not present proposals deviating from the agreements of the parliamentary groups of the cabinet parties at plenary sessions, nor shall they vote for such proposals.
5. Clearly local issues and what can be defined as matters of conscience may be exempted from these rules. Concerning such matters, the procedure will be agreed upon in advance at a negotiation between the leaders of cabinet party parliamentary groups, separately in each case.
6. The minister concerned will be informed immediately of any amendments to legislative bills and to the introductory argumentation presented in favour of them. Budgetary amendments and changes in supplementary budgets will be agreed on jointly with cabinet.

With such disciplinary rules in place, cabinets rarely need to fear major trouble in connection with the parliamentary debate on government bills and resolutions. In fact, it may seem that the centre of gravity in parliamentary politics has decisively shifted towards the cabinet. This is both true and not quite true. It is true in the sense that the opportunities of the parliamentary minority, that is, the opposition, to influence overall policy have become restricted indeed. On the other hand, several developments have had the effect of intensifying the interaction of cabinet and parliament.

'In times of stable majority parliamentarism, the opposition MPs unequivocally and pointedly have the role of a bystander', writes Jaakko Nousiainen, a leading authority on Finnish parliamentarism (2006: 310). With the unchallenged majority status of cabinets and because of the abolition of the power of parliamentary minorities to defer legislation, there is now little need to negotiate with the opposition about policy decisions. Parliamentary negotiations take place among the cabinet parties and among the opposition parties rather than between government and opposition. The policy influence of the opposition concerns details at best; overall, policy is determined by cabinet in rather a sovereign manner. Although opposition parties do seek co-operation where they can, they are more often than not divided by a number of important policy differences. An active and visible 'shadow cabinet' of the British variety is not part of the Finnish parliamentary scene; there is, as Arter has pointed out, no formal leader of the opposition (2006: 184). What they have of policy influence, opposition MPs usually wield through work in parliamentary committees. At plenary sessions, by contrast, opposition activity often has a declaratory character; when the roll is called, the opposition invariably loses. Although the role of an opposition party is today highly frustrating, the largest opposition party has customarily refrained from sustained and harsh criticism of government policy. A strategic need to keep the channels of communication open between the major parties has been the cause of this cautiousness. With the flexible coalitions based on party size rather than ideological position, the next election may bring about a government based on one of the major parties in government and the leading opposition party. The True Finn party group has, however, introduced a more offensive rhetoric in parliamentary debates. Interestingly enough, the Centre Party has not followed the True Finn example but opted for a clearly more conciliatory and constructive tone.

With the increased longevity of Finnish cabinets the time-horizon of parliamentary politics is today radically different from that of the first four post-war decades. In earlier times, the focus of cabinet parties was, to a large extent, on producing as many positive outcomes for their particular supporter groups as possible and as rapidly as possible. To put it differently: government decisions were distributive and targeted and often of an *ad hoc* character. Today, cabinets can usually rely on governing for a full four years, which is why it makes sense to try to implement a long-term policy agenda. The cabinet programme that the participating parties agree on before the cabinet is appointed is today not just a document required by convention but an instrument that guides overall cabinet policy (Myllymäki 2010: 235). All of this indicates that cabinet politics in contemporary Finland is different from the distributive 'pork-barrel' politics of earlier decades. In Matti Wiberg's words, parties today 'participate in government more to further long-term national policy-making than to fight for acute group interests' (2009: 19).

The use of top-down budgeting as of 1991 has had a similar effect on inter-party bargaining in cabinet. As of that year, the overall fiscal framework is determined annually before embarking on the details of the budgetary process. This imposes a ceiling on the total expenditures in the coming fiscal year and, naturally, restricts the freedom of manoeuvre of individual ministers and parties in cabinet (Tiili 2008: 80–2). Inside cabinet and central government administration, frame budgeting enhances the influence of the Ministry of Finance over other government sectors. The top officials at this ministry responsible for overall government budget planning have become central players in the budgetary process and their influence is felt everywhere in Finnish government administration (Wiberg 2009: 46; Murto 2010).

Power and influence within the cabinet are also distributed in a different way than was the case in earlier decades. On the one hand, power inside cabinet has been centralised in matters of major political importance. To begin with, the position of the prime minister has been strengthened. The old constitution did not define the prime minister's powers at all. It simply stated that there was to be a cabinet for the general management of state affairs 'including a Prime Minister and a necessary number of other ministers' (Section 2). According to the 2000 constitution

> The Prime Minister directs the activities of the Government and oversees the preparation and consideration of matters that come within the mandate of the Government. The Prime Minister chairs the plenary meetings of the Government (Section 66).

The 2003 Law on the State Council (cabinet) strengthens the prime minister's powers further (Myllymäki 2010: 197). According to Section 3, he oversees the implementation of the cabinet programme and presides at the meetings of the four standing committees required by law. He also leads the preparation of matters to be decided by the European Union (Murto 2010).

Overall, the collegiate character of cabinet decision-making has given way to a pattern of small groups of ministers having disproportionate influence over major issues. For one, membership in cabinet standing committees furnishes a minister with an influence that his colleagues outside committees do not possess. These committees convene to prepare major issues in foreign and security policy, EU affairs, fiscal matters and economic policy, respectively. Even when they are staffed with the maximum number of members allowed by the cabinet statute, none of them includes more than half of the cabinet ministers. In these crucial areas in Finnish politics, policy-preparation is restricted to a fairly limited cabinet elite. Despite the fact that standing committees lack formal powers of decision, their proposals become *de facto* official cabinet policy. In fact, even inside these committees, a small elite of three or four ministers often agrees on the main content of government policies in their respective areas.

When deciding politically significant and controversial questions that cut across policy sectors, the elite nature of cabinet decision-making has become still more pronounced. The party leaders of cabinet parties meet to resolve or prevent conflicts arising from real or expected controversies between ministers representing various sectors or parties. The trend over time has been towards an increased role for cabinet party leader meetings as an overall policy broker (Wiberg 2009: 45–6).

The heightened role of the standing committees and informal party-leader meetings has brought Finland closer to the prevalent pattern in the rest of northern Europe. The pattern of conflict resolution is 'cabinet dominated' rather than 'cabinet external' (Bergman et al. 2006: 195). Meanwhile, the policy agenda of the cabinet as a collegiate body has become more formalised and restricted to major issues and matters that are required by law to be formally dealt with at the cabinet plenary meeting. Plenary meetings are highly formalised and limited to the actual decisions on each matter on the agenda. They do not allow for debate on alternatives or for political controversy. Such aspects of the issues must be settled before the matters reach the plenary meeting. For more than half a century, the cabinet 'evening class'[12] provided an informal setting in which cabinet ministers could discuss issues at hand and resolve inter-party differences before issues reached the formal decision stage. However, these meetings have become more formalised during recent decades. At the same time, a wider range of participants, including parliamentary party leaders, has been allowed to participate in evening classes. They have therefore lost much of their earlier importance as a pre-decision arena for political negotiations within the cabinet (Myllymäki 2010: 62; Murto 2010; Arter 2006: 137). Instead, the importance of cabinet standing committees, party-leader meetings, ad hoc gatherings and deliberation in the various ministries has grown. Arguably, Arter's assessment in the early 1980s that the cabinets represent 'meetings of the whole government' rather than comprising 'a ministerial élite' (1984: 101) does seem not entirely accurate today.

The role of preparation and decision-making within ministries represents a contrast to the overall centralisation of power in cabinet politics. An increasing number of issues are decided in the ministries rather than at the level of the cabinet as a whole (Myllymäki 2010: 54). As of 1994, the cabinet plenary meeting only deals with issues that are explicitly defined by the cabinet statute as matters to be decided at the plenary meeting. All other matters are decided by the individual ministers (Wiberg 2009: 41). With this procedural change, the number of items on the plenary agenda was rapidly halved. From 2000 on the number of matters has again risen, but this is, as is evident from Table 4.5, mainly due to that fact the new constitution transferred the power to issue decrees from president to cabinet.

Of course, most of the issues that, according to law, must be decided at the plenary are of considerable political significance. Nevertheless, the matters left to the ministers to decide are far from mere technical details. Therefore, while political power in major issues has been centralised in the cabinet, there has been a parallel decentralisation of power, enhancing the influence of individual ministers in sectoral matters.

---

12. Thus called jokingly because the meetings were normally held in the evening.

Table 4.5: Number of matters decided at cabinet plenary meetings, 1993–2008 (selected years)

	1993	1994	1997	1999	2000	2002	2004	2006	2008
All decisions	1281	802	676	596	872	940	851	907	901
Of which cabinet decrees	–	–	–	–	279	309	289	268	279

Source: Wiberg 2009: 130.

The strategic effect of these parallel processes of centralisation and decentralisation is that it is in the interest of individual ministers to have as many matters as possible decided at ministry level. When issues become 'cabinet matters', the influence of the cabinet elite preponderates. Especially for ministers not included in this elite, ministerial decisions therefore represent a central channel of political influence. The problem with this strategy from the point of view of ministers and parties is that it largely coincides with the wishes of the ministerial bureaucracy. Civil servants in the ministries are often wary of the 'politicisation' that occurs when issues are dealt with at the level of the entire cabinet. Whether concerned about the interests of their particular sector, about long-term policy development and consistency or about the role of expertise in policy-making, bureaucrats tend to fear situations in which issues became highly publicised and subject to political controversy. They will therefore endeavour to persuade their minister to adopt the point of view of their administrative sector in handling ministerial issues. Frequently, this harmony in outlook between ministers and bureaucrats is easy to achieve. That is, for instance, the case with Centre Party agricultural ministers and their ministries; ministers and top administrators belong to the same 'agricultural-political complex'; they have known each other long and tend to think alike. In the case of less self-evident ministerial appointments, the unity of outlook is of course less given. On the other hand, in these cases ministers frequently represent minor cabinet parties and are perhaps in particular need of the backing of their ministries. Wiberg cites a frequently proffered notion according to which it takes a ministry a month to get a new minister 'house-broken'. After this time the 'the minister no longer works primarily to implement the cabinet programme but to defend the interests of his ministry as defined by the ministry's top officials' (Wiberg 2008: 178).

The decentralisation of cabinet decision-making clearly enhances the influence of the administrative elite in Finnish politics. In an environment where policy differences between consecutive cabinets are incremental and cabinets rely on solid majorities, ministry bureaucrats can safely apply themselves to long-term policy planning. An editorial in the national daily *Hufvudstadsbladet*, in October 2010, points to the questionable practice of top ministerial officials presenting policy plans that reach far beyond the next election. These plans affect party positions in the electoral campaign and are highly influential when the programme of the new cabinet is forged. The difference as compared to, for instance, Sweden, is that the ministry viewpoints are not just presented by ministers or politically appointed officials but by senior civil servants at large (Lindén 2010: 16). A column in the same newspaper by a renowned Finnish economist living in Sweden noted the tendency of media to turn to the administrative elite in the finance ministry for analyses of Finnish economic policy. The media simply expect these top civil servants to have a more profound policy impact than ministers or party leaders. Again, the difference as compared to Sweden is underlined (Vartiainen 2010: 11).

The blurring of the distinction between political and administrative functions is also, in a sense, a by-product of the economic depression of the early 1990s. When the Aho cabinet was being formed in 1991, it was apparent that the country was headed for the most severe economic downturn since the Great Depression. In these exceptional circumstances, the parties decided to invite the permanent secretaries of the ministries to participate in the cabinet-programme negotiations. By the mid-1990s, Finland had weathered the acute economic crisis. The top bureaucrats, however, had gained seats in the negotiations on cabinet programmes and they hung on to them. Ever since that time, the right of permanent secretaries to influence the cabinet programme that they and their administrative colleagues are supposed to help implement has been, *de facto*, recognised by political parties.

Governing together – or apart?

In the first three or four post-war decades, Finnish cabinet politics were unstable and conflictual. While they lasted, however, cabinets very much governed as a collective. Since then, cabinets have become stable and politics has become orderly. Paradoxically, the parties and ministers that form the cabinet govern much less in the shape of collegiate deliberative and decision-making bodies. The cabinet plenary meeting is a formal arena for decisions which does not allow for debate. Matters must be negotiated and settled politically before they reach the plenary. Politically significant and/or controversial matters are settled at the cabinet elite level, rather than collectively by the cabinet as a whole. This goes both for the deliberations and the negotiations that precede the decision stage. These take place between ministers and bureaucrats in the various sectors and in committees and working groups in the cabinet. None of these arenas include the cabinet as a whole. Some forums, especially the Cabinet Standing Committee for Economic Policy, have disproportionate policy influence. When difficult political problems arise, cabinet party leaders tend to take over; once again, only a minority of the ministers is involved. Other issues have increasingly been transferred to ministry level, where they are often handled with limited contact across sectors. Ministers tend to focus on defending the interests of their particular sector. A tacit principle of 'non-intervention' seems to have established itself in the relations between ministerial sectors. Prime ministers have, in fact, encouraged this mode of cabinet policy-management (Tiili 2004: 137–8).

Minna Tiili, who has analysed the internal performance of Finnish cabinets, draws the rather disheartening conclusion that cabinets in Finland today only rarely function as genuine collegiums as was the intention of the constitution. Ministers share an equal responsibility for the decisions taken in the name of the cabinet but they clearly are not equal in terms of power and influence. In fact, Tiili points out that decision-making is no longer even *collective*, in the sense that ministers would be present when important decisions are taken (Tiili 2004: 137–8). The parallel processes of centralisation and decentralisation have rendered cabinet politics increasingly fragmented.

Cabinets as arenas for political power and as social networks have undergone a major change in the past two or three decades. Leading ministers and top civil servants have seen their power enhanced; other ministers are the potential losers. As the collective contacts within the cabinet have become less frequent, strong personal ties between cabinet ministers do no longer automatically come about. Ministers simply do not see each other as often as they used to (Wiberg 2009: 35). The weakening of cabinet collegiality thus goes hand in hand with the attenuation of the social network of which ministers used to be part.

Cabinet termination

Cabinets are terminated when they are replaced by a new government, either a political one or, in times of political crisis, a caretaker cabinet. Above, Nousiainen's criteria for cabinet transitions have been followed. Consequently, new cabinets have been counted either when there has been an election between two cabinets, or a new prime minister has been appointed, or the majority/minority status of a cabinet has changed.

Elections are either scheduled or early. Between 1906 and 1954, regular parliamentary elections were held every three years. After that, the maximum period between elections has been four years (Tarasti and Taponen 1996: 59). Until 1991, the president had the constitutional right to dissolve parliament and call for early elections. That year, a constitutional reform ordained that the president could call early elections only 'in response to a reasoned proposal by the Prime Minister, and after having heard the parliamentary groups' (Section 25 of the Finnish Constitution).

Several other causes related to parliament may lead to cabinet transition. The cabinet may be defeated by a parliamentary vote of no confidence, either when the cabinet itself actively seeks to test its parliamentary support or as a result of a motion of no confidence by MPs. New cabinets can also come about when parties in parliament expand the party-political base of a cabinet without actually voting the incumbent government out of office.

Cabinets may also shift for reasons connected to the cabinets themselves. Prime ministers may choose to step down for political or private reasons. In Finland, prime ministers occasionally run for the office as President of the Republic; if they are successful, they have to resign as prime minister. Cabinets may also resign due to a cabinet crisis, that is, the inability of the cabinet parties to agree on major policy issues.

Before the 2000 Constitution was adopted, the president had extensive powers pertaining to the formation, appointment and dismissal of cabinets. As the cabinets were much more tied to the will of the president, relations between cabinet and president could be the cause of cabinet resignations. Presidential elections could also occasionally cause the resignation of a cabinet.

Besides reasons connected to these three central government institutions, cabinet politics during an extended period of time reflected the country's external relations, above all its relations with the Soviet Union/Russia. Foreign-policy problems sometimes developed into general crises affecting Finnish politics at large, which is why this category can be singled out as a separate group of causes behind cabinet transitions in Finland.

Matti Wiberg has classified cabinet resignations in Finland between 1944 and 2005 according to these groups of causes. To his data, figures on the cabinets in 2005–11 have been added (Table 4.6).

The figures in Table 4.6 describe two radically different political climates. The by-now-familiar pattern of increased stability is once again apparent from the table. In the early post-war decades, cabinets resigned frequently and for a variety of reasons. There were political crises between the parties, manifested in the relations between parliament and cabinet, between the parties in cabinet, or both. Such crises are conspicuous by their absence in the latter period. To a large extent, cabinet resignations in one way or another involved the president. The president dissolved parliament and called for early elections four times in 1944–82; in three instances, it was Kekkonen who did this as president (Nousiainen 1992b: 215–16). There have been no early elections since the Kekkonen years. Three prime ministers resigned during 1944–82 in order to assume the presidency; this has not occurred a single time since then.

Table 4.6: Causes of cabinet resignations, 1944–2011

	1944–82	1982–2011	1944–2011
Reasons related to parliament			
Scheduled elections	5	9	14
Early elections	4	–	4
Vote of no confidence	3	–	3
Expanded cabinet basis	1	–	1
Reasons related to cabinet			
Prime minister elected president	3	–	3
Prime minister resigns	1	2	3
Internal cabinet crisis	6	–	6
Reasons related to president			
Disagreement with president	2	–	2
Presidential elections	2	–	2
Reasons related to foreign relations	3	–	3
Total	30	11	41

Source: for 1944–2005, Wiberg 2009: 24; for 2005–2011, calculated by author.

Disagreements with the president caused cabinet resignations in the former period, as did presidential elections; these reasons too seem to have ceased to apply. Finally, the foreign policy, supremely led by the president in 1944–82, seems no longer to be a field that gives rises to cabinet resignations.

The fundamental change in Finnish politics following the transition from Kekkonen to Koivisto in 1982 is highlighted in a particularly pronounced manner when examining the causes of cabinet resignations before and after that watershed year.

Conclusion

The introductory section of this chapter formulated several questions about the causes and effects of the transition to stable oversized majority cabinets in Finland. The analysis above has sought answers to these queries. It is now time to sum up the main findings that have been highlighted empirically.

What were the most important forces behind the transition to the present form of coalition politics? Finnish government politics has gained stability as a result of a general move from a conflictual societal and political practice to a highly consensual style of politics. The change in the parliamentary sphere was preceded by an earlier transition in the labour market and in economic policy. The waning of presidential interventions in parliamentary affairs since the Kekkonen years is another important factor behind this change. Similarly, the fact that foreign policy no longer provides instruments for determining the fate of coalitions, parties and individual politicians has levelled the playing field of the parliamentary game. The propensity for forming oversized coalitions is a long-term feature in Finnish politics, caused in part by the strong mechanisms for parliamentary minorities that existed until the mid-1990s. Before the 1980s, however, even oversized cabinets were vulnerable to internal crises and presidential interventions that regularly led to their termination and replacement by minority or non-political cabinets.

How has it affected the parties and the relations between them? The ideological rivalry between parties has become significantly weaker. Parties appear to be willing to enter into coalition with any of the other parties. They are therefore careful not to exclude themselves from any imaginable coalition; consequently, they rarely attack each other so fiercely, in connection with campaigns or debates, that this would pre-empt a given coalitional pattern.

What strategies are available to parties, given the prevalence of oversized coalitions? As oversized coalitions rarely need to fear major trouble on the part of parliament, and from the opposition in particular, the sole channel of major political influence is cabinet membership. Each major party needs to cultivate sufficiently functional contacts with the two other main parties, while at the same time encouraging any policy disagreements between them. Whether the spectacular victory of the populist True Finns in 2011 will change this pattern, it is too early yet to tell. Minor parties wishing to be included in cabinet must present themselves as reasonable, constructive and flexible. Since it is the consistent strategy of major cabinet parties never to allow a minor party to become pivotal, minor parties are sometimes compelled to sacrifices even in issues of central importance to them.

How is policy determined and in what ways can parties act to further their political goals and the interests of their constituents? To influence policy, parties must belong to the cabinet. Even inside cabinet, power is far from evenly distributed. An 'elitisation' of cabinet decision-making has taken place. The prime minister's influence has grown, as has that of the group of cabinet party leaders. Membership in cabinet standing committees is also an important instrument of political influence. Outside this cabinet elite sphere, ministers can hope to have policy influence through decisions within their ministries; the number of matters that are decided at this level has clearly risen. Targeted 'pork barrel' policies aimed at furthering the interests of given constituencies have generally become more difficult to achieve, as cabinet policy-making has become more tied to the long-term goals expressed in the cabinet programme.

What is the role of the political opposition? It is today very difficult for the parliamentary opposition to exert an influence on overall cabinet policy. Cabinets can count on solid majorities in parliament and are almost never dependent on the co-operation of opposition parties to get legislation approved. The abolition of the right of a third of the MPs to defer legislation beyond the next election was an important constitutional change in this regard. Opposition parties are rarely united by common policy agendas; in fact, the opposition is often internally more heterogeneous than the cabinet coalition. On the other hand, those parties that do not have cabinet status as their apparent first priority may benefit from the situation. Populist parties frequently gain a following since they seem to be more clearly critical of the cabinet than other parties.

How well do parties manage to control and direct the government bureaucracy? The influence of the leading government bureaucrats has been clearly expanded during recent decades. Given the width and heterogeneity of government coalitions the viewpoints and expertise of civil servants frequently function as a 'neutral' starting point for policy-making. The permanent secretaries of ministries today wield a major influence not only on individual decisions but on the cabinet programme at large. The role of the top officials of the finance ministry is particularly pronounced in Finnish cabinet politics. Overall, the top government bureaucracy is probably the group of actors whose influence has been enhanced most as Finnish politics has gained in stability.

How, then, have these changes affected politics and society in Finland more generally? Is it possible to pass an overall verdict whether the transformation of government politics has been positive or negative from the point of view of the Finnish nation at large? These questions are of course fundamentally important but it is very difficult to provide clear-cut answers to them. What the impact of politics and policy is on the general social development of a country is always hard to assess in a definite manner. One cannot turn back the clock, choose an alternative course of development and assess its effects – such social experimentation is out of reach for social scientists. Neither can the effects of politics and policy be separated from those of other factors, economic trends in particular. In the case of small, open economies such as Finland, the role of international economic conditions is always crucial. Whether the development of Finnish society primarily reflects these external economic factors, a combination of them and domestic policy, or first and foremost political choices at home, will remain a moot question.

These analytical difficulties aside, many would argue that the by-now long era of government stability has had a number of beneficial effects on Finnish society. In the past decades, Finland has faced several crises and challenges successfully. The processes of de-regulation, globalisation and modernisation of the public sector have touched upon the very basic tenets of the socio-economic order in Finland. The economic depression of the first half of the 1990s, as well as the financial crisis from 2008 onwards, shook the foundations of economic security in Finland. Despite the length and seriousness of the recession, a look at other EU member states readily reveals that Finland has handled these challenges in a way that compares favourably with most other countries.[13] It is very difficult to see how the fragile and conflict-prone governments of earlier decades could have faced these crises with a similar determination and ensuing success. They simply lacked both the longevity and the collective commitment that it takes to resolve a serious national crisis.

Whilst the overall assessment of government performance in recent decades is, arguably, positive, we also have to inquire about effects from a democratic perspective. How would one assess Finland during recent decades with the aid of such central criteria as popular sovereignty, political accountability and legitimacy? To what extent have the changes that have been described in this chapter enhanced democracy in Finland? In what respects are their consequences problematic?

Here, too, the assessment must in several ways be positive. If the basic chain of democratic governance is perceived so that the people elect their representatives to parliament and parliament controls the cabinet, contemporary Finnish politics compares favourably with earlier periods. Once presidential interventions and chronic political instability ceased to disturb the parliamentary chain of command – much helped by the demise of foreign-policy concerns as a central determinant – the role of parties and elections became clearer in Finnish politics. Parties today hold the key to cabinet-formation; they cannot hide behind the president like they used to. Elections have a direct bearing on how cabinets are formed in contemporary Finland.

However, consensual politics in a fragmented multi-party system such as the Finnish one creates several problems of accountability. Multi-party coalitions are, in fact, always problematic from the point of view of accountability. Who should the citizens hold accountable if they are dissatisfied with government policy, and whom should they reward if they are happy with it? The prime minister's party? All cabinet parties according to a given ratio? In Finland, these perennial problems connected with multi-party cabinets are made worse by the fact that all parties at all times try to cultivate their relations with presumptive cabinet partners. The opposition is weak and tame, its members hope to become cabinet parties as soon

---

13. http://www.hoecd.org/eco/surveys/economic-survey-finland.htm

as possible and they rarely present a truly alternative programme as compared to that of the incumbent cabinet. 'The lack of real alternatives' was long the perennial criticism against the dominant pattern in Finnish parliamentary politics. If the more confrontational style of parliamentary politics introduced by the True Finns brings about a change in this regard, their advent would indeed be a historical dividing line.

With the stabilisation of cabinet politics and the waning of fundamental ideological differences, parties have paved the way for a stronger administrative predominance in Finnish politics. This, in turn, has further enhanced long-term planning as a guide for political decision-making. While this may have several positive consequences in terms of the cognitive basis of decisions and policy consistency, it adds to the already blurred picture of political accountability.

Chapter Five

Voters Amidst Change

with Heikki Paloheimo

A Finnish voter from, say, 1960 would find today's social and political landscape bewildering. To begin with, the electorate itself looks radically different from a few generations ago. The population segments that were the original basis of party-formation have seen their relative magnitude change dramatically. The economic means available to most voters today, as well as their general level of education, were restricted to the small proportion that formed the upper echelons of society in the first post-war decades. Today's citizens live in a society that is highly integrated with its international environment and increasingly heterogeneous in cultural terms. The shadow of the neighbouring great power no longer looms large in the political life of the country.

The parties that contest the field have been remarkably resilient in the face of these changes. To be sure, newcomers have challenged the traditional parties on a number of occasions and several of the original parties have seen their popular following change considerably. Still, Finland, along with many other west European countries, testifies to Lipset and Rokkan's famous thesis about the freezing of party systems. Surprisingly many of the parties that dominated the field in the 1920s are still around in one form or another.

To an astonishingly high degree, then, politics is still the matter of the 'same old parties'. How these parties behave is, by contrast, very different from the political patterns of the first post-war decades. Most parties are eager to participate in government with more or less any other party; to achieve this, they play down major ideological differences and are willing to go to great lengths to find compromises with other parties. The dominant role of the president in the parliamentary game long gone, parties are free to forge these often highly unorthodox alliances as they choose. Increasingly, the role of party organisations has become that of campaign machines instead of popular movements based on mass membership. Campaign costs have skyrocketed, and several parties have experienced highly embarrassing scandals related to political finance. The same old parties they may be but, even more, it may appear as if parties are now all the same.

How have voters reacted to this mix of persistence and change? How has political participation been affected? What changes have occurred in the electoral choices made by citizens? Do parties get their popular support from segments of the population other than those they used to rely on? Are voters increasingly replacing party evaluations with a focus on candidates and party leaders? How, finally, has citizens' relationship with politics at large been affected by the transformations described earlier in this book? Do citizens view democracy in a different way from a few decades ago? How do they perceive their own capacity to comprehend the political process?

These questions form the core of this final empirical chapter of the book. They will be approached in a fashion similar to the earlier chapters. Systematic empirical analysis, to a considerable degree cast in both comparative and longitudinal terms, forms the backbone of the text. The conditions for this kind of analysis have clearly improved in recent years. Comparative data at both aggregate and individual levels are available to a steadily growing extent. As for detailed survey data, for a long time, Finland compared unfavourably to its Nordic neighbours, Germany and the US (Bengtsson *et al.* 2014: 8). As of 2002, however, there is a permanent National Election Study Program (FNES)[1] in Finland. In combination with evidence from occasional earlier surveys, FNES data provide a sufficient basis for analyses of main trends over time.

Electoral participation

Modern representative democracies are [...] built upon the electoral process. The voters' choice between competing parties or candidates is still the primary basis of public access and influence in contemporary democracies [...] participation in elections is typically the most common form of citizen political engagement.

Thus wrote Russell Dalton and Mark Gray in their chapter in a highly acclaimed edited volume about the transformations of democracy, about a decade before this book was written (2003: 23). Despite a growing interest in democratic innovations allowing for various forms of deliberative democracy and direct citizen participation, few would question that free and fair elections will continue to be a cornerstone of the democratic form of government. For practical reasons, democracy in large societies tends to be representative rather than direct. It is difficult to picture an organising principle for representative democracy that does not, in one way or another, involve elections. Even proponents of participatory and deliberative conceptions of democracy usually acknowledge the importance of electoral democracy (Dahl 1989: 340; Thompson 2008: 512).

What about the importance of participation in elections, of voter turnout? Most analysts seem to agree that high levels of electoral participation are desirable. To be sure, the extremely high levels of electoral participation that preceded the collapse of democracy in Weimar Germany and some other countries in interwar Europe suggested that a high turnout may be a sign of dangerously heightened social conflict. Today, however, most experts view low rather than high levels of turnout as a problem for democracy. The greater the percentage of those who do not participate in elections, the more risk that the results of an election reflect the preferences of only some of the population groups in a society. Correspondingly, when large groups of citizens do not turn out to vote, voting tends to become socially skewed. For instance, well educated citizens turn out more than people with lower levels of education. If differences between social groups are considerable, this may raise questions about the representativeness of the elected officials. All in all, therefore, a high electoral turnout is normally seen as a desirable goal (Abramson 1995: 913–20).

---

1.   http://www.vaalitutkimus.fi/en/vaalitutkimus_suomessa.html

Table 5.1: Voter turnout in parliamentary elections in 23 stable democracies (% of voting-age population)

	Average turnout 1960–79 per cent A	Average turnout 2000–09 per cent B	Difference B–A	Countries with norms on compulsory voting
United Kingdom	74.6	57.9	−16.7	
France	67.1	50.9	−16.2	
Canada	70.2	55.5	−14.7	
Austria	88.6	74.1	−14.5	*
Finland	*82.4*	*68.8*	*−13.6*	
Italy	94.3	82.1	−12.2	*
The Netherlands	86.8	77.3	−9.5	*
Israel	81.6	72.3	−9.3	
Ireland	77.1	67.9	−9.2	
Switzerland	47.2	38.5	−8.7	
Germany	84.0	75.9	−8.1	
Japan	71.1	63.5	−7.6	
New Zealand	83.3	76.5	−6.8	
Sweden	85.5	79.3	−6.2	
Norway	81.4	76.4	−5.0	
USA	51.2	46.5	−4.7	
Denmark	86.6	83.0	−3.6	
Iceland	89.2	86.9	−2.3	
Belgium	87.7	86.0	−1.7	*
Australia	84.6	83.1	−1.5	*
Luxembourg	89.5	90.4	0.9	*
Malta	80.8	96.8	16.0	
Mean	**79.3**	**72.3**	**−7.0**	

Source: IDEA 2002 and http://idea.int

Notes: In some nations, citizens must register before Election Day. In other countries, including Finland, citizens who have reached the stipulated voting age are registered automatically by the authorities. In countries without automatic voter-registration, voting turnout as a percentage of voting-age population is normally much lower than turnout as a percentage of registered voters.

Countries marked with an asterisk have rules on compulsory voting. In Australia and Belgium citizens are obliged to present an acceptable reason for not voting. At least in principle, citizens may face a penalty as a result of non-voting without an acceptable reason. In Greece, Italy and Luxembourg, non-voting is not sanctioned effectively. In Austria, voting is compulsory only in Tyrol and even there, non-voting does not lead to penalties. In The Netherlands, compulsory voting was abolished in 1967.

When turnout in stable democracies since 1960 is surveyed during two separate periods (Table 5.1), a generally declining trend is clearly visible. In the 1960s and 1970s, mean electoral turnout was nearly 80 per cent; in the 2000s, it was just a couple of points above seventy. Among the 23 democracies surveyed, only Malta and Luxembourg deviate from the general pattern. As for Finland, turnout in the sixties and seventies was roughly three points higher than the average for stable democracies; in the 2000s it was approximately three and a half points *below* average. This means that the decline in turnout in Finland has been steeper than in most comparable states. Figure 5.1 shows the historical development of electoral turnout in Finland.

In general terms, electoral participation in Finland peaked in the 1960s and 1970s. This goes for both parliamentary and municipal elections. Kekkonen's prolonged presidency led to a tacit protest in the form of lower turnout in presidential elections in the 1970s. Koivisto's ascent to the presidency inspired a heightened popular interest in presidential elections. From 1982 to 2012, turnout in presidential elections was higher than in other elections. Overall, however, voter turnout rose until the 1960s; from the early 1980s on, one can speak of a general decrease in electoral participation in Finland over time.

Socio-economic correlates

High levels of turnout presuppose an extensive political mobilisation of all main segments of the population. In such cases, differences in turnout between

Figure 5.1: Voter turnout in national and local elections in Finland (%)

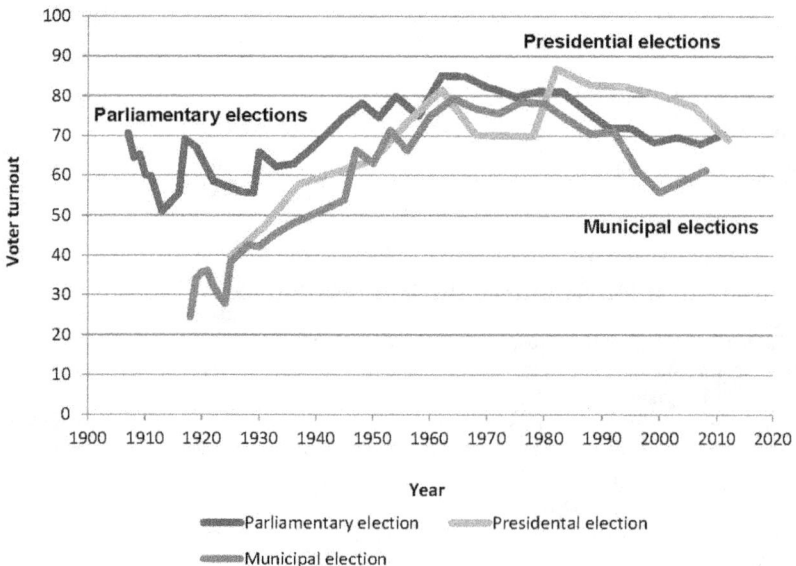

Source: Statistics Finland, national election statistics

population segments remain small. At lower levels of turnout, various groups typically display uneven rates of political participation. Early Finnish studies of electoral participation (Allardt and Bruun 1956; Pesonen and Sänkiaho 1979) pointed to patterns similar to those demonstrated by international research. Among other things, men were found to be somewhat more active as voters than women; citizens with higher levels of education were more active than those with less education; citizens in the age bracket 40 to 55 years were more active than other age groups; and middle-class voters were more active than citizens belonging to the working class. As turnout increased, however, the importance of socio-economic factors as determinants of electoral participation waned. This is evident from Table 5.2.

Table 5.2: Voter turnout in parliamentary elections in Finland 1975–2011 (estimates for demographic groups)

	1975–83	1987–91	1995–99	2003	2007	2011
Number of cases (N)	(5,933)	(4,831)	(7,444)	(2,659)	(1,417)	(1,285)
Voting turnout (% of voting age population)	80.6	74.3	70.1	69.7	67.9	70.5
Gender						
Men	81.1	73.6	68.7	67.6	65.8	69.6
Women	80.3	74.9	71.4	71.6	69.9	71.3
Difference	*0.8*	*−1.3*	*−2.7*	*−4.0*	*−4.1*	*−1.7*
Men by age group						
18–24	76	64	59	51	38	49
25–39	82	73	59	69	64	50
40–59	83	80	73	69	64	77
60	81	74	85	72	78	83
Range	*7*	*16*	*26*	*21*	*40*	*34*
Women by age group						
18–24	77	64	68	59	52	49
25–39	82	76	61	71	65	66
40–59	82	79	79	71	73	71
60	77	78	83	79	76	82
Range	*5*	*15*	*15*	*20*	*24*	*33*
Education						
Primary School	79	74	67	63	61	62
Vocational school	83	70	67	65	62	59
Vocational institute	84	77	74	75	73	78
University	85	82	83	84	87	87
Range	*6*	*12*	*16*	*21*	*26*	*28*

Table 5.2 (continued)

	1975–83	1987–91	1995–99	2003	2007	2011
Occupational group						
Farmers	81	87	83	75	73	n/a
Blue-collar workers	79	67	60	63	59	55
White-collar workers	85	80	75	77	74	85
Entrepreneurs and self-employed workers	78	72	76	75	73	77
Pensioners	80	82	79	75	75	78
Students	80	67	62	68	61	64
Unemployed	73	67	63	57	50	46
Others	78	73	66	57	57	71
Range	*12*	*20*	*21*	*20*	*25*	*39*
Household income						
I (lowest) income quartile	79	74	69	62	60	54
II quartile	81	73	68	73	69	65
III quartile	83	75	73	74	70	77
IV (highest) income quartile	86	80	76	71	83	83
Range	*7*	*7*	*8*	*12*	*23*	*29*
Nagelkerke R^2	0.02	0.08	0.10	0.08	0.16	0.19

Notes: Figures on voting turnout as percentage of voting-age population and voting turnout by gender originate from voting registries. They are exact figures of voting turnout among persons entitled to vote and living in Finland. Results by age group, education, socio-economic group and household income are estimates based on survey data. Survey data have been weighted so that voting turnout of both genders is fixed to the real voting turnout of men and women in the elections concerned.

The Nagelkerke R^2 measures are results of logistic regression analyses where voting turnout is explained by the socio-demographic factors presented in the table. The Nagelkerke R^2 statistics may be interpreted in the same way as R^2 measures in ordinary regression analyses. The higher the value of R^2, the better the dependent variable can be explained with the independent variables used in the model.

Data: 1975–83: FSD1003, FSD1006, FSD1007, FSD1012, FSD1013; 1987–91: FSD1014, FSD1015, FSD1029, FSD1030, FSD1033; 1995–99: FSD1032, FSD1034, FSD1037, FSD1042; 2003: FSD1260, FSD2024; 2007: FSD2269; 2011: FSD2653.

Of the periods surveyed in Table 5.2, 1975–83 displays a high level of turnout. During that period, differences in turnout between demographic groups were small. Consequently, demographic factors were not particularly important as statistical determinants of electoral participation. As turnout started to drop rapidly from the early 1980s on, the importance of these factors grew in a concomitant fashion. Today, age, education, occupation and income all offer statistically significant explanations of why some individuals turn out to vote while others do not. In each of these categories, there has been a basically linear increase of differences in turnout. Younger citizens vote less than middle-aged and older Finns; the drop in the lowest age brackets has been marked indeed. This goes hand in hand with Hanna Wass's finding that the youngest voter groups know the party choices of their parents clearly less often than older voters (Wass 2007: 11). Low education similarly leads to low turnout, higher levels of education to more active electoral participation.[2] White-collar employees vote much more actively than blue-collar workers. Less than half of those out of work turn out to vote; the decline is sharp compared with the first period with all of 73 per cent of unemployed citizens still participating. Similarly, high-income earners are active voters; voting activity declines linearly as we move towards lower income brackets. Overall, the decline of electoral participation very much corroborates international findings about the importance of social status. When turnout is high, the importance of such factors as explanations of participation is relatively limited; with declining participation, their explanatory power increases rapidly (Franklin 2002).

Gender differences are less marked but their development is interesting. The 1987 election was the first one in which women voted more actively than men. From then on, the difference between women and men continued to grow until the 2011 election. That year, the rise to prominence of the True Finns mobilised previously passive male citizens, in particular. It is highly uncertain whether this group of male voters will continue to participate as actively as in the 2011 election.

Other determinants

Demographic and socioeconomic factors can be viewed as basically objective descriptions of voter characteristics. They describe survey respondents in respects in which the likelihood of error is small. It is, of course, imaginable that respondents exaggerate or understate matters pertaining to, say, their education or income. The risk that respondents interpret survey questions on these points differently or fail to understand them is, nevertheless, limited. This section, by contrast, examines factors that involve a larger measure of subjective interpretation. The question is to what extent differences in electoral participation among citizens are attributable to such factors as political interest, efficacy, knowledge and the perceived polarisation of the party field.

Interest in politics is one of the most common judgmental questions posed in political surveys. Finnish surveys before 2003 included this question a couple of times, which makes a time series covering nearly three decades possible. The regular FNES surveys since 2003 have included this item every time.

It is, of course, no surprise that politically interested citizens vote more actively than those who take little or no interest in politics. What is noteworthy is the development over time. In 1983, slightly over half of the respondents who considered themselves completely uninterested in politics said that they had voted

2. Moreover, a 2011 study by Mattila and others found that a high education level led to active electoral participation irrespective of personality traits, whereas these were found to influence turnout among voters with less education.

Table 5.3: Interest in politics and voter turnout (%)

	1983	1991	2003	2007	2011
Very interested	87	90	87	87	95
Rather interested	88	77	82	76	79
Not much interested	83	68	62	57	53
Not at all interested	51	44	39	27	21
Correlation between interest and voter turnout[1]	0.31	0.29	0.35	0.35	0.46

Data: FSD1011 (1983), FSD1018 (1991), FSD2269 (2007), FSD2653 (2011).
Notes: Based on the survey question: 'How interested are you in politics?' Estimates of voter turnout have been calculated by weighting the survey data so that voter turnout among men and women equals their officially registered electoral participation.
[1] Cramer's V.

in the previous parliamentary election. In 2011, not much more than a fifth of the respondents in this category said they had voted. At the same time, electoral participation has remained high or even increased among those who are very interested in politics. The two middle categories display declining turnout but the decrease is much sharper in the lower than the upper category. Consequently, political interest explains electoral participation to a growing degree. The sense of civic duty that apparently persuaded many uninterested citizens to go to the polls seems to have lost much of its power to motivate. At the high tide of electoral participation, people's collective identities were clearer and stronger and, as a result, pressures concerning electoral participation were more marked than nowadays. In a 1977 survey, 86 per cent of the respondents fully agreed with the statement 'voting in elections is a civic duty'. In the last decades, collective identities have become more vague and obscure; as a result, collective pressures towards electoral participation have been eroded somewhat. In the 2007 FNES survey, the corresponding figure was 66 per cent.

When Campbell, Gurin and Miller in 1954 introduced the concept of *efficacy* they characterised it in the following manner:

> Sense of political efficacy may be defined as the feeling that individual political action does have, or can have, an impact upon the political process, i.e., that it is worth while to perform one's civic duties. It is the feeling that political and social change is possible, and that the individual citizen can play a part in bringing about this change (quoted in Gabriel 1998: 359).

It is easy to see that efficacy may have a strong bearing on the propensity of an individual to participate in politics. Defined in the above manner, efficacy is more or less identical with a judgment whether or not participation makes any difference. Low efficacy should bring about little or no participation.

Soon enough, however, researchers found that efficacy consists of two aspects, which may be closely related but must be regarded as analytically separate. *Internal efficacy* denotes a sense of individual citizen competence: 'I as a citizen possess the necessary personal qualifications to influence the political process by participating in it'. Such citizens do not feel that politics is too complicated for them to understand. They feel that they are reasonably well informed and at least equally as competent as anyone else to judge political matters; they may even feel that they would be personally qualified to hold public office if need be (Craig, Niemi and Silver 1990).

External efficacy pertains to the individual's perception of the political system: 'The system is open to citizen influence and responds to the needs and opinions expressed by the citizens'. As emphasised by Gimpel, Lay and Schuknecht (2003: 17), the sense of external efficacy 'is not simply a reflection of what one thinks of incumbent officeholders at a given moment; it reflects a more enduring attitude toward the system'.

Most studies have pointed to a clearly positive association between efficacy and political participation (Harris 1999: 81). It is, however, not particularly common to look for combined effects of internal and external efficacy. The present study does just that. A measure based on the sum of the following two survey items is used to gauge political efficacy: 1) 'Sometimes, politics seems so complicated that a person like me can't really understand what is going on'; and 2) 'People like me don't have any say in what the government and parliament do'. Table 5.4 shows that the correlation of political efficacy and voter turnout has increased over time. In 1983, the difference in turnout between voters with a strong political efficacy and those whose efficacy was weak was 12 percentage points. By the 2000s, this difference had roughly doubled.

Closely related to political interest and efficacy is the question of political knowledge. Citizens who are knowledgeable about politics are probably more likely to be interested in politics and feel that they understand the way politics works. Unlike these aspects, however, empirical observations about political knowledge do not need to depend on the respondents' own perceptions; it can

Table 5.4: Political efficacy and voter turnout

	1983	1991	2003	2007	2011
Strong efficacy	88	76	82	79	82
Rather strong efficacy	82	72	78	72	76
Rather weak efficacy	79	70	66	67	73
Weak efficacy	76	64	51	57	60
Correlation between political efficacy and voter turnout[1]	0.10	0.10	0.24	0.15	0.19

Data: FSD1011 (1983), FSD1018 (1991), FSD2269 (2007), FSD2653 (2011).
[1] Cramer's V.

be *tested* by researchers. A number of Finnish electoral surveys have included various knowledge questions: respondents are asked to choose between several response alternatives, of which one for each question is correct. It is, of course, possible that even some correct answers are based on guesswork rather than solid knowledge but it is unlikely that a large portion of respondents provide correct answers to most or all questions without any knowledge at all. The specific content of the questions has varied from survey to survey but the answers can readily be converted into a commensurable four-grade scale over time.

As was to be expected, turnout rises linearly with higher levels of political knowledge. Less than half of the respondents with poor political knowledge reported that they had voted. This was the case throughout the twenty-year period surveyed. Similarly, very high levels of turnout are to be found among citizens with a good level of political knowledge. The pattern is rather stable over time; if anything, the differences between citizens with low and high levels of knowledge have tended to rise.

The fourth question highlighted in this section is whether the perceived visibility of political alternatives has an effect on citizens' propensity to vote. The idea is that if the parties and their programmes are perceived to be clearly distinct, this should inspire voting more than if parties are deemed to be more or less alike. Informed by Russell Dalton's study of party-system polarisation (2008), an ordinal-scale variable was constructed on the basis of the following survey question: 'In politics people sometimes talk of left and right. Where would you place party A on a scale from 0 to 10 where 0 means the left and 10 means the right?' By combining the answers that respondents gave for each of the parties represented in parliament, overall scores for their perception of the polarisation of the Finnish party field could be calculated.

Once again, there is a reasonably clear pattern over time. In 1979, there was no difference in turnout between those citizens who viewed the ideological differences between parties as large and those who thought the differences were small. Three decades later, turnout among the former was approximately 20 percentage points higher than among the latter. Those who could not provide answers to the survey questions on which Table 5.6 is based have voted less than

Table 5.5: Political knowledge and voter turnout

	1991	2003	2007	2011
Good knowledge	83	82	86	87
Rather good knowledge	78	81	74	78
Rather poor knowledge	69	65	70	74
Poor knowledge	48	40	48	47
Correlation between political knowledge and voter turnout[1]	0.27	0.32	0.28	0.35

Data: FSD1018 (1991), FSD1260 (2003), FSD2269 (2007), FSD2265 (2011).
[1] Cramer's V.

Table 5.6: Image of party polarisation and its effect on voter turnout

	1979	1983	2003	2007	2011
Strong polarisation	81	84	78	78	82
Rather strong polarisation	88	83	73	78	76
Rather weak polarisation	84	83	73	69	75
Weak polarisation	81	78	65	58	66
Don't know	70	60	36	32	54
Correlation between party polarisation and voter turnout	0.5	0.18	0.22	0.27	0.22

Data: FSD1006 (1979), FSD1012 (1983), FSD1260 (2003), FSD2269 (2007) and FSD2653 (2011).

other citizens throughout the period. In 2007, a mere third of the respondents in this category reported that they had voted. This figure was, however, clearly higher in 2011, probably thanks to the mobilisation brought about by the True Finns among previous non-voters. Overall, it is clear that those voters who see marked differences between the party alternatives are today much more inclined to vote than those who view the parties as being rather similar.

Finally, the combined effects of the factors examined in this section are surveyed in a regression analysis (Table 5.7).

Political interest is the most consistently significant factor in explaining variations in turnout; its overall relevance has grown over time. Save for political efficacy, the other factors attain high levels of significance on most occasions, too.

Table 5.7: Logistic regression analyses of voter turnout

	2003	2007	2011
Political interest	2.22	1.98	2.87
	***	***	***
Political efficacy	1.14	1.12	1.15
	*		
Party polarisation	1.39	1.33	1.15
	***	***	*
Political knowledge	1.54	1.37	1.51
	***	***	***
Nagelkerke R^2	0.22	0.22	0.26
(N)	(1,411)	(1,407)	(1,285)

Data: FSD2269 (2007) and FSD2653 (2011).
Note: Regression coefficients are odds ratios (e^B). Overall goodness-of-fit of the models is measured with the Nagelkerke R^2 coefficient.

Electoral participation: Conclusions

Together with the data on party membership presented in Chapter Three, the evidence on electoral participation paints a somewhat disconcerting picture of the state of electoral democracy in Finland. Participation in elections has declined rapidly, in fact more rapidly than in most comparable states. With the rising levels of abstention from voting, the differences between those groups of citizens who vote and those who abstain have increased markedly. To a growing extent, the typical voter is middle-aged or older, well educated and a medium-to-high-income earner. Non-voters typically display opposite values on these indicators. Of particular concern is the rapid drop in turnout among the youngest voter cohorts; in particular, young voters with low levels of education tend to abstain *en masse* (Martikainen and Wass 2002; Martikainen, Martikainen and Wass 2005). Moreover, the differences between citizens who take an interest in politics and those who are uninterested have grown; the latter are increasingly likely not to vote at all. The same goes for political efficacy and political knowledge, although their effects on turnout are not quite as strong. Citizens who feel that they comprehend politics and view the political system as open and responsive, are more likely to vote than those who harbour opposite sentiments.

All in all, then, it seems that electoral participation in Finland is increasingly confined to citizens who fare relatively well in Finnish society. The typical voter is strong in terms of socio-economic resources, knowledge and subjective citizen competence. The opposite characteristics describe the typical non-voter. It is difficult to avoid seeing a parallel to a more general theme in contemporary debate, that about Finland as a 'two-thirds society'. That which is held to be true of economic and social well-being seems to apply to electoral participation in like manner.

Electoral choice

Party choice

The Finnish party system is fragmented but relatively stable. The emergence of new parties has not changed its structure in a definite manner. The quantitatively most significant change is the decline of the extreme left. The 2011 election vote-share of the Left Alliance is not much more than a third of the top achievements of its predecessor in the 1940s and 1950s. The Centre Party was weakened by the electoral success of the populists in the 1970s and 1980s and again, and most spectacularly, in 2011. Overall, however, the past three decades have been characterised by the even competition between the Social Democrats, the Centre Party and the Conservatives.

Table 5.8: Proportion of votes cast for different parties in parliamentary elections, 1945–2011

	Soc Dem	Cent	Cons	Left P	Green	Swe	Chr Dem	Pop	Lib	Others
1945	25.1	21.3	15.0	23.5	–	7.9	–	–	5.2	2.0
1948	26.3	24.2	17.1	20.0	–	7.3	–	–	3.9	1.2
1951	26.5	23.2	14.6	21.6	–	7.3	–	–	5.7	1.1
1954	26.2	24.1	12.6	21.6	–	6.8	–	–	7.9	0.6
1958	23.2	23.1	15.3	23.2	–	6.5	–	–	5.9	2.8
1962	19.5	23.0	15.0	22.0	–	6.1	–	2.2	6.3	5.9
1966	27.2	21.2	13.8	21.1	–	5.7	0.5	1.0	6.5	2.9
1970	23.4	17.1	18.0	16.6	–	5.3	1.1	10.5	6.0	2.0
1972	25.8	16.4	17.6	17.0	–	5.1	2.5	9.2	5.2	1.2
1975	24.9	17.6	18.4	18.9	–	4.7	3.3	3.6	4.3	4.3
1979	23.9	17.3	21.7	17.9	–	4.3	4.8	4.6	3.7	1.8
1983	26.7	17.6	22.1	13.5	1.4	4.9	3.0	9.7	–	1.1
1987	24.1	17.6	23.1	13.6	4.0	5.6	2.6	6.3	1.0	2.1
1991	22.1	24.8	19.3	10.1	6.8	5.5	3.1	4.8	0.8	2.7
1995	28.3	19.8	17.9	11.2	6.5	5.1	3.0	1.3	0.6	6.3
1999	22.9	22.4	21.0	10.9	7.3	5.1	4.2	1.0	0.2	5.0
2003	24.5	24.7	18.6	9.9	8.0	4.6	5.3	1.6	0.3	2.5
2007	21.4	23.1	22.3	8.8	8.5	4.6	4.9	4.1	0.1	2.2
2011	19.1	15.8	20.4	8.1	7.3	4.3	4.0	19.1	–	1.9
Average for 1991–2011	23.1	21.8	19.9	9.8	7.4	4.9	4.1	5.3	0.3	3.4

Party abbreviations:
Soc Dem   Social Democratic Party.
Cent   From 1907 to 1965 Agrarian Union, thereafter the Centre Party.
Cons   National Coalition.
Left P   From 1945 to 1990 Finnish People's Democratic Union (FPDU), from 1991 on Left Alliance (LA).
Green   Green League.
Swe   Swedish People's Party in Finland.
Chr Dem   From 1966 to 2002 Finnish Christian League, thereafter Finnish Christian Democrats.
Pop   From 1958 to 1966 Small Farmers' Party, from 1966 to 1995 Finnish Rural Party, thereafter True Finns.
Lib   From 1918 to 1950 National Progressive Party, from 1951 to 1965 Finnish People's Party, from 1965 to 1983 Liberal People's Party. In the parliamentary election of 1983 the Liberal People's Party was a member organisation of the Centre Party. From 1987 to 2002 Liberal People's Party, thereafter the Liberals.

Table 5.9: Proportion of votes cast for different parties in 2007 parliamentary election, by socio-demographic group

	Cent	Cons	Soc Dem	Left P	Green	Swe	Chr Dem	Pop	Others	All	
All valid votes	23.1	22.3	21.4	8.8	8.5	4.9	4.6	4.1	2.3	100	
Gender											
Men	23	23	23	10	6	3	4	5	2	100	(528)
Women	24	22	20	8	11	7	5	3	0	100	(528)
Age											
18–24	16	19	16	10	23	1	5	8	0	100	(73)
25–39	25	19	15	6	14	4	4	11	3	100	(229)
40–59	26	22	19	12	9	6	4	3	0	100	(352)
60+	21	26	29	8	3	5	5	2	2	100	(403)
Education											
Primary school	20	18	27	10	11	3	5	5	2	100	(256)
Vocational school	30	14	26	13	5	7	3	4	0	100	(322)
Vocational institute	23	30	19	4	8	5	5	5	2	100	(319)
University	18	33	11	10	15	5	8	1	1	100	(158)
Social class											
Working class	18	4	34	18	7	5	3	8	3	100	(296)
Lower-middle class	31	16	20	7	9	9	2	5	1	100	(128)

Table 5.9 (continued)

	Cent	Cons	Soc Dem	Left P	Green	Swe	Chr Dem	Pop	Others	All	
Middle class	26	29	19	4	9	4	5	3	0	100	(447)
Upper-middle class	14	49	7	7	10	2	9	2	1	100	(134)
No class at all or don't know	36	18	16	9	11	7	2	2	0	100	(45)
Family income											
I income quartile	30	7	27	10	9	8	4	4	2	100	(173)
II income quartile	24	19	25	10	9	6	4	4	1	100	(263)
III income quartile	26	23	18	12	6	3	4	6	3	100	(270)
IV income quartile	17	40	16	6	10	4	6	2	0	100	(236)

Note: For party abbreviations, *see* Table 5.8 with legend.
Data: Distribution of all valid votes from the official election registry. Data by gender, age, education, social class and family income from the Finnish National Election Study 2007, FSD2269.

Where in the Finnish population do the parties have their main bases of support? What, if any, are the main trends in this regard? Table 5.9 gives a detailed picture of the social bases of party support in the 2007 election.

In terms of gender and age, the supporters of the main parties do not seem radically different. However, when it comes to education, social class and income, the differences are reasonably clear. Conservative voters are wealthier, more educated and belong to the highest social classes significantly more than those citizens who vote for the Centre Party and, in particular, the Social Democrats. The Green voters present a different picture. Here it is precisely gender and age that seem important; a typical Green voter is a woman not older than 24 years. For the smaller parties, the sample is so limited that definite conclusions are difficult to draw.

How, if at all, did these patterns change with the spectacular success of the True Finns in 2011? Table 5.10 sheds light on this question.

The table indicates that the True Finns probably won voters from all major parties, although the Centre Party's losses stand out more than those of the others. According to Suhonen (2011: 623) individual-level data do not lend decisive support to the notion that it was the Centre Party in particular that lost voters to the True Finns. Nevertheless, the Centre Party did particularly poorly among the youngest voters, down 6 percentage points since the 2007 election. Overall, however, the socio-economic profiles of the traditional parties changed surprisingly little. Apart from the gender dimension – the True Finns stand out as a male-dominated party – the socio-economic profile of the populists does not deviate very much from those of the Centre Party and the left parties. A particular success for the True Finns lies in their strong showing among the youngest voters.

What are the more general trends in the social bases of support of political parties in Finland? In the following, focus will be on two variables: social class and income. As shown in Tables 5.9 and 5.10, these variables attained different values among the voters of the largest parties. Data for the past two decades illustrate trends in the importance of these factors for the party choice of Finnish voters.

No linear trend can be discerned concerning the importance of these two socio-economic factors for party choice in Finland. However, social class seems to have lost at least some of its explanatory power over the years. This would seem to indicate that the voters of the various parties have become more alike in terms of their subjective class affiliation. As for income level, its importance has been relatively stable, although the correlations are not particularly strong. The significance of income declined from 1991 to 2003. In the two most recent elections it was again slightly higher. The highest impact of income on party choice is, nevertheless, to be found at the beginning of the period.

Party choice presents an interesting contrast to some of the data presented above concerning electoral participation. While the socio-economic differences between voters and non-voters have increased, the adherents of the various parties have, if anything, become more alike in socio-economic terms. What has this development meant to the party loyalty of Finnish voters? Table 5.13 sheds some light on this question.

Table 5.10: Proportion of votes cast for different parties in 2011 parliamentary election, by socio-demographic group

	Cent	Cons	Soc Dem	Left P	Green	Swe	Chr Dem	Pop	Others	All
All valid votes	15.8	20.4	19.1	8.1	7.3	4.3	4.0	19.1	1.9	100
Gender										
Men	16	21	20	7	6	4	2	22	2	100 (520)
Women	16	20	18	9	9	5	6	16	1	100 (500)
Age										
18–24	10	15	12	14	16	4	0	18	12	100 (74)
25–39	16	20	15	7	16	4	2	18	3	100 (216)
40–59	14	18	18	10	6	4	6	23	1	100 (315)
60+	19	23	23	6	2	5	4	17	1	100 (415)
Education										
Primary school	16	16	21	9	6	5	2	20	5	100 (208)
Vocational school	18	12	21	12	3	3	6	25	2	100 (269)
Vocational institute	17	23	21	6	7	4	3	19	1	100 (363)
University	11	33	12	8	15	6	6	11	0	100 (181)
Social class										
Working class	9	6	31	16	3	3	2	29	2	100 (263)
Lower-middle class	22	8	24	7	5	4	8	20	3	100 (117)
Middle class	20	25	14	5	9	6	4	17	1	100 (423)
Upper-middle class	9	51	9	3	10	4	5	8	1	100 (145)
No class at all or don't know	21	3	17	13	13	3	6	17	6	100 (71)

Table 5.10 (continued)

	Cent	Cons	Soc Dem	Left P	Green	Swe	Chr Dem	Pop	Others	All	
Family income											
I income quartile	18	6	20	12	11	3	3	23	5	100	(144)
II income quartile	18	15	24	10	4	5	5	19	1	100	(250)
III income quartile	14	23	20	7	7	3	3	23	1	100	(241)
IV income quartile	15	29	14	7	10	5	3	16	1	100	(291)

Note: For party abbreviations, *see* Table 5.8 with legend.
Data: Distribution of all valid votes from the official election registry. Data by gender, age, education, social class and family income from the Finnish National Election Study 2011, FSD2653.

Table 5.11: Correlations between social class and party choice, by party, 1991–2011

	1991	1995	1999	2003	2007	2011
Soc Dem	0.38	0.29	0.23	0.25	0.19	0.15
Cent	0.14	0.10	0.16	0.15	0.11	0.12
Cons	0.45	0.34	0.35	0.24	0.31	0.31
Left P	0.20	0.25	0.22	0.19	0.21	0.14
Green	0.12	0.07	0.08	0.07	0.04	0.11
Swe	0.08	0.10	0.09	0.10	0.09	0.06
Chr Dem	0.11	0.07	0.05	0.07	0.07	0.08
Pop	0.14	0.09	0.08	0.15	0.12	0.10

Data: FSD1029 (1991), FSD1032 (1995), FSD1042 (1999), FSD1260 (2003) and FSD2269 (2007), FSD2653 (2011).
Notes: For party abbreviations, *see* Table 5.8 with legend.
Data on social class are based on the following survey question: 'To which social class would you say that you belong?'
The answers have been coded into four groups: a) working class b) lower-middle class, c) middle class + upper-middle class d) no class at all or don't know. Correlations are Cramer's V scores.

Table 5.12: Correlations between income group and party choice, by party, 1991–2011

	1991	1995	1999	2003	2007	2011
Soc Dem	0.09	0.06	0.03	0.07	0.11	0.06
Cent	0.05	0.07	0.08	0.04	0.11	0.02
Cons	0.23	0.18	0.20	0.16	0.26	0.22
Left P	0.07	0.07	0.05	0.07	0.07	0.04
Green	0.13	0.08	0.10	0.06	0.05	0.10
Swe	0.08	0.06	0.09	0.08	0.05	0.06
Chr Dem	0.11	0.09	0.05	0.08	0.09	0.03
Pop	0.18	0.12	0.03	0.09	0.09	0.06

Data: FSD1029 (1991), FSD1032 (1995), FSD1042 (1999), FSD1260 (2003) and FSD2269 (2007), FSD2653 (2011).
Notes: For party abbreviations, *see* Table 5.8 with legend.
Correlations are Cramer's V scores.
Income group of the family divided in four quartiles.

Figure 5.2: Correlations between social class and party choice and between income and party choice, 1991–2011; values of Cramer's V

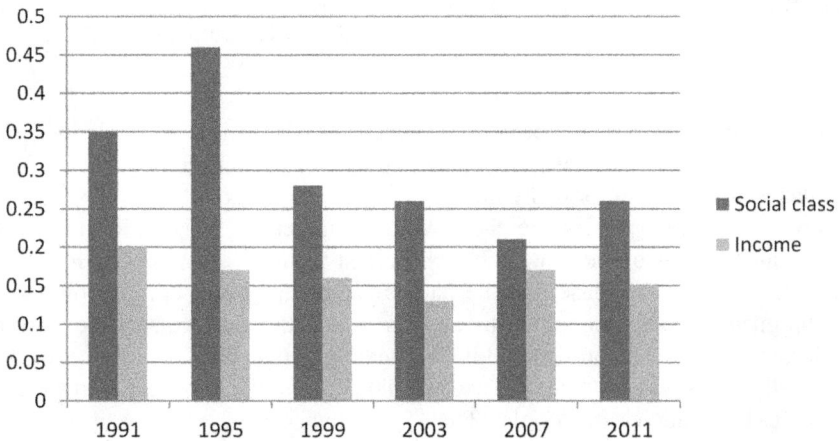

Data: FSD1029 (1991), FSD1032 (1995), FSD1042(1999), FSD1260 (2003), FSD2269 (2007), FSD2653 (2011).
Notes: Social class in four groups: a) working class, b) lower-middle class, c) middle class + upper middle class, d) no class at all or cannot say.
Income: family income in quartiles.

Table 5.13: Party loyalty of voters in parliamentary elections, 1975–2011

	Soc Dem	Cent	Cons	Left P	Green	Chr Dem	Swe	Pop	All voters
1975	88	80	84	91	–	75	81	42	74
1979	85	86	88	85	–	72	88	40	79
1983	89	86	93	78	–	48	82	56	76
1987	90	88	89	76	68	87	75	48	73
1991	73	85	72	81	67	79	86	44	66
1995	73	64	57	67	53	52	74	24	61
1999	61	79	78	78	70	84	67	43	66
2003	70	71	74	51	49	43	79	22	67
2007	71	81	88	78	53	67	79	52	50
2011	62	68	74	54	44	65	70	79	64
Average for 1975–2011	76	79	80	74	58	67	78	45	68

Data: FSD1002 (1975), FSD1005 (1979), FSD1010 (1982), FSD1013 (1986), FSD1016 (1990), FSD1018 (1991), FSD1031 (1995), FSD1038 (1999), FSD1260 (2003), FSD2269 (2007), FSD2653 (2011).
Notes: Party loyalty by party measures what percentage of those who cast their votes for a given party in a given election did so in the next election as well. For example, the value 62 for the Social Democrats in the 2011 election should be read: 62 per cent of the respondents who cast their vote for the Social Democrats in 2007 supported this party in the election of 2011, too.

Once again, a definite linear trend cannot be discerned. Nevertheless, the general course of development is reasonably clear. Save for the populists, whose popular following is notoriously unstable, and, to some extent, for the Christian Democrats, Finnish parties are faced with an increasingly volatile electorate. A growing portion of the voters switch parties from election to election, thus shrinking the electoral base that the parties can safely count on. Together with the diminishing socio-economic differences among the adherents of the various parties, this makes electoral competition demanding indeed.

Finally, some words about the exceptional success of the populist True Finns in the 2011 election seem in order. The 15 percentage-point advance of the party represents one of the greatest victories ever scored by a Finnish party. Studies by Sami Borg (2012) and David Arter (2013a and 2013b) present a picture of the dynamics of this success. Apparently, the rise to prominence of the True Finns was due to a confluence of both long- and short-term factors. On the one hand, there was a growing dissatisfaction, going back several decades, with the way parliamentary politics had been handled by the three largest parties. On the other hand, True Finn support was boosted by two spectacular crises, one of them Finnish, the other European, in the years immediately preceding the election. The debate and indignation created by the way party and electoral finance had been handled (*see* Chapter Three) by some of the main parties clearly lent credibility to the True Finns' criticism of 'old parties' as an elite interested only in itself. The European financial crisis and, in particular, the aid packages to Greece and Portugal, made large parts of the electorate more receptive to the EU-critical stance of the True Finns (Borg 2012).

Equally important, the nomination process was an apparent success. The fact that the Party was able to present a slate of candidates in all fourteen mainland constituencies was in itself a success. Moreover, the absence of a large number of incumbents apparently inspired True Finn candidates to campaign actively and attract attention, despite being previously unknown (Arter 2013a and 2013b).

In terms of sources of support, the True Finns in 2011 won voters from all main parties. Both in relative and absolute terms, the Social Democrats and the Centre Party lost most voters to the populists. Equally important, the True Finns were able to mobilise previous non-voters and attract large portions of first-time voters. From a social and demographic point of view, Finnish populism stands out as a male-dominated lower- and middle-class movement. Attitudinally, the wish to shake up a party system viewed as immobile and elitist seems to have been the most important driving force. The oft-mentioned anti-immigration and anti-EU sentiments clearly also played a role; but they were apparently less important than the critical attitude towards established parties in general.[3] In ideological terms, True Finn voters represent the centre rather than the extremes of the continuum; they are definitely not right-wing as concerns social and economic policy (Borg 2012). They are worried about the future of Finland as a Nordic welfare state, which they think the established parties are sacrificing at the altars of marketisation, European integration and globalisation.

Personalised choice?

Parliamentary politics is conditioned by the electoral success of political parties. The relative strength of parties in parliament resulting from elections largely determines the basis on which governments can be formed. Parties are, however, represented in parliament and cabinet by individual politicians of flesh and blood. To what extent do voters' choices at the polls reflect their perceptions of individual politicians, their merits and flaws? Is the importance of individual politicians increasing; may these assessments in fact be more important to voters than parties and other collective identities?

A persistent notion about political development during the past several decades is that politics in the democratic west has become *personalised*. According to this idea, individual politicians have become more important to voters, at the expense of parties, ideologies and collective solidarity. Naturally enough, journalistic accounts of politics have found this perspective particularly appealing. The personalisation thesis has, however, also resonated well with large parts of

---

3. An earlier study by Elina Kestilä (2006: 185–6), however, revealed that anti-immigrant attitudes co-vary with several of the socio-economic characteristics of typical True Finn voters.

the political science community, as is evident from the following quotations from renowned scholars in the field:

> [...] people vote differently from one election to another, depending on the particular persons competing for their vote. Voters tend increasingly to vote for a person and no longer for a party or a platform. This phenomenon marks a departure from what was considered normal voting behavior under representative democracy, creating an impression of a crisis in representation [...] (Manin 1997: 219).

> Although the growing importance of personal factors can also be seen in the relationship between each representative and his constituency, it is most perceptible at the national level, in the relationship between the executive and the electorate. Analysts have long observed that there is a tendency towards the personalization of power in democratic countries (*ibid.*).

> The growing tendency to aggregate around individual politicians produces a personalization of politics reflecting the atomization of power, which breaks up into many competing centers that conflict and cooperate with each other and seek a political authority, exercised and personified by a single individual, with which to identify. These changes are part of a circular process in which power flows from the party structure, the traditional intermediary of political consensus, to individual politicians, resulting in a lessening of the ability of parties to manage political institutions and, in turn, a decline of the institutions' ability to act effectively (Swanson and Mancini 1996: 10).

> [...] the personalization of politics will remain a – and perhaps *the* – central feature of democratic politics in the twenty-first century (McAllister 2007: 585).

A growing body of research has subjected the personalisation thesis to empirical scrutiny. Although much systematic research still remains to be done, the evidence is extensive enough to permit a few general conclusions. Although examples of the decisive influence of party leaders and individual candidates on the outcome of elections can readily be found, a general and linear trend towards more personalised politics cannot be demonstrated. To be sure, the focus of media presentations and electoral campaigns has increasingly been on party leaders in particular. However, when it comes to the importance of party leaders to voter choices, systematic evidence simply does not permit a conclusion that there is an increase in recent decades. As to the role of individual candidates for voter choices, the evidence is mixed, at best (for a review, *see* Karvonen 2010).

For two reasons, Finland is an interesting case in this regard. First, unlike almost all comparable cases, the electoral system compels the voter to choose not just between parties but between individual candidates representing the party of their choice (*cf.* Bengtsson *et al.* 2014: 81–102). Has the choice of candidates begun to weigh more heavily over the years? Is voting in Finland, in other words, more candidate-centred than it used to be? Second, as was shown in Chapter Four, the role of the prime minister has become more pronounced in Finnish politics, due to the reform process that culminated in the 2000 Constitution. As the leader of the party that receives the highest share of parliamentary seats is very likely to be the prime minister of the subsequent post-election government, Finnish elections, much more than earlier ones, decide who is to be the next prime minister. An interesting question, therefore, is whether voters attach more importance to the qualities of the various party leaders than they used to.

These two aspects – the importance to voters of individual candidates and party leaders – form the focus of this section. Most of the empirical evidence originates from surveys and therefore reflects the subjective views of the respondents. To a certain extent, however, use will also be made of register data on the distribution of preference votes among candidates.

The most obvious question to ask is of course whether it is party or candidate that matters more to voters when they cast their votes. This item has been included in a number of electoral surveys since 1983; in the FNES surveys from 2003 on, it has been asked in connection with each parliamentary election. Table 5.14 shows how the answers to this question have changed over the years.

Until 2007, there was a steady, albeit by no means dramatic, increase in the share of those who reported that candidate weighed more heavily than party. That year, the share of these respondents for the first time was more than 50 per cent. However, the 2011 election brought about a change in this regard. Quite evidently, the massive challenge from the populist True Finns is the main explanation. On the one hand, those who opposed the True Finns probably felt that it was important to mark their sympathies for parties challenged by the populists. On the other hand– and perhaps even more importantly – populist voters tended to

Table 5.14: Importance of party and candidate to Finnish voters, 1983–2011, selected years (%)

	1983	1991	2003	2007	2011
Party more important	52	51	49	48	55
Candidate more important	42	43	47	51	44
Cannot say	6	6	4	1	1
Total	100	100	100	100	100
(N)	(993)	(1,141)	(1,004)	(1,172)	(1,124)

Sources: Pesonen *et al.* 1993: 724 (1983 and 1991), FSD1260 (2003), FSD2269 (2007), FSD2653 (2011).
Note: Based on the following survey question: 'In the final analysis, which was more important to you, party or candidate?'

emphasise their party choice. To be sure, in the electoral district (Uusimaa) where the immensely popular True Finn leader Timo Soini was a candidate, many voters cast their votes for him – and therefore for the True Finns as a party – because of his personal appeal. In the rest of Finland, voters did not have this choice and, moreover, many of the candidates were new and fairly unknown. This may explain why the supporters of the True Finns probably tended to emphasise party over candidate when asked this question.

Unfortunately, there is precious little in the way of comparative data that would help put the Finnish evidence into perspective. The exception is a few Irish electoral surveys that have contained similar items (*see* Karvonen 2010: 56; Karvonen 2012: 48). The two countries have different electoral systems and the survey questions have not been formulated in an entirely identical manner. Nevertheless, it seems that the emphasis on candidates is stronger and has grown more in Ireland than in Finland. In 1979, 51 per cent of the Irish respondents said party was more important and 46 per cent said candidate was more important, while 4 per cent could not say. In 2011, the corresponding figures were 23, 70 and 7 per cent, respectively.

This difference between Finland and Ireland persists when the question is formulated in a different way. Inspired by Irish election studies, the 2011 FNES survey contained the following item: 'If the candidate for whom you voted had represented another party, would you still have voted for him/her?' Table 5.15 shows the responses to this question compared to similar questions in two Irish surveys.

Clearly fewer Finnish than Irish voters would be willing to support the candidate of their choice irrespective of the party affiliation of the candidate. Only one in ten Finnish voters indicate that party affiliation does not matter to them, while more than

Table 5.15: To what extent is candidate choice dependent on party affiliation of candidates? Comparisons between Ireland and Finland (%)

Ireland 2002	If this candidate* had been running for any of the other parties would you still have given a first-preference vote to him/her?			
	No	Yes	Depends on party	
	38	46	16	
Ireland 2011	If this candidate* had been running for any of the other parties would you still have given a first-preference vote to him/her?			
	No	Yes	Depends on party/ Cannot say	
	35	32	33	
Finland 2011	If the candidate for whom you voted had represented another party, would you still have voted for him/her?			
	No	Yes	Yes, if the party was suitable to me	Cannot say
	56	10	32	2

* *The candidate to whom the respondent had given his/her first-preference vote.*
Sources: Ireland 2002: Marsh 2007: 523; Ireland 2011: data provided by Professor Michael Marsh; Finland 2011: FSD2653.

half of them, in fact, seem to choose party first and candidate after that. The middle position – that a candidate might be considered if he or she ran for *some* but not *any* other party – is also acceptable to many voters in both Finland and Ireland.

Overall, Table 5.15 nuances the data presented in Table 5.14. When voters say that candidate matters more than party they do not necessarily mean that they are willing to consider the candidates of all parties in an unprejudiced manner. Rather, they perhaps indicate that they give the choice of candidate more or less thought when they vote. If this is a correct interpretation, then the data indicate that the importance of candidates grew until the rise to prominence of the True Finns in 2011. Again, it is difficult to determine whether the 2011 election signified a new trend or merely a temporary deviation.

Which voters, then, are party-oriented and which voters stress the importance of candidate? Table 5.16 examines the demographic, socio-economic and political

Table 5.16: Relative importance of party and candidate in Finnish parliamentary elections of 2007 and 2011, in light of explanatory factors (%)

	2007			2011		
	Party more important	Candidate more important	N	Party more important	Candidate more important	N
All	48	52	1,156	56	44	1,113
Gender						
Woman	48	52	590	55	45	545
Man	49	51	566	56	44	568
Age						
18–24	47	53	79	65	35	75
25–34	42	58	160	59	41	159
35–44	44	56	150	48	52	155
45–54	41	59	208	49	51	169
55–64	51	49	248	56	44	217
65+	57	43	311	59	41	338
Education						
Elementary	47	53	89	57	43	81
Secondary	51	49	193	64	36	149
Vocational	47	53	395	52	48	295
Intermediate	46	54	266	60	40	282
Professional	46	54	80	56	44	108
Academic	53	47	168	50	50	199
Interest in politics						
No interest	36	64	42	33	67	27
Limited interest	39	61	295	52	48	198
Some interest	50	50	579	54	44	598
Great interest	58	42	240	64	36	289

Table 5.16 (continued)

	2007			2011		
	Party more important	Candidate more important	N	Party more important	Candidate more important	N
Political knowledge						
Weak	42	58	207	51	49	270
Fair	44	56	390	54	46	300
Good	53	47	321	56	44	335
Excellent	54	46	240	63	37	209
Party identity						
None	7	83	82	37	63	74
Weak	28	72	196	39	61	234
Fairly strong	44	56	427	53	47	417
Strong	67	33	450	72	28	385
Left-right self-placement						
Left	65	35	109	63	37	120
Leans left	53	47	184	58	42	177
Centre	41	59	252	47	53	232
Leans right	42	58	315	52	42	307
Right	59	41	253	66	34	220
Party choice						
Cent	44	56	242	45	55	162
Soc Dem	54	46	244	54	46	193
Cons	55	45	210	61	39	204
Left	49	51	91	53	47	81
Green	44	56	109	55	45	74
Swe	66	34	50	73	27	44
Chr Dem	43	57	63	59	41	41
True F	39	61	38	67	33	195

Sources: FSD2269 (2007) and FSD2653 (2011).
Note: Based on the following survey question: 'In the final analysis, which was more important to you, party or candidate?'

characteristics of these two groups of respondents. Included are the two most recent parliamentary elections in Finland.

Table 5.16 bears witness to both continuity and change between 2007 and 2011. To begin with, it is interesting to note the *absence* of a statistically significant correlation at both elections:

- The *gender* of voters lacks explanatory power on both occasions: men and women stress party and candidate to the same extent.

A few factors turned out to possess statistically significant explanatory power[4] in connection with both elections. These factors represent *continuity* between two elections that differed from each other in many other respects:

- *The oldest voter categories* primarily emphasised the importance of party.
- Voters who took a considerable *interest in politics* similarly stressed party over candidate.
- The same goes for voters with *high levels of political knowledge*.
- The *less established the party preference* of a voter, the more he/she stressed the importance of candidate.
- *Self-placement on the left-right scale* also played a role: voters close to the middle of the scale stressed candidate, whereas left- and right-wing voters emphasised party.
- *Party choice* had a similar effect: those who voted for the Social Democrats, the Conservatives and the Swedish People's Party emphasised party, whereas Centre Party voters stressed candidate.

The following observations signal *change* between 2007 and 2011:

- *The youngest voters* emphasised party much more in 2011 than four years earlier.
- The same goes for *the least educated voters*: level of education was not a statistically significant factor in 2007, which it was in 2011.
- A corresponding change had occurred among voters with a *low level of political knowledge*.
- Green, Christian and True Finn voters emphasised the importance of candidate in 2007. The importance of party to these voter groups had grown considerably four years later; in the case of the True Finns, this change was rather remarkable.

All in all, the results convey a rather clear picture of party-centred and candidate-centred voting. The most stable part of the electorate – citizens with a high degree of interest in politics and good political knowledge – regard the party as of central importance. These voter segments also turn out actively to vote. Voters with opposite characteristics – limited political interest and poor knowledge of politics – emphasise the role of candidates more. These generalisations are still valid but they were put to a test at the 2011 election. Thanks to the landslide victory of the True Finns, the party won scores of votes from segments that typically had emphasised candidate rather than party previously. In 2011, however, it seems that most True Finn voters supported them as a party instead of focusing on candidates as individuals (with the obvious exception of Timo Soini in the Uusimaa district). Should the support for the True Finns turn out to be as unstable as that of its populist predecessors, it may well be that the figures on party *vs.* candidate will return to their pre-2011 levels.

What, if any, are the changes in the long-term distribution of votes on individual candidates? If the thesis about the personalisation of politics holds true,

---

4.   The value of chi square was significant on at least the .05 level.

one might expect the distribution of candidate votes to look different today than in earlier periods. More specifically, personalisation would predict the following. If voters attach greater importance to the qualities of individual candidates, the channels that provide information about candidates and their qualities will play an increasingly significant role in the political process. Access to such channels – visibility in the media and the public sphere – is always unevenly distributed among candidates. Those candidates that have such access will, therefore, have an increasing advantage over other candidates. Over time, therefore, we can expect *an increasing concentration of candidate votes on the most popular candidates.*

Table 5.17 would indeed seem to indicate that the 2000s have witnessed a certain concentration of candidate votes on the most popular candidates. The figures peaked in 2007, when Sauli Niinistö, later President of the Republic, received a completely unprecedented 60,563 personal votes in the district of Uusimaa. Four years later, Niinistö was no longer a candidate but the share of the most popular candidates still remained at a fairly high level compared to earlier decades. Populist leader Soini and Alexander Stubb, a highly popular Foreign Minister, both received more than 40,000 personal votes in the Uusimaa district. Apparently, there seems to be a tendency today towards a concentration of votes on a few extremely popular candidates in the largest electoral districts. Although this by no means indicates a pervasive process of personalisation, it lends the thesis a degree of support.

Journalistic accounts of politics and elections often regard the role of *party leaders* as decisive.[5] In this view, the personal popularity of party leaders is seen as the key factor for electoral success; it is party leaders who 'win' or 'lose' elections.

Table 5.17: Share of the most popular candidates of all valid votes, 1975–2011 (%)

Election year	Candidate with most personal votes	5 candidates with most personal votes	10 candidates with most personal votes	20 candidates with most personal votes
1975	0.8	3.1	5.3	9.3
1979	0.9	3.1	5.8	9.1
1983	0.8	3.3	6.0	10.3
1987	0.6	2.8	5.1	8.8
1991	0.8	3.6	6.1	9.9
1995	0.7	3.0	5.6	9.7
1999	1.1	3.4	5.8	10.1
2003	0.9	3.6	6.1	10.2
2007	2.2	5.0	7.2	11.5
2011	1.5	4.8	7.2	10.9

Sources: Statistics Finland, Electoral statistics 1975–2011.

---

5.   On 28 August 1996, the UK daily *Observer* ran a telling headline: 'Never mind the policies, just feel the leaders'. Quoted in King 2003b: 2.

The importance of party leaders is assumed to have grown during recent decades and to continue to do so. Systematic empirical research on stable parliamentary democracies tells a different story: 'Voters' evaluations of party leaders appear to be as important or unimportant now as when they were first measured by the series of surveys we have been analyzing. Nothing much seems to have changed', Curtice and Holmberg write after having surveyed six west-European democracies during nearly four decades (2005: 251–2). Other scholars (Holmberg and Oscarsson 2004; Karvonen 2010; King 2003a) have reached similar conclusions.

In the Finnish case, however, the role of party leaders deserves closer scrutiny because of the effects of the constitutional-reform process of the 1990s. Today, much more than under the 1919 Constitution, Finnish parliamentary elections are referenda of sorts on the next prime minister. In practice, with the sole exception of the 2011 election, three parties have competed for the position as the largest party: the Social Democrats, the Centre Party and the Conservatives. The following account will therefore be limited to these three parties.

A number of surveys have asked the question whether and to what extent party leaders are believed to influence the electoral success of their respective parties. Do citizens believe that a given party leader boosts his/her party's electoral success, has little impact or in fact diminishes the party's electoral following? Table 5.18 shows how respondents have viewed the role of the leaders of the three largest parties from 1984–2007.

Table 5.18: Citizens' views of impact of leaders of three largest parties on electoral fortunes of their parties, 1984–2007 (mean index values)

Year	Mean value of index	N
1984	0.83	1,198
1988	0.75	1,047
1990	0.71	977
1992	0.91	836
1994	0.75	1,520
1995	0.85	1,455
1996	0.87	1,042
1997	0.89	1,367
2000	0.83	1,517
2007	1.00	1,027

Sources: FSD2276 (1984–1990), FSD2274 (1992–2000), FSD2269 (2007).
Note: Index from 0 to 2 based on answers to the survey question 'How is party X affected by the fact that it is led by NN?' The index is a sum variable for which response alternatives have been coded as follows: increases support a great deal 2, increases support somewhat 1, no effect 0, reduces support somewhat 1, reduces support a great deal 2.

It is important to note that the measure used concerns the *extent* but not the *direction* of the assumed party-leader effects on electoral support. Thus, the table does not differentiate between negative and positive effects; if persons are important, this should work both ways. The figures for the individual years are somewhat difficult to compare, as respondents tend to ascribe recently selected party leaders lower values than to more experienced leaders – whom, of course, they know better. The time-period covered is, however, so long that such effects should be evened out. An overall trend does not seem to exist: estimations of the impact of party leaders have varied somewhat from year to year but it would be inaccurate to speak of a general increase. Still, it is noteworthy that the index value for 2007 is the highest one ever measured. This was the only year in the time series during which the effects of the new constitution on government-formation were unequivocal. Parliament had resolved, in 2002, that the task of forming a government after an election under the new constitution would first go to the leader of the party that had the largest number of parliamentary seats. This led to a heightened interest in the personal competence of the leaders of the three main parties. The figure for 2007 most likely reflects this increased focus on party leaders in the public debate.

Table 5.19 shows that there is a growing tendency to emphasise the suitability of the party leader as prime minister among those voters who vote for the three established main parties. For many years, it is from among these three parties that prime ministers have been chosen. In 2011, more than half of the supporters of these parties considered the suitability of the party leader as prime minister to be a factor of considerable or decisive importance to their party choice. While the development in the 2000s has by no means been dramatic, it does match the expectation that the role of party leaders as prime ministerial candidates has become more pronounced.

To sum up: the conclusion concerning the alleged personalisation of politics in the Finnish case seems to support the thesis somewhat more than in many comparable

Table 5.19: Importance of influencing choice of prime minister to Conservative, Social Democratic and Centre Party voters in 2003, 2007 and 2011 (%)

		2003	2007	2011
How much was your choice of party influenced by the suitability of the party's leader as prime minister?	Decisively	20	21	23
	Considerably	24	24	30
	To some extent	26	22	24
	Not at all	28	32	22
	Cannot say	1	1	1
	Total	100	100	100
	(N)	590	704	564

Sources: FSD 1260 (2003), FSD2269 (2007) and FSD2653 (2011).
Note: Suitability as prime minister: responses to the survey question 'to what extent was your choice of party affected by the following factors?' Response alternative: 'The leader of the party was in my view most suitable as prime minister.'

cases. To a degree, the conclusion must depend on how the effects on the True Finn offensive in 2011 are interpreted. In 2011, more voters than in previous elections stressed party over candidate as a motive for electoral choice. If one sees the True Finn landslide as a typical 'flash phenomenon', one may argue that the tendency to stress the importance of candidates is likely to return to its earlier levels. If that is the case, then Finland can be seen as an affirmative case from the point of view of the personalisation thesis. The most popular candidates receive growing shares of all candidate votes and the role of party leaders is becoming more prominent as a motive behind party choice. The changes are gradual and proceed at a moderate pace – but they are there. They match the changes in parliamentary politics brought about by the constitutional reform and they also go hand in hand with the growing alienation from parties to which many of the analyses in this book have pointed.

Citizens and the political system

The evidence presented thus far in this chapter points to changes in Finnish voter behaviour that seem to match many of the expectations created by the earlier chapters. Electoral participation has declined more rapidly than in most comparable countries. Electoral volatility has grown and the socio-economic determinants of party choice have lost some of their explanatory power. A gradual shift towards a more personalised way of viewing politics seems to have taken place.

Are these trends confined to the relationship between parties and voters; do they therefore manifest themselves only in the electoral context? Or are they indications of a more fundamental change in political life, meaning that the relationship between citizens and the political system at large has been altered in recent decades? These are the queries addressed in this final empirical section of this chapter.

A question of fundamental importance is, of course, how citizens view democracy as a system. Do citizens, irrespective of their attitude towards incumbent governments and leaders, view democracy as a desirable political order? If this is the case, they are likely to respect its principles even if they dislike current leaders and policies. In countries where the legitimacy of democracy as a system is strong, outbursts of generalised discontent that threaten the democratic order are not likely.

Citizen attitudes towards democracy are often gauged with the aid of the following item from the World Value Surveys: 'Democracy may have its problems, but it's better than any other form of government'. The FNES surveys have included this item as of 2003; prior to that, Finnish respondents were asked this question twice in the World Value Surveys.

In the 2000s, 90 per cent or more of the Finns have viewed democracy as the best political system imaginable; the share of such respondents has grown over the years. The two most recent surveys demonstrate a particularly marked growth in the share of 'strong democrats', that is, persons who completely agree with the statement. In the mid-1990s, the acceptance of democracy was somewhat lower. The most apparent reason is that Finland was going through the most severe economic crisis since the Great Depression. Overall, the general acceptance of democracy is about the same as in most west European nations and stronger than

Figure 5.3: Democracy may have its problems, but it's better than any other form of government

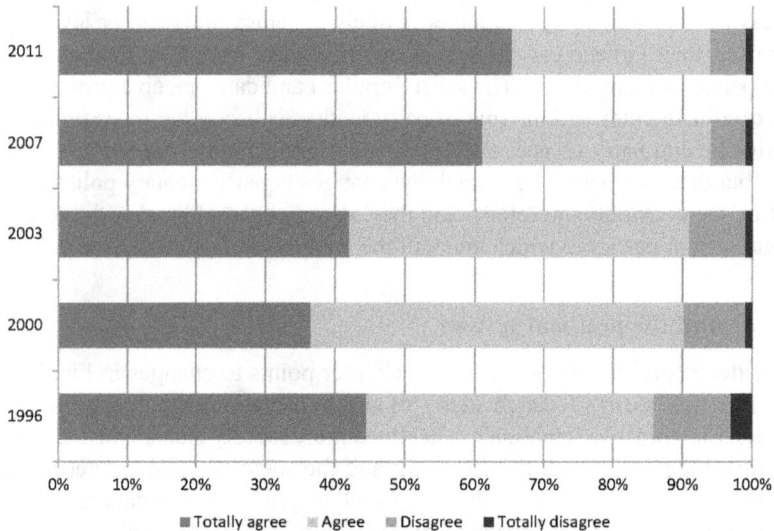

Data: FSD0152 (1996), FSD0157 (2000), FSD1260 (2003), FSD2263 (2007), FSD2653 (2011)

in most east European countries. In Finland's Nordic neighbours, this share is, however, slightly higher still.[6]

Democracy as a principle may be held in high esteem but this does not necessarily translate into support for those institutions without which democratic processes cannot be carried out. Legislative institutions are needed to make rules; a civil service must be in place to carry out government policy; courts must function in order to provide rule adjudication. These government institutions must be examined by independent media and they must interact with free organisations such as parties and interest groups. All these institutions are needed to make democracy work. If citizens view them or several of them with great distrust, this may create problems for democracy as such.

Throughout the democratic west, trust in political and public institutions tends to be lower than the general acceptance of democracy itself. When measured on a scale from zero to 10 (0 = no trust, 10 = complete trust), the following averages were found for 24 European countries: the police 5.6; the legal system 4.8; the parliament 4.3; politicians 3.4; and political parties 3.4 (Grönlund and Setälä, 2012: 528). Finland, along with the other Nordic countries, displayed the highest level of institutional trust. How has institutional trust in Finland evolved over time? Table 5.20 sheds some light on this question.

---

6.   http://www.wvsevsdb.com/wvs/WVSAnalizeQuestion.jsp

Table 5.20: Trust in political and public institutions in Finland, in 1990, 2000 and 2008 (% of those trusting a great deal or quite a lot)

	1990	2000	2008
National parliament	34	42	42
Civil service	33	40	46
Legal system	66	67	73
Trade Unions	32	54	48
Press	38	36	42

Data: European Values Study 1990, 2000 and 2008.
Note: Response alternatives were: a great deal, quite a lot, not very much, not at all.

Trust in political and public institutions in Finland has been strengthened over time. In 1990, an average of roughly 40 per cent of the respondents said they trusted the institutions in question. Eighteen years later, this figure was around 50 per cent. This finding goes hand in hand with the strengthened legitimacy of democracy as a fundamental principle, demonstrated in Figure 5.3. A negative trend concerning the fundamentals of the Finnish system of government cannot be documented; in fact, it is the other way around.[7]

Whether citizen trust in politicians and parties should be viewed as part and parcel of the legitimacy of the political system is a difficult question. On the one hand, if large parts of the citizenry view parties as entirely untrustworthy, this may have negative effects on system legitimacy as a whole. On the other hand, it is very difficult to tell whether citizens can differentiate between the *right* of politicians and parties to make decisions and *which policies* they pursue once elected into office. Nevertheless, it is interesting to see whether Finnish citizens view parties and politicians differently from citizens elsewhere. European Social Survey data can be used to put Finland into a broader comparative perspective (Table 5.21).

Table 5.21 shows that trust in politicians and parties in western Europe has generally declined in the 2000s. Finland is part of this pattern. The decline in trust has been slightly faster in Finland than in western Europe at large but, generally, the figures for Finland have been close to European averages. The highest levels of trust are to be found in Germany and – somewhat surprisingly – in Greece (but this was, of course, before the massive financial crisis). Scandinavia displays, perhaps equally surprisingly, relatively low levels of trust. Trust is somewhat higher in Finland than elsewhere in Scandinavia but the differences are small. Overall, the development of citizen trust in politicians and parties in Finland appears to be in line with many of the other indicators measuring citizen engagement in party

---

7.   Interestingly enough, when Bengtsson and Mattila studied the support of alternatives such as referenda and government by experts to existing political institutions in Finland, the support of such alternatives was found to be strongest among least educated and least politically knowledgeable citizens. These groups are, of course, least likely to vote or engage in politics in general. *See* Bengtsson and Mattila 2009.

Table 5.21: Average trust in politicians and parties in western Europe in the 2000s

Country	Trust in politicians 2002	Trust in politicians 2004	Trust in politicians 2010	Trust in parties 2004	Trust in parties 2010
Austria	5.4	4.8	n/a	4.8	n/a
Belgium	4.5	3.8	3.3	3.8	3.3
Switzerland	4.8	4.5	2.9	4.4	2.8
Germany	7.0	6.1	5.8	6.2	5.8
Denmark	3.6	3.1	3.0	3.1	3.0
Spain	4.0	3.5	3.6	3.5	3.7
Finland	*4.8*	*4.3*	*3.6*	*4.3*	*3.6*
France	3.6	3.9	3.4	3.9	3.4
UK	4.9	4.0	4.6	4.1	4.6
Greece	6.1	5.2	5.3	5.2	5.3
Ireland	4.8	4.8	4.9	4.9	4.9
Luxembourg	3.4	3.2	n/a	3.2	n/a
The Netherlands	5.6	4.0	3.5	4.0	3.5
Norway	4.9	3.8	3.0	3.8	3.0
Portugal	3.6	4.4	4.1	4.4	4.2
Sweden	4.7	4.2	2.9	4.2	2.9
ALL	5.0	4.2	3.9	4.2	3.9

Source: European Social Survey: http://nesstar.ess.nsd.uib.no/webview
Note: Based on ESS survey questions: 'How much do you personally trust politicians/political parties? 0 means you do not trust politicians/political parties at all, and 10 means you have complete trust.'

politics presented in this book. It is clear, however, that Finland is part of a general European pattern rather than a deviant case in this regard.

If democracy and its institutions are generally accepted by Finnish citizens, then perhaps the growing distance between citizens and parties is a reflection of a general de-politicisation of the people? In other words, people may think that democracy is a good principle and its institutions reasonably trustworthy but they are simply losing interest in politics. Many things compete for people's attention and one hypothesis is that we have entered a less political era than, say, the 1960s and 1970s, when electoral participation and party membership peaked. Figure 5.4 contains evidence that sheds light on this question.

Figure 5.4 emphatically belies the notion that a declining interest in politics lies behind the behavioural patterns observed earlier in this study. Interest in politics has grown linearly in the roughly three decades the data cover. In 1979, a little over 40 per cent of the survey respondents said they were very interested or rather interested in politics; in 2011, the corresponding figure was approximately 30 percentage points higher.

Figure 5.4: Interest in politics

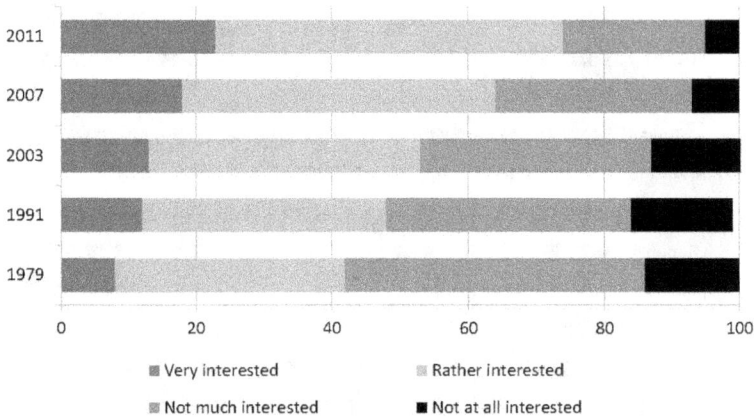

Sources: Pesonen *et al.* 1993: 179 (years 1966 and 1991), FSD1004 (1977), FSD1013 (1986), FSD0153 (1996), FSD1260 (2003) and FSD2269 (2007)
Note: Based on the survey question 'How interested are you in politics?'

Thus far, little seems to indicate that the decline in electoral participation and party activity, demonstrated earlier in this book, has begun to affect citizens' attitudes toward democratic governance more generally. More than nine out of ten Finns support democracy as the foundation of government and politics and this share is growing over time. Confidence in central democratic institutions is on a comparatively high level and growing rather than diminishing. To be sure, confidence in politicians and parties displays the opposite trend. This was, however, to be expected, and Finland is a rather typical west European case in this regard. Political interest among Finnish citizens displays a growth over time: which seems surprising, given the decline in electoral participation and party membership.

There is, however, one aspect of politics where Finnish responses in comparative surveys display patterns that are clearly different from not just their Nordic neighbours but from western Europe more generally. Finns seem to find politics difficult to understand. When the 2008 European Social Survey asked 'How often does politics seem so complicated that you can't really understand what is going on?', Finns, along with respondents from eastern, southern and south-east Europe were among those who said this was often the case. Citizens of other Nordic countries, as well as throughout western Europe, found it easier to comprehend politics (Figure 5.5).

A reasonable explanation of this rather unexpected result might be that the level of political knowledge in Finland is low; Finns may simply be politically more ignorant than citizens in comparable countries. Alas, political knowledge is notoriously difficult to measure in a comparative perspective (*cf.* Grönlund and Milner 2006, 389–90). Still, what little there is of comparative evidence

Figure 5.5: Politics is too complicated to understand

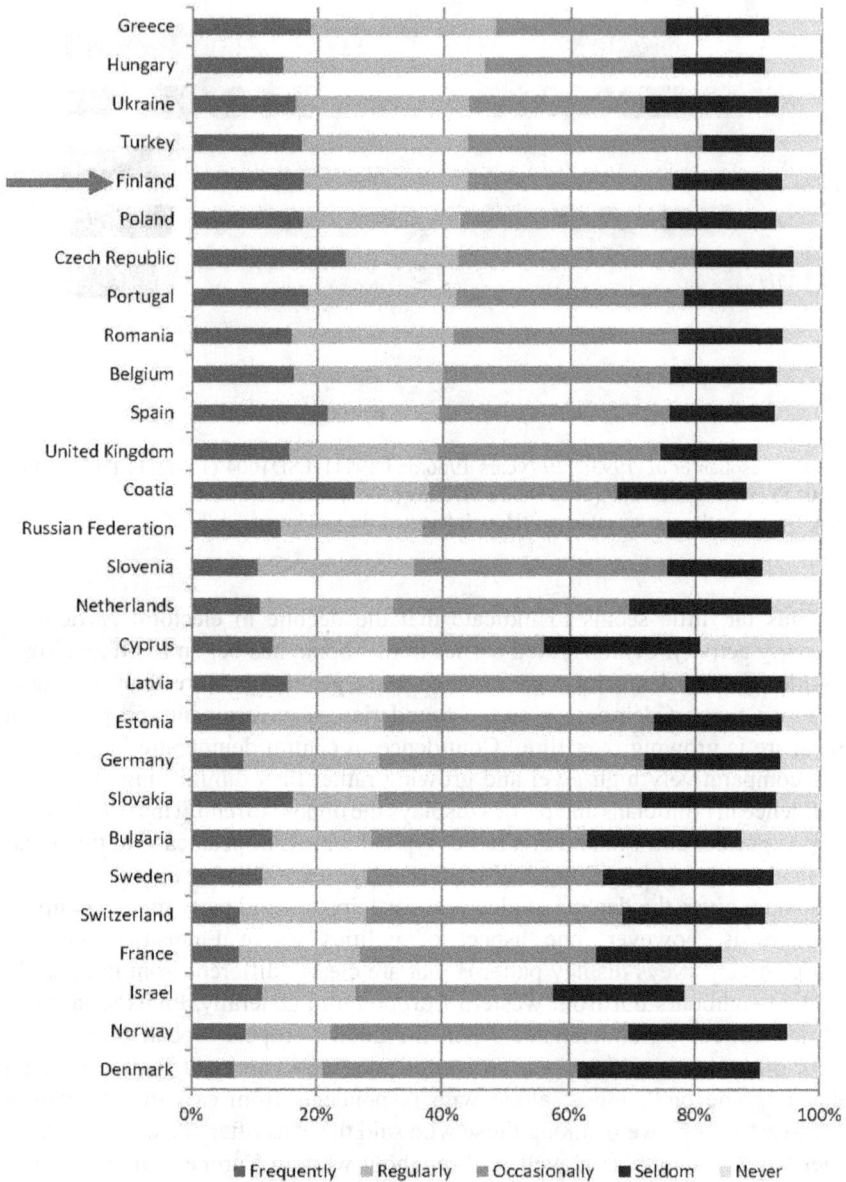

Source: European Social Survey round 4 – 2008, http://nesstar.ess.nsd.uib.no/webview/
Note: Based on the ESS survey question 'How often does politics seem so complicated that you can't really understand what is going on?'

seems to indicate that the level of political knowledge in Finland resembles that of elsewhere in Scandinavia; Nordic citizens, in turn, appear politically knowledgeable compared to citizens in other countries (Grönlund 2007: 409). Moreover, the high level of education in Finland and the internationally renowned performance of Finnish schools would also seem to gainsay the hypothesis of large-scale political ignorance.

A more credible explanation is that Finnish politics in fact *is* difficult to understand compared to the political life of many other nations. The consensual style of campaigning and governing depicted in Chapters Three and Four makes it difficult for citizens to judge what the political alternatives offered in elections really are. Which campaign promises can parties and candidates be expected to live up to? What are the alternative government coalitions on offer at the election? Why does one particular coalition get chosen over other possible alternatives? Whom should citizens hold accountable for policy when the merits and flaws of a government are judged at the next election? These are fundamental questions that need to be answered in order for the citizen to be able to form a picture of the political process. Yet, answers remain vague to basically all these questions in Finland. Parties typically refrain from campaign promises that might render their participation in future government coalitions difficult. In particular, they rarely rule out any of the other parties beforehand as cabinet partners.[8] In a similar vein, coalition parties are collectively responsible for government policy and they are bound by strong formal commitments to explicit rules of parliamentary behaviour. In a word, it is very difficult for citizens to tell where the parties stand on crucial issues, what the main lines of political conflict are and who is really responsible for the way the country is governed. Should the success of the True Finns compel parties to be more outspoken in their future campaigns, this would indeed signify an important change in Finland's political culture.

Moreover, constitutional change since the early 1990s probably adds to citizens' confusion. Older voters have been accustomed to thinking in terms of a president with far-reaching powers and a will to use these powers extensively. Although most citizens understand that the presidency means less than it used to, it probably remains unclear exactly how complete the parliamentarisation of the Finnish system of government has been. The relatively high turnout in recent presidential elections suggests that citizens still expect the president to have a central role in the political process at large – which simply is not compatible with the current constitution. Finland's EU membership, including widely differing notions about the division of labour between the Union and the Member States, most likely adds to this confusion.

---

8. It was a rare exception that the Greens announced during their 2011 campaign that they would not participate in a coalition including the True Finns.

Conclusions

Voting behaviour and citizen attitudes in Finland have undergone marked changes in the last several decades. Some of these changes are understandable in light of the vast social and political developments described in earlier chapters of this book; some others seem more surprising or paradoxical. It is perhaps easy to understand why electoral participation has declined more in Finland than in most west European countries. The intensity of the structural and political divisions that had shaped the Finnish party system led to a high level of electoral participation in the 1960s and 1970s. With the rapid weakening of these divisions, including the disappearance of one of the strongest communist movements in the west, the incentives to turn out to vote were diminished. Declining turnout, in turn, caused electoral participation to become socially biased; it is the more educated, more informed and more well-to-do citizens that today clearly participate most actively in elections. The very same structural transformation of Finnish society has also given rise to an increasing homogeneity in the support of political parties. The explanatory power of socio-economic factors *vis-à-vis* party choice is on the wane. To some extent, the role of individual politicians (candidates and party leaders) has been accentuated at the expense of parties when citizens make electoral choices.

The growing distance between electoral politics and citizens has not given rise to a more sceptical citizen attitude towards democracy and its main institutions. Democracy as a principle and its central institutions enjoy growing support among the citizens. Moreover, it would be incorrect, despite declining turnout and party activity, to speak of a general political apathy among Finns. Citizen interest in politics has grown over a considerable period of time. By contrast, Finns do feel that politics is frequently difficult to understand; in this respect, they differ from citizens elsewhere in western Europe. It seems reasonable to attribute this feature of Finnish politics to the consensual style of politics which has been predominant in Finland for the past four decades.

Chapter Six

Conclusion: Politics in a Changing Society

Finland is a Nordic country with a vulnerable geopolitical location. If one wishes to come up with a parsimonious explanation of main patterns in Finland's political and social history, these are the two factors one should bear in mind. The centuries of common history with Sweden left the Finnish nation with fundamental features – social, cultural, legal, mental – that are distinctly Nordic in character. The Nordic states have a long history of open borders and organised co-operation; they continue to influence each other when it comes to developing their societies further. Thus, when societies are compared internationally, the Nordic countries tend to cluster close together, whether they be measured in terms of social trust (Bäck 2011: 85), gender equality,[1] corruption[2] or government performance (Holmberg and Rothstein 2012: 314).

'We can't do anything about geography.' These oft-quoted words usually attributed to Finnish president (1946–1956) J. K. Paasikivi express a condition that sets Finland apart from its Scandinavian neighbours. Time and again, developments in Russia have influenced Finnish politics, in fact, impinged on the foundations of Finland's sovereign existence. More often than not, these developments have occurred beyond Finland's control; Finland has not been able to do much to influence or avert their occurrence. The history of independent Finland starts with the Civil War of 1918; it is not explicable except in terms of the Bolshevik Revolution in Russia. The early 1930s saw the rise of a right-wing extremist movement in Finland that nearly led to the demise of Finnish democracy. Without the Soviet-instigated labour unrest in the late 1920s, this movement would scarcely have attained the scale and influence it in fact did. The wars of 1939–40 and 1941–44 were, of course, a result of Finland's vulnerable strategic position. Similarly, the long post-war years in the shadow of the Soviet Union – the period of 'Finlandization' – reflected the geopolitical realities that remain somewhat of a constant in Finnish political history. Each of these externally determined circumstances had an impact also on party-formation, inter-party relations and voter alignments.

These two factors have tended to pull Finnish politics in opposite directions. The features that Finland shares with its Nordic neighbours have made for developments similar to those throughout Scandinavia. The geopolitical pressures from Russia account for aberrations from this path. The net effect is a zigzag course of sorts, whereby Finland has frequently seemed to be drifting away from the Nordic course – only to return to it, often in an astonishingly short period

---

1. http://www.ssfindex.com/cms/wp-content/uploads/indicator8.pdf
2. http://www.transparency.org/cpi2012/results

of time. The violent and traumatic Civil War of 1918 certainly set Finland apart in a Scandinavian comparison. Against this backdrop, it seems surprising that a social democratic cabinet was allowed to take office merely eight years after the 'White' victory over the 'Reds'. Right-wing extremism elsewhere in Scandinavia was a far cry from the powerful Lapua movement in Finland in the early 1930s. Nevertheless, by the second half of the 1930s, Finland had opted for the same 'red–green' compromise between the Social Democrats and the Agrarians that had secured the democratic form of government against extremist pressures from both right and left among its Scandinavian neighbours. In the midst of the Cold War, with accusations about Finlandization mounting, Finland systematically and persistently engaged in far-reaching Nordic co-operation that decisively affected its welfare policies, social structures and popular values.

These cross-pressures also explain another typical feature of Finnish politics and society, a phenomenon that might be termed 'the late-but-rapid syndrome'. Russian resistance held back the gradual enfranchisement of the population that took place in the other Nordic countries in the late nineteenth century. Once this resistance was overcome, in 1906, Finland introduced a representation reform that was much more radical than elsewhere in Scandinavia. Similarly, industrialisation and economic modernisation were delayed much longer than in most of western Europe; once they got under way, however, Finland basically went direct from an agricultural to a post-industrial society.

In post-war Finnish politics, marked swings of the pendulum have occurred several times. The Social Democratic and Conservative resistance against Kekkonen as president was a source of heightened political conflict throughout his first six-year period. During the rest of his prolonged rule, no major party seriously challenged his position. Inter-party relations were marked by suspicion and conflict in the first three post-war decades, only to be replaced by a consensual style of politics in an astonishingly short period of time. The long years of the Cold War had had Finland walking a tightrope between Soviet suspicions and Finland's need to safeguard its western social order. Upon the collapse of the Soviet Union, Finland resolutely proceeded to integrate itself with the core of west European co-operation – in fact, with far fewer reservations than neighbouring Sweden and Denmark. As in physics, the position of the political pendulum is explained by how far to the opposite side it was when the swing started.

The absence of bipolar dynamics

In a striking contrast to neighbouring Sweden, in particular, parliamentary politics in Finland is not a rivalry between two ideologically opposed blocs (Arter 2006: 262–6). This may seem surprising, as Finland has, indeed, had her fair share of ideological polarisation. Up until the end of the 1970s, Finland had one of the largest communist-dominated parties in the west. In elections between 1945 and 1979, the Finnish People's Democratic League mustered an average of 20 per cent of the vote. Meanwhile, there was a Social Democratic Party with fairly stable support from about a quarter of the electorate. From a purely numeric point of view, cabinets dominated by the political left were not out of the question during this period. No clear-cut leftist cabinets came about, however. Cabinets with both the FPDL and the SDP did occur but these always included bourgeois parties as well. President Kekkonen also strove to foster co-operation between the left and the centrist parties. Moreover, the two parties on the left were wary and suspicious of each other, as they were rivals both in electoral terms and in the labour-market arena. As we have seen, cabinets tended to be short-lived during this period.

From around 1980 on, the FPDL's popularity began to plummet. Already in August 1968 the party had split over the Soviet Union's intervention in Czechoslovakia (Mäkelä 1987: 181). Other internal differences followed, creating an insurmountable barrier between the 'majority' and the 'minority'; the party was dissolved definitively in 1990. The Left Alliance founded on its ruins that year has not been able to halt the downward trend and the party has dwindled in terms of both membership and vote shares. The 8 per cent of the vote it won in the 2011 represents a historical low point for the extreme left in Finnish politics. The Social Democrats have managed to hold their ground somewhat better, although their support in the two most recent elections has fallen short of their 25 per cent average in earlier elections and their showing in the most recent polls has been clearly below 20 per cent.

The weakening of the left has had pervasive effects on parties and parliamentary politics as well as on the electorate. It is, in fact, a key element in the pattern of parliamentary politics characteristic of Finland. If the parties of the left wish to govern, they must do this in co-operation with at least one, but usually several bourgeois parties. The left-right distinction offers no basis for viable coalitions in Finnish parliamentary politics. This, in turn, compels the parties on the left to consider their relations with other parties before each election. If they wish to be eligible for a cabinet coalition, they must refrain from attacking the main bourgeois parties too fiercely. The disappearance of divisive campaign slogans and propaganda goes hand in hand with the decline of the left.

For voters, the blurring of the programmatic differences presents several challenges. If the parties are 'all the same', why vote at all? In particular, why vote for a party on the extreme left if its programme is basically no different from that of the Social Democrats? After the collapse of communism, the Left Alliance has been compelled to disavow all ties with Soviet-style socialism. The problem is that by so doing, it has narrowed the ideological margin between itself and the Social Democrats decisively. The demise of a communist-dominated left-wing party created a large segment of politically homeless voters. The decline of the vote shares of the extreme left has coincided with an identical drop in voter turnout.

The decline of parties and electoral participation

In Finland, as elsewhere in the democratic west, political parties face considerable challenges. Party-membership has declined rapidly and many major parties have lost more than half of their members in recent decades. Citizens' identification with parties has been attenuated and their trust in parties and politicians is low. A growing number of voters switch parties from election to election.

These are all features that Finland shares with most comparable countries. Explanations of these phenomena must be sought in circumstances common to all these cases rather than in features that set Finland apart in an international comparison. As for electoral participation, the decline has been particularly marked in Finland; Finland does not stand in a category of its own but it is one of the cases where turnout has clearly fallen more than the average for stable western democracies. It does not seem far-fetched to attribute some of this rapid decline to the dramatic changes in Finnish society described above. When turnout peaked in the 1960s, Finland was a polarised society in which citizens had motive not just to vote *for* something but, equally important, *against* other 'camps' perceived as hostile. As was just noted, the demise of communism left a large segment of the electorate politically homeless; by the same token, it left many other voters without a clearly defined enemy. Fewer and fewer citizens felt that they were presented with a real choice in elections. All of this has sped up the downward trend in electoral participation.

When turnout declines, it becomes socially skewed. Voting is no longer clearly perceived as a civic duty. Those who are weak in terms of cognitive resources and interest in politics – aspects that go hand in hand with education and socio-economic resources – tend increasingly not to turn out to vote at all. For those who do vote, the role of party leaders and individual candidates has been accentuated.

Much has been written and said about the 'crisis' or 'decline' of parties, but it is too early yet to proclaim the end of parties in Finland or elsewhere. Still, Finnish parties and electoral politics are clearly plagued by increasing problems of popular legitimacy.

Recurrent waves of populist protest

As noted earlier, the dramatic success of the True Finns in the 2011 election represents the third wave of populist protest in post-war Finnish politics. The impressive victories scored by the Rural Party in 1970 and 1972 had roots in interrelated social, economic and political changes. The country was in the midst of a rapid structural transformation, entailing a massive flow of migration from rural northern and eastern Finland to the urban areas of the south and to neighbouring Sweden. Agricultural production in peripheral parts of Finland had been based on small, often minuscule, farms that were kept alive with government subsidies long after they had become economically unviable. Once the floodgates opened, however, these farms and economic activity based on primary production were hit heavily and hard. Hundreds of thousands of Finns left their homes for the suburbs of southern Finland or the industrial centres of Sweden. In 1965, just a few years before the great wave of migration, the Agrarians had changed their party name to Centre Party, thus signalling their attempt to transform from a farmers' party into a catch-all party, with an intention to establish itself as a main contender in urban centres as well. Particularly among those voters who remained in the countryside of eastern and northern Finland, the Rural Party succeeded in establishing itself as the representative of the 'forgotten people', who were, allegedly, ignored by other parties including the Centre Party (Toivonen 2011: 82–3).

Although the Rural Party started to crumble due to internal differences almost immediately after its electoral success, it was able to stage a comeback in the 1983 election. By that time, the effects and downsides of urbanisation were clearly visible and the party made considerable inroads among voters in the southern suburbs. Its decision to participate in cabinets, however, illustrated the dilemma of populist rhetoric *versus* executive responsibility. Once in power, the populists had to refrain from the kind of wholesale promises that had characterised their electoral campaigns. Their voters were disenchanted and the party melted into insignificance in a matter of a few years.

The third wave of populism was slower in coming but all the more powerful once it occurred. In 2011, the True Finns surged from 5 to 19 per cent of the vote and became the third largest party in parliament. The road to this renaissance for populism in Finnish politics was paved with the cumulative effects of Finnish EU membership (from 1995 on) and with the experience from a long period of co-operation between the three largest parties, of which two always participated in cabinet. Meanwhile, the urbanisation process had continued unabated and Finnish society had felt the effects of globalisation, both in the economic sphere and in the form of non-European immigration. The losers in this social transformation – those who felt that their jobs and social security were under attack – became the source of strength for the True Finns. Both of the two traditional popular mass parties – the Centre Party and the Social Democrats – lost voters to the populists.

These recurrent waves of populism in Finnish politics must be seen as one of the most characteristic consequences of the rapidity and thoroughness of the social transformation in the country. The changes have affected the lives of hundreds of thousands of voters and many of these citizens can be persuaded that 'established parties' have chosen to ignore them in order to safeguard their positions in the parliamentary game. The combination of rapid social change and the relative immobility of the party system repeatedly create 'political space' for a populist alternative. The two first waves of populism proved short-lived. Although it is too early yet to tell whether the True Finns will repeat this pattern, populist parties tend to be inherently unstable and vulnerable to internal disagreements. Moreover, much of the True Finn support stems from voter segments whose electoral participation is sporadic at best. The likelihood that these citizens again become politically disenchanted and 'homeless' is much greater than in the case of citizens whose participation in elections is regular and duty-based. On the other hand, at the time of writing (February 2014) the True Finns' standing in the polls (17.8 per cent[3]) attests to a perhaps unexpectedly stable popularity. Be that as it may: the rise to prominence of the True Finns illustrates a pattern that seems to be characteristic of Finnish political culture.

Politics behind the veil of consensus

Arguably, the long years of fundamental political stability, including the predominance of surplus majority cabinets have had several highly positive effects on Finnish politics and society. The social progress during this period and

---

3.   http://svenska.yle.fi/artikel/2014/01/29/partikartan-oforandrad

the relative financial health that Finland has maintained despite an increasingly volatile international economy would hardly have been possible without a consensus about the foundations of economic and social policy. Had Finnish politics continued with the high level of conflict characteristic of the first three post-war decades, it would probably also have been politically impossible to agree on the shift from semi-presidential to parliamentary rule that was completed in the 2000 constitution. This shift created a much stronger connection between parliamentary elections and subsequent cabinet-formation than earlier. Much more than in the Kekkonen years, election results and party negotiations in parliament affect government-formation. Elections today are, to a certain extent, referendums on the next prime minister. Although political accountability is always problematic in a fragmented multi-party system dependent on coalition cabinets, it is no exaggeration to say that 'elections matter' much more than under the old constitution.

Forming cabinets consisting of numerous parties with widely varying ideological histories requires a large degree of compromise on the part of the participating actors. Governing in oversized multi-party coalitions demands a collective commitment to the agreed-on cabinet programme, both in cabinet and in parliament. The more diverse the coalition, the stronger the requirement of internal discipline among cabinet parties. All of this plays into the hands of the central government bureaucracy. For cabinet parties, policy proposals by administrative officials may be easier to accept than suggestions that clearly emanate from other parties. Consensus spells compromise and discipline; and it is often bureaucrats who can provide the basis for policy-compromises. As cabinets are stable, the kind of long-term planning bureaucrats tend to favour becomes practicable.

For the citizens, however, this mode of politics entails several problems. While most Finns have been reasonably satisfied with the concrete performance of governments, they find it difficult to make informed choices and judgments about politics. Paradoxically, although Finns display a high level of education, a considerable political knowledge and a growing interest in politics, their internal efficacy – that is, their subjective citizen competence – is rather low. They frequently find politics difficult to comprehend. The reason is, in fact, that Finnish politics *is* demanding from the point of view of any outside observer. Election campaigns are vague and void of clear and definite policy promises. The political alternatives on offer at elections tend to remain blurred. The assignment of responsibility in a system based on heterogeneous multi-party coalitions is extremely difficult. Voters find it difficult to know whom to thank or punish for past political performance. The multi-layered institutional setting in which politics takes place – parliament, president and the European Union – adds to citizen bewilderment.

Consensual government produces long- and short-term results that the majority of Finnish citizens probably find positive. However, it also accounts for the continued decline in electoral participation and a deepening sentiment of an impenetrable veil between citizens and the governing elite.

Still frozen after all this change?

No party system is immutable. Old parties do disappear; new parties do gain positions in the political arena. Still, many parties have proven to be remarkably resilient in the face of major social changes. The Finnish party system bears testament to the continued relevance of Lipset and Rokkan's observation about 'the freezing of the major party alternatives' (1967: 50) in west European democracies. Of the six party families represented in the parliament elected in 1922, only the Liberals were absent in the parliament elected in 2011. Despite the appearance of new contenders, including the spectacular breakthrough of the True Finns, the five 'constituent parties' from the early period of Finnish independence still mustered two-thirds of the vote in the most recent election.

In light of changes such as the True Finn victory in 2011, one might be tempted to predict the demise of the frozen party system of Finland. With the accumulated social change that has largely obliterated the structural foundations of the party system, together with electoral shocks such as the one in 2011, in this view, parties cannot simply continue as if nothing fundamental has happened. A reorganisation of the entire party field is necessary if one wishes to have a supply of party alternatives that matches the divisions in the electorate.

If a party system for Finland were to be created from scratch today, the result would surely be a set of parties quite different from those represented in parliament. Above all, a new system would have to reflect a cleavage that is becoming increasingly salient but cuts right across most of the existing parties: that between internationalism and a form of nationalism. With the exception of the True Finns, and in varying proportions, all parties display politicians, activists and supporters who see European integration, economic internationalisation and increasing cultural pluralism as positive for Finland and others who view them as a threat. True, motives may vary from party to party. A neo-liberal may welcome internationalisation from the point of view of economic efficiency, whereas an environmentalist may see it as the only workable solution to problems such as global warming. Similarly, globalisation may be seen as a threat from the point of view of the Nordic model of social welfare or the future of Finnish agriculture, while somebody perhaps simply dislikes the idea of continued immigration. The central point is, in any case, that this distinction that divides popular opinions in a clearly measurable fashion still does not constitute an organising principle for the party system itself.

Should the True Finn victory in 2011 be seen as the first step toward a reorganisation of the Finnish party system along the nationalism/globalisation divide? Quite clearly, the populist message based on a critical stance *vis-à-vis* the EU, a restrictive view on immigration and an emphasis on national culture resonated well with a sizable portion of the electorate. How likely are others to follow suit, resulting in a reorganisation of the party field? The question is in two parts, and so should the answer be. Surely, the Social Democrats, in particular, have tried to challenge the populists in their home court by, *inter alia*, presenting a tougher image on EU issues. However, the step towards actual party amalgamations or splits is a long one. In fact, it is probably so long that it will take more than just an occasional electoral shock to bring about a change.

As shown in Chapter Two, external impulses have, in several instances, had an impact on party-formation in Finland. In practice, this has meant that events in Russia have had repercussions in Finland. Of course, development in Russia remains just as difficult to predict as upheavals in Russian history have always proven to be. Most certainly, major changes in Russia would be felt clearly in Finnish politics. The scenario that is perhaps most likely– that Russia opts for an even more outwardly aggressive course than at present – would bring Finns together across political and social divides but it would not necessarily make an impact on the way politics is organised in Finland.

This must, however, remain purely speculative. What we do know of Russia's importance is that Finland's eastern neighbour has all but ceased to be a bone of contention among parties. Party leaders and representatives from the Left Alliance to the Conservatives voice critical opinions about Russia. For instance, conditions for human rights in Russia are criticised frequently, without any apparent fear of reprisals. It is hard to see how *Ostpolitik* might reappear as a factor that affects party-formation and inter-party relations.

Today, a more relevant external determinant of Finnish politics is the European Union. Needless to say, the 2010s have been a turbulent period for the EU, the European Monetary Union in particular. The eurozone has been shaken to its core. For a while, one of the possible scenarios was that the EMU would split into several smaller units or even be dissolved altogether. Although this does not seem highly likely at the time of writing, the fundamental economic, structural and institutional problems in the eurozone are anything but solved.

The most marked change in Finnish politics for several decades, the rise of the True Finns, was decisively fuelled by the crisis in the EU. Should the attempts to rescue the eurozone definitively fail, this would certainly amount to purgatory for Finnish parties and governments. It is not unthinkable that a European crisis of these proportions would turn out to be a shock sufficient to bring about a reorganisation of the Finnish party system.

Bibliography

Abramson, P. R. (1995) 'Participation, Political', in Lipset, S. M. (ed.) *The Encyclopedia of Democracy: Volume III*, London: Routledge, pp. 913–21.

Alapuro, R. (1985) 'Yhteiskuntaluokat ja sosiaaliset kerrostumat 1870-luvulta toiseen maailmansotaan', in Valkonen, T., Alapuro, R., Alestalo, M., Jallinoja, R. and Sandlund, T. (eds) *Suomalaiset: Yhteiskunnan rakenne teollistumisen aikana*, Porvoo: WSOY, pp. 36–100.

— (1988) *State and Social Revolution in Finland*, Berkeley: University of California Press.

Allardt, E. and Bruun, K. (1956) 'Characteristics of the Finnish non-voter', *Transactions of the Westermarck Society*, vol. III, Copenhagen: Ejnar Munkgaard, pp. 55–76.

Anckar, D. (1971) *Partiopinioner och utrikespolitik. En studie av partipolitiska pressopinioner kring ett antal händelser i Finlands utrikespolitik 1955–1965*, Åbo: Åbo Akademi.

— (1974), *Analys av partiers beteende: en fallstudie i partistrategi*, Åbo: Åbo Akademi.

— (2000) 'Jäähyväiset semipresidentialismille', *Politiikka* 42(1): 9–14.

Andeweg, R. B. and Irwin, G. A. (2005) *Governance and Politics of The Netherlands*, Houndsville, Basingstoke, Hampshire: Palgrave Macmillan.

Arter, D. (1984) *The Nordic Parliaments: A Comparative Analysis*, London: C. Hurst & Company.

— (1987) *Politics and Policy-Making in Finland*, Brighton, Sussex: Wheatsheaf Books.

— (1999a) 'From class party to catchall party?: The adaptation of the Finnish Agrarian-Center Party', *Scandinavian Political Studies*, 22(2): 157–79.

— (1999b) *Scandinavian Politics Today*, Manchester: Manchester University Press.

— (2006) *Democracy in Scandinavia: Consensual, majoritarian or mixed?* Manchester: Manchester University Press.

— (2009) 'Money and voters: the cost of election for first-time Finnish MPs', *Politiikka* LI(1): 17–33.

— (2011) 'The Michael Marsh question: how do Finns do constituency service?', *Parliamentary Affairs*, 64(1): 129–52.

— (2012a) 'Analysing "successor parties": the case of the True Finns', *West European Politics*, 35(4): 803–25.

— (2012b) '"Big Bang" elections and party system change in Scandinavia: farewell to the "enduring party system"?', *Parliamentary Affairs* 65: 822–44.

— (2013a) 'How the True Finns won a seat in Etelä-Savo – and why it is important to know', *Politiikka*, LV(4): 207–22.

— (2013b) 'The "hows", not the "whys" or "wherefores": the role of intra-party competition in the 2011 breakthrough of the True Finns', *Scandinavian Political Studies*, 36(2): 99 –120.

Bäck, H. and Larsson, T. (2006) *Den svenska politiken. Struktur, processer och resultat*, Malmö: Liber.

Bäck, M. (2011) *Socialt kapital och politiskt deltagande i Europa*, Åbo: Åbo Akademi University Press.

Becker, U. (2003) *Smallcons Project. A Framework for Socio-Economic Development in Europe? The consensual political cultures of the small West European states in comparative and historical perspective* (No. HPSE–CT–2002–00134) Deliverable 1. State-Of-The-Art Report (unpublished).

Bell, D. (1960) *The End of Ideology: On the exhaustion of political ideas in the fifties*, New York: The Free Press.

Bengtsson, Å. and Mattila, M. (2009) 'Direct democracy and its critics: support for direct democracy and "stealth" democracy in Finland', *West European Politics*, 32(5): 1031–48.

Bengtsson, Å., Hansen, K. M. Harðarson, Ó. Þ. Narud, H. M. and Oscarsson, H. (2014) *The Nordic Voter: Myths of exceptionalism*, Colchester: ECPR Press.

Bergman, T., Müller, W. C. Strøm, K. and Blomgren, M. (2006) 'Democratic delegation and accountability: cross national patterns', in Strøm, K., Müller, W. C. and Bergman, T. (eds) *Delegation and Accountability in Parliamentary Democracies*, Oxford: Oxford University Press, pp. 109–220.

Bobbio, N. (1996) *Left and Right: The significance of a political distinction*, Cambridge: Polity Press.

Borg, S. (ed.) (2012) 'Perussuomalaiset' *Muutosvaalit 2011*, Helsinki: The Ministry of Justice, pp. 191–210.

Browne, E. C., Frendeis, J. P. and Gleiber, D. W. (1986) 'The process of cabinet dissolution: an exponential model of duration and stability in western democracies', *American Journal of Political Science*, 30: 628–50.

Bryce, J. (1921) *Modern Democracies*, London: Macmillan.

Budge, I., Klingemann, H. -D. Volkens, A. Bara, J. and Tanenbaum, E. (2001) *Mapping Policy Preferences: Estimates for parties, electors, and governments 1945–1998*, Oxford: Oxford University Press.

Cain, B. E., Dalton, R. J. and Scarrow, S. E. (eds) (2003) *Democracy Transformed: Expanding political opportunities in advanced industrial democracies*, Oxford: Oxford University Press.

Carlson, T. (2000) *Partier och kandidater på väljarmarknaden. Studier i finländsk politisk reklam*, Åbo: Åbo Akademi University Press.

Christensen, H. S. (2011) *Political Participation Beyond the Vote: How the institutional context shapes patterns of political participation in 18 Western European democracies*, Åbo: Åbo Akademi University Press.

Colomer, J. M. (ed.) (2004) *Handbook of Electoral System Choice*, Houndmills, Basingstoke, Hampshire: Palgrave Macmillan.

Craig, S. C., Niemi, R. and Silver, G. E. (1990) 'Political efficacy and trust: A report on the NES pilot study items', *Political Behavior,* 12(3): 289–314.

Curtice, J. and Holmberg, S. (2005) 'Party leaders and party choice', in Thomassen, J. (ed.) *The European Voter: A comparative study of modern democracies*, Oxford: Oxford University Press, pp. 235–53.

Dahl, R. A. (1989) *Democracy and its Critics:*, New Haven and London: Yale University Press.

D'Alimonte, R. (2008) 'Italy: a case of fragmented bipolarism', in Gallagher, M. and Mitchell, P. (eds) *The Politics of Electoral Systems*, Oxford: Oxford University Press, pp. 252–76.

Dalton, R. J. (2004) *Democratic Challenges, Democratic Choices: The erosion of political support in advanced industrial democracies*, Oxford: Oxford University Press.

— (2008) *The Good Citizen. How a younger generation is reshaping American politics*, Washington, DC: CQ Press.

Dalton, R. J. and Anderson, J. (eds) (2010) *Citizens, Context, and Choice: How context shapes citizens' electoral choices*, Oxford: Oxford University Press.

Dalton, R. J., Farrell, D. M. and McAllister, I. (2011) *Political Parties & Democratic Linkage. How Parties Organize Democracy*, Oxford: Oxford University Press.

Dalton, R. J. and Gray, M. (2003) 'Expanding the electoral marketplace', in Cain, B. E., Dalton, R. J. and Scarrow, S. E. (eds) *Democracy Transformed?: Expanding Political opportunities in advanced industrial democracies*, Oxford: Oxford University Press, pp. 23–43.

Dalton, R. J. and Wattenberg, M. P. (eds) (2002a) *Parties Without Partisans. Political change in advanced industrial democracies*, Oxford: Oxford University Press.

— (2002b) 'Unthinkable democracy: Political change in advanced industrial democracies', in R. J. Dalton and M. P. Wattenberg (eds) *Parties Without Partisans. Political change in advanced industrial democracies*, Oxford: Oxford University Press, pp. 3–18.

De Winter, L. and Dumont, P. (2008) 'Uncertainty and complexity in cabinet formation', in Strøm, K. Müller, W. C. and Bergman, T. (eds) *Cabinets and Coalition Bargaining: The democratic life cycle in Western Europe*, Oxford: Oxford University Press, pp. 122–57.

Dogan, M. (2001) 'Class, religion, party: triple decline of electoral cleavages in Western Europe', in Karvonen, L. and Kuhnle, S. (eds) *Party Systems and Voter Alignments Revisited*, London: Routledge, pp. 93–114.

Duverger, M. (1951) *Les partis politiques*, Paris: Armand Colin.

Elf, M. (2007) 'Social structure and electoral behavior in comparative perspective: the decline of social cleavages in Western Europe revisited', *Perspectives on Politics*, 5(2): 277–94.

Farrell, D. M. (1997) *Comparing Electoral Systems*, Houndmills, Basingstoke, Hampshire: Macmillan.

Flora, P., with Kuhnle, S. and Urwin, D. (1999) *State Formation, Nation-Building, and Mass Politics in Europe: The theory of Stein Rokkan*, Oxford: Oxford University Press.

Franklin, M. (2002) 'The Dynamics of Electoral participation', in LeDuc, L. Niemi, R. and Norris, P. (eds) *Comparing Democracies 2*, London and Thousand Oaks, CA: SAGE, pp. 148–68.

Fukuyama, F. (1998) *The End of History and the Last Man*. New York: Avon Books.

Gabriel, O. W. (1998) 'Political efficacy and trust', in van Deth, J. W. and Scarborough, E. (eds) *The Impact of Values*, Oxford: Oxford University Press, pp. 357–89.

Gallagher, M., Laver, M. and Mair, P. (2001) *Representative Government in Modern Europe. Institutions, parties, and governments*, New York: McGraw-Hill.

— (2011) *Representative Government in Modern Europe*, London: McGraw-Hill.

Gallagher, M. and March, M. (eds) (1988) *Candidate Selection in Comparative Perspective*, London: SAGE.

Gimpel, J. G., Lay, J. C. and Schuknecht, J. E. (2003) *Cultivating Democracy: Civic environments and political socialization in America*, Washington, DC: Brookings Institution Press.

Grönlund, K. (2007) 'Knowing and not knowing: the internet and political information', *Scandinavian Political Studies*, 30(3): 397–418.

Grönlund, K. and Milner, H. (2006) 'The determinants of political knowledge in a comparative perspective', *Scandinavian Political Studies*, 29(4) 386–406.

Grönlund, K. and Setälä, M. (2012) 'In honest officials we trust: institutional confidence in Europe', *American Review of Public Administration*, 42(4): 523–42.

Hakovirta, H. (1975) *Suomettuminen*, Jyväskylä: Gummerus.

Hallberg, P., Martikainen, T. Nousiainen, J. and Tikkanen, P. (2009) *Presidentin valta: Hallitsijanvallan ja parlamentarismin välinen jännite Suomessa 1919–2009*, Helsinki: WSOY.

Harris, F. C. (1999) *Something Within: Religion in African-American Political Activism*, Oxford: Oxford University Press.

Hazan, R. Y. and Rahat, G. (2010) *Democracy Within Parties: Candidate selection methods and their political consequences*, Oxford: Oxford University Press.

Helander, V. (1990) 'Från minoritetsskydd till minoritetsvälde?', in Karvonen, L. and Ståhlberg, K. (eds) *Festskrift till Dag Anckar, 50 år den 12 februari 1990*, Åbo: Åbo Academy Press, pp. 34–55.

Holmberg, S. and Oscarsson, H. (2004) *Väljare: Svenskt väljarbeteende under 50 år*, Stockholm: Norstedts juridik.

Holmberg, S. and Rothstein, B. (2012) 'Access to safe water', in Holmberg, S. and Rothstein, B. (eds) *Good Government: The relevance of political science*, Cheltenham: Edward Elgar, pp. 303–16.

Häikiö, M. (1993) *Presidentin valinta: Miten valtionpäämiehet on Suomessa valittu, millaisiin poikkeusmenetelmiin valinnoissa on turvattu ja miksi presidentin toimikautta jatkettiin kokonaan ilman vaalia vuonna 1973*, Porvoo: WSOY.

Hyvämäki, L. (1954) *Vaaran vuodet*, Helsinki: Otava.

IDEA (2002) *Voter turnout since 1945: A global report*, Stockholm: International Institute for Democracy and Electoral Assistance.

Inglehart, R. (1997) *Modernization and Postmodernization: Cultural, economic, and political change in 43 societies*, Princeton, NJ: Princeton University Press.

Inglehart, R. and Norris, P. (2004) *Rising Tide: Gender equality and cultural change around the world*, Cambridge: Cambridge University Press.

International Historical Statistics: Europe 1750–2005, Mitchell, B. R. (ed.) Houndmills, Basingstoke, Hampshire: Palgrave Macmillan.

Isaksson, G. -E. (2011) 'Presidentialisation of Parliamentary Systems: reality or illusion?' in Persson, T. and Wiberg, M. (eds) *Parliamentary Government in the Nordic Countries at a Crossroads*, Stockholm: Santérus Academic Press, pp. 223–44.

—   (2013) *Regering eller opposition? Regeringsbildningar i Norden och i Västeuropa under sex årtionden*, Stockholm: Santérus förlag.

Jahn, D. (2011) 'Conceptualizing left and right in comparative politics: towards a deductive approach', *Party Politics*, 17(6): 745–65.

Jansson, J. -M. (1992) *Från splittring till samverkan: Parlamentarismen i Finland.* Helsingfors: Söderströms.

—   (2000) *Från regeringsformen till grundlagen*, Helsingfors: Söderströms.

Jungar, A. -C. (2000) *Surplus Majority Government: A comparative study of Italy and Finland*, Uppsala: Acta Universitates Upsaliensis.

—   (2002) 'A case of a surplus majority government: the Finnish Rainbow Coalition', *Scandinavian Political Studies*, 25(1): 57–84.

Kantola, J. (2012) 'Warriors for democracy. Scandal as a strategic ritual of journalism', in Allern, S. and Pollack, E. (eds) *Scandalous: The mediated construction of political scandals in four Nordic countries*, Göteborg: Nordicom, pp. 73–86.

Karvonen, L. (1996) 'Christian parties in Scandinavia: victory over the windmills?', in Hanley, D. (ed.) *Christian Democracy in Europe*, London: Pinter, pp. 121–41.

—   (2000) 'Finland: from conflict to compromise', in Berg–Schlosser, D. and Mitchell, J. (eds) *Conditions of Democracy in Europe, 1919–1939: Systematic case studies*, Houndmills, Basingstoke, Hampshire: Macmillan, pp. 129–56.

—   (2003) 'Kekkonens ställning: Fyra kritiska test', *Finsk Tidskrift* 8–9/2003: pp. 573–88.

—   (2010) *The Personalisation of Politics: A study of parliamentary democracies*, Colchester: ECPR Press.

—   (2012) 'Att välja parti och att välja person', *Sphinx Yearbook*, Helsingfors: The Finnish Society of Sciences and Letters, pp. 41–54.

Karvonen, L. and Berglund, S. (1980) 'Partier, pengar, demokrati: Det offentliga partistödets effekter i Sverige och Finland', in Anckar, D. and Berglund, S. (eds) *Planerad demokrati: Styrka och dilemma*, Åbo: Stiftelsens för Åbo Akademi forskningsinstitut, pp. 89–112.

Karvonen, L., Djupsund, G. and Carlson, T. (1995) 'Political language' in Karvonen, L. and Selle, P. (eds) *Women in Nordic Politics: Closing the gap*, Aldershot: Dartmouth, pp. 343–79.

Karvonen, L. and Rappe, A. (1991) 'Social structure and campaign style: Finland 1954–1987', *Scandinavian Political Studies*, 14(3): 241–59.

Karvonen, L. and Selle, P. (eds) (1995), *Women in Nordic Politics. Closing the gap*, Aldershot: Dartmouth.

Katz, R. S. and Mair, P. (1995) 'Changing Models of party organization and party democracy: The emergence of the cartel party', *Party Politics*, 1(1): 5–28.

Kauppalehti June 13, 2011.

Kestilä, E. (2006) 'Is there a demand for radical right populism in the Finnish electorate?', *Scandinavian Political Studies* (29)3: 169–91.

King, A. (ed.) (2003a) 'Conclusions and implications', *Leaders' Personalities and the Outcomes of Democratic Elections*, Oxford: Oxford University Press, pp. 210–21.

—   (ed.) (2003b) 'Do leaders' personalities really matter?', *Leaders' Personalities and the Outcomes of Democratic Elections*, Oxford: Oxford University Press, pp. 1–43.

Kirby, D. (2006) *A Concise History of Finland*, Cambridge: Cambridge University Press.

Kirchheimer, O. (1966) 'The transformation of the Western European party systems', in LaPalombara, J. and Wiener, M. (eds) *Political Parties and Political Development*, Princeton, NJ: Princeton University Press, pp. 177–200.

Klingemann, H. -D., Volkens, A., Bara, J., Budge, I. and McDonald, M. (2008) *Mapping Policy Preferences II: Estimates for parties, electors, and governments in Eastern Europe, European Union and OECD 1990–2003*, Oxford: Oxford University Press.

Komiteanmietintö 2009: 1 *Ehdotus laiksi ehdokkaan vaalirahoituksesta*, Helsinki: Ministry of Justice.

—   2009: 3 *Puoluerahoituksen avoimuus*, Helsinki: Ministry of Justice.

Kyntäjä, T. (1993) *Tulopolitiikka Suomessa: Tulopoliittinen diskurssi ja instituutiot 1960–luvulta 1990–luvun kynnykselle*, Helsinki: Gaudeamus.

Laakso, S. (1975) *Hallituksen muodostaminen Suomessa: Tutkimus HM 36 §:n taustasta, genetiikasta, tulkinnasta ja soveltamiskäytännöstä*, Vammala: Suomalainen lakimiesyhdistys.

Laqueur, W. (1980) *The Political Psychology of Appeasement: Finlandization and other unpopular essays*, New Brunswick, NJ: Transaction Books.

Laver, M. and Schofield, N. (1990) *Multiparty Government: The politics of coalition in Europe*, Oxford: Oxford University Press.

Lehtinen, L. (2002) *Aatosta jaloa ja alhaista mieltä: Urho Kekkosen ja SDP:n suhteet 1944–1981*, Helsinki: WSOY.

Lindén, C. -G. (2010) 'Regeringens program redan klart', *Hufvudstadsbladet* October 23, 2010, p. 16.

Lipset, S. M. (2001) 'Cleavages, parties and democracy', in Karvonen, L. and Kuhnle, S. (eds) *Party Systems and Voter Alignments Revisited*, London: Routledge, pp. 3–10.

Lipset, S. M. and Rokkan, S. (eds) (1967) 'Cleavage structures, party systems and voter alignments: an introduction', *Party Systems and Voter Alignments*, New York: The Free Press, pp. 1–64.

Lundell, K. (2004) 'Determinants of candidate selection: the degree of centralization in comparative perspective', *Party Politics* 10(1): 25–47.

— (2005) *Contextual Determinants of Electoral System Choice. A macro-comparative study 1945–2003*, Åbo: Åbo Akademi University Press.

Mair, P. (1997) *Party System Change: Approaches and interpretations*, Oxford: Oxford University Press.

— (2001) 'The freezing hypothesis: an evaluation', in Karvonen, L. and Kuhnle, S. (eds) *Party Systems and Voter Alignments Revisited*, London: Routledge, pp. 27–44.

Majander, M. (2004) *Pohjoismaa vai kansandemokratia? Sosialidemokraatit, kommunistit ja Suomen kansainvälinen asema 1944–51*, Helsinki: Suomalaisen kirjallisuuden seura.

— (2013) 'Yksinäinen sheriffi, filosofikuningas', in Tiihonen, S., Pohls, M. and Korppi–Tommola, J. (eds) *Presidentti johtaa. Suomalaisen valtiojohtamisen pitkä linja*, Helsinki: Kustannusosakeyhtiö Siltala, pp. 213–36.

Mäkelä, J. (1987) 'The radical left and the communist party in Finnish politics', in Mylly, J. and Berry, R. M. (eds) *Political Parties in Finland: Essays in history and politics*, Turku: University of Turku, Political History, pp. 151–86.

Manin, B. (1997) *The Principles of Representative Government*, Cambridge. Cambridge University Press.

Marsh, M. (2007) 'Candidates or parties? Objects of electoral change in Ireland', *Party Politics*, 13(4): 500–27.

Martikainen, P., Martikainen, T. and Wass, H. (2005) 'The effect of socioeconomic factors on voter turnout in Finland: a register-based study of 2.9 million voters', *European Journal of Political Research*, 44: 645–69.

Martikainen, T. and Wass, H. (2002) *Äänettömät yhtiömiehet. Osallistuminen vuosien 1987 ja 1999 eduskuntavaaleihin*, Vaalit 2002: 1, Helsinki: Tilastokeskus.

Mateo Diaz, M. (2005) *Representing Women? Female legislators in West European parliaments*, Colchester: ECPR Press.

Matland, R. and Studlar, D. T. (2004) 'Determinants of legislative turnover: a cross-national analysis', *British Journal of Political Science*, 34: 87–108.

Mattila, M. (1997) 'From qualified majority to simple majority: the effects of the 1992 change in the Finnish constitution', *Scandinavian Political Studies*, 20(4): 331–45.

Mattila, M. and Raunio, T. (2002) 'Government formation in the Nordic countries: the electoral connection', *Scandinavian Political Studies*, 25(3): 259–80.

Mattila, M. and Sundberg, J. (2012) 'Vaalirahoitus ja vaalirahakohu', in Borg, S. (ed.) *Muutosvaalit 2011*, Helsinki: Ministry of Justice, pp. 227–39.

Mattila, M., Wass, H., Söderlund, P., Fredriksson, S., Fadjukoff, P. and Kokko, K. (2011) 'Personality and turnout: results from the Finnish longitudinal studies', *Scandinavian Political Studies*, 34(4): 287–307.

McAllister, I. (2007) 'The personalization of politics', in Dalton, R. J. and Klingemann, H. -D. (eds) *Oxford Handbook of Political Behaviour*, Oxford: Oxford University Press, pp. 571–588.

Meguid, B. M. (2010) *Party Competition between Unequals: Strategies and electoral fortunes in Western Europe*, New York: Cambridge University Press.

Meinander, H. (2008) *Kekkografi och andra historiska spånor*, Keuru: Söderströms.

Meinander, N. (1983) *Finland mognar*, Borgå: Söderströms.

Merkl, P. H. (1970) *Modern Comparative Politics*, New York: Holt Rinehart & Winston.

Michels, R. (1915) *Political Parties: A sociological study of the oligarchical tendencies of modern democracy*, New York: The Free Press.

Mickelsson, R. (2007) *Suomen puolueet: Historia, muutos ja nykypäivä*, Tampere: Vastapaino.

Mitchell, P. and Nyblade, B. (2008) 'Government formation and cabinet type', in Strøm K., Müller, K. C. and Bergman, T. (eds) *Cabinets and Coalition Bargaining: The democratic life cycle in Western Europe*, Oxford: Oxford University Press, pp. 85–122.

Murto, E. (1994) *Pääministeri: Suomen pääministerin rooli 1917–1993*, Helsinki: Hallintohistoriakomitea.

— (2010) 'Valtioneuvosto Suomen poliittisessa järjestelmässä', in *Suomen poliittinen järjestelmä – verkkokirja*, http://blogs.helsinki.fi/vol–spj/valtioneuvosto/, accessed 1 June 2010.

Müller, W. C. (2008) 'Austria: A complex electoral system with subtle effects', in Gallagher, M. and Mitchell, P. (eds), *The Politics of Electoral Systems*, Oxford: Oxford University Press, pp. 397–416.

Müller, W. C., Bergman, T. and Ström, K. (eds) (2008) 'Coalition theory and cabinet governance: an introduction', *Cabinets and Coalition Bargaining: The democratic life cycle in Western Europe*, Oxford: Oxford University Press, pp. 1–50.

Müller, W. C. and Strøm, K. (2008) 'Coalition agreements and cabinet governance', in Ström, K., Müller, W.C. and Bergman, T. (eds) *Cabinets and Coalition Bargaining: The democratic life cycle in Western Europe*, Oxford: Oxford University Press, pp. 159–200.

Mylly, J. (1987) 'The emergence of the Finnish multi–party system. A comparison with developments in Scandinavia, 1870–1920', in Mylly, J. and Berry, R. M. (eds) *Political Parties in Finland: Essays in history and politics*, Turku: University of Turku, Department of Political History, pp. 9–27.

Myllymäki, A. (2010) *Suomen pääministeri – presidentin varjosta hallitusvallan käyttäjäksi*, Helsinki: Talentum.

Nousiainen, J. (1992A) *Politiikan huipulla. Ministerit ja ministeristöt Suomen parlamentaarisessa järjestelmässä*, Porvoo: WSOY.

—— (1992B) *Suomen poliittinen järjestelmä*, Porvoo: WSOY.

—— (2000) 'From semi-presidentialism to parliamentary government: political and constitutional development in Finland', in Karvonen, L. and Ståhlberg, K. (eds) *Festschrift for Dag Anckar on his 60th Birthday on February 12, 2000*, Åbo: Åbo Akademi University Press, pp. 337–52.

—— (2006) 'Suomalainen parlamentarismi', in Jyränki, A. and Nousiainen, J. *Eduskunnan muuttuva asema. Suomen eduskunta 100 vuotta*, Helsinki: Edita, pp. 180–357.

Oscarsson, H. and Holmberg, S. (2013) *Nya svenska väljare*, Stockholm: Norstedts Juridik.

Paloheimo, H. (2001) 'Divided government in Finland: from a semi-presidential to a parliamentary democracy', in Elgie, R. (ed.) *Divided Government in Comparative Perspective*, Oxford: Oxford University Press, pp. 86–105.

—— (2003) 'The rising power of the prime minister in Finland', *Scandinavian Political Studies*, 26(3): 219–44.

—— (2007) 'Eduskuntavaalit 1907–2003', in Ollila, A. and Paloheimo, H. *Kansanedustajan työ ja arki*, Helsinki: Edita, pp. 174–379.

—— (2009) 'Puoluejärjestelmän lohkeamat ja ristiriitaulottuvuudet', in Mickelsson, R. (ed.) *Puolueiden tulevaisuus*, Helsinki: Ministry of Justice, pp. 15–61.

Paloheimo, H. and Raunio, T. (2008) 'Puolueiden rooli ja tehtävät demokratiassa', in *Suomen puolueet ja puoluejärjestelmä*, Porvoo: WSOY, pp. 11–25.

Paloheimo, H., Reunanen, E. and Suhonen, P. (2005) 'Edustuksellisuuden toteutuminen', in Paloheimo, H. (ed.) *Vaalit ja demokratia Suomessa*, Porvoo: WSOY, pp. 252–89.

Paloheimo, H. and Sundberg, J. (2009) 'Vaaliliitot eduskuntavaaleissa 1945–2007', in Borg, S. and Paloheimo, H. (eds) *Vaalit yleisödemokratiassa*, Tampere: Tampere University Press, pp. 206–42.

Panebianco, A. (1988) *Political Parties: Organization & Power*, Cambridge: Cambridge University Press.

Pedersen, M. N. (1983) 'Changing patterns of electoral volatility: explorations in explanations', in Daalder, H. and Mair, P. (eds) *West European Party Systems: Continuity and change*, London: SAGE, pp. 29–66.

Pernaa, V. (2012) 'Vaalikamppailu mediassa', in Borg, S. (ed.) *Muutosvaalit 2011*, Helsinki: Ministry of Justice, pp. 29–42.

Pesonen, P. (1995) 'The evolution of Finland's party division and social structure', in Borg, S. and Sänkiaho, R. (eds) *The Finnish Voter*, Tampere: Finnish Political Science Association, pp. 9–22.

—   (2001) 'Change and stability in the Finnish party system', in Karvonen, L. and Kuhnle, S. (eds) *Party Systems and Voter Alignments Revisited*, London: Routledge, pp. 115–37.

—   (2004) 'Dangerous curves in Finnish politics: a sweet victory and a sour honeymoon', *Journal of Social Research*, 2: 275–95.

Pesonen, P. and Riihinen, O. (2002) *Dynamic Finland: The political system and the welfare state*, Helsinki: Finnish Literary Society.

Pesonen, P. and Sänkiaho, R. (1979) *Kansalaiset ja kansanvalta*, Porvoo–Helsinki–Juva: WSOY.

Pesonen, P., Sänkiaho, R. and Borg, S. (1993) *Vaalikansan äänivalta: Tutkimus eduskuntavaaleista ja valitsijakunnasta Suomen poliittisessa järjestelmässä*, Porvoo: Werner Söderström Osakeyhtiö.

Petersson, O, von Beyme, K., Karvonen, L., Nedelmann, B. and Smith, E. (1999) *Democracy the Swedish Way. Report from the democratic audit of Sweden 1999*, Stockholm: SNS Förlag.

Pharr, S. J. and Putnam, R. D. (eds) (2000) *Disaffected Democracies: What's Troubling the Trilateral Countries?*, Princeton: Princeton University Press.

Puoskari, M. (2002) 'Suomalaisten ministereiden sosiaalinen tausta ja rekrytoituminen vuosina 1983–2001', *Politiikka*, 44(4): 328–42.

Rappe, A. (1996) 'Party propaganda in motion: Finland 1954–1991', *Scandinavian Political Studies*, 19(4): 329–59.

Rasch, B. E. (2011) 'Why minority governments? Executive-legislative relations in the Nordic countries', in Persson, T. and Wiberg, M. (eds) *Parliamentary Government in the Nordic Countries at a Crossroads*, Stockholm: Santérus Academic Press, pp. 41–62.

Raunio, T. (2008) 'Finland: one hundred years of quietude', in Gallagher, M. and Mitchell, P. (eds), *The Politics of Electoral Systems*, Oxford: Oxford University Press, pp. 473–90.

Rautkallio, H. (1992) *Novosibirskin lavastus: Noottikriisi 1961*, Helsinki: Tammi.

Rentola, K. (1997) *Niin kylmää että polttaa: Kommunistit, Kekkonen ja Kreml 1947–1958*, Helsinki: Otava.

Reunanen, E. and Suhonen, P. (2009) 'Kansanedustajat ideologisella kartalla', in Borg, S. and Paloheimo, H. (eds) *Vaalit yleisödemokratiassa*, Tampere: Tampere University Press, pp. 325–56.

Riker, W. H. (1962) *The Theory of Political Coalitions*, New Haven, CT: Yale University Press.

Rintala, M. (1962) *Three Generations: The extreme right in Finnish politics*, Bloomington, IN: Indiana University Press.

Rokkan, S. (1970) *Citizens, Elections, Parties. Approaches to the comparative study of the processes of development*, Oslo: Universitetsforlaget.

Rose, R. and Urwin, D. W. (1970) 'Persistence and change in Western party systems since 1945', *Political Studies*, 18(3): 287–319.

Ruostetsaari, I. (2000) 'From political amateur to professional politician and expert representative: parliamentary recruitment in Finland since 1863', in Best, H. and Cotta, M. (eds) *Parliamentary Representatives in Europe 1848–2000: Legislative recruitment and careers in eleven European countries*, Oxford: Oxford University Press, pp. 50–87.

Ruostetsaari, I. and Mattila, M. (2002) 'Candidate-centred campaigns and their effects in an open list system: The case of Finland', in Farrell, D. M. and Schmitt–Beck, R. (eds) *Do Political Campaigns Matter? Campaign effects in elections and referendums*, London: Routledge, pp. 92–107.

Saalfeld, T. (2008) 'Institutions, chance, and choices: the dynamics of cabinet survival', in Strøm, K., Müller, W. C. and Bergman, T. (eds) *Cabinets and Coalition Bargaining. The democratic life cycle in Western Europe*, Oxford: Oxford University Press, pp. 327–68.

Salminen, E. (1979) *Aselevosta kaappaushankkeeseen: Sensuuri ja itsesensuuri Suomen lehdistössä 1944–1948*, Keuruu: Otava.

Sartori, G. (1994) *Comparative Constitutional Engineering: An inquiry into structures, incentives and outcomes*, London: Macmillan.

— (2005) *Parties and Party Systems. A framework for analysis*, Colchester: ECPR Press. (reprint of the 1976 original edition).

Schattschneider, E. E. (1942) *Party Government*, New York: Rinehart.

Seiler, D. -L. (1986) *De la comparaison des partis politiques*, Paris: Economica.

Shugart, M. S. (2001) 'Electoral efficiency and the move to mixed-member systems', *Electoral Studies* 20(2): 173–93.

Smith, G. (2011) *Democratic Innovations. Designing institutions for citizen participation*, Cambridge: Cambridge University Press.

Soikkanen, T. (1987) 'Changing bourgeois parties in a changing Finnish society', in Mylly, J. and Berry, R. M. (eds) *Political Parties in Finland: Essays in history and politics*, Turku: University of Turku, Department of Political History, pp. 58–97.

Somit, A., Wildenmann, R., Boll, B. and Römmele, A. (eds) (1994) *The Victorious Incumbent: A threat to democracy?*, Aldershot: Hampshire: Dartmouth.

Strøm, K., Müller, W. C. and Bergman, T. (eds) (2006) *Delegation and Accountability in Parliamentary Democracies*, Oxford: Oxford University Press.

Suhonen, P. (2011) 'Mistä perussuomalaiset tulevat?', in Wiberg, M. (ed.) *Populismi*, Helsinki: Edita, pp. 61–81.

Sundberg, J. (1985) *Svenskhetens dilemma i Finland: Finlandssvenskarnas samling och splittring under 1900-talet*, Helsingfors: Finska Vetenskaps–Societeten.

— (1995) 'Organizational structure of parties, candidate selection and campaigning', in Borg, S. and Sänkiaho, S. (eds) *The Finnish Voter*, Tampere: Finnish Political Science Association, pp. 45–65.

— (1996) *Partier och partisystem i Finland*, Helsingfors: Schildts.

Sundberg, J. (1999) 'The enduring Scandinavian party system', *Scandinavian Political Studies*, 22(3): 221–41.

— (2005) 'Finlandssvenskt väljarbeteende – en tillbakablick', in Bengtsson, Å. and Grönlund, K. (eds) *Den finlandssvenska väljaren*, Vasa: Samforsk, pp. 5–22.

— (2008) 'Puolueiden organisaatiot ja suhteet etujärjestöihin', in Paloheimo, H. and Wiberg, M. (eds) *Suomen puolueet ja puoluejärjestelmä*, Helsinki: WSOY, pp. 61–83.

Sundberg, J. and Gylling, C. (1992), 'Finland', in Katz, R. S. and Mair, P. (eds) *Party Organizations: A Data Handbook*, London: SAGE Publications, pp. 273–316.

Suomi, J. (1992) *Urho Kekkonen: 1956–1962, kriisien aika*, Helsinki: Otava.

— (1994) *Presidentti: Urho Kekkonen 1962–1968*, Helsinki: Otava.

Swanson, D. L. and Mancini, P. (1996) 'Politics, media, and modern democracy: introduction', in Swanson, D. L. and Mancini, P. (eds) *Politics, Media, and Modern Democracy: An international study of innovations in electoral campaigning and their consequences*, Westport, Connecticut: Praeger, pp. 1–28.

Tarasti, L. (2010) *Vaaliehdokkaiden ja puolueiden rahoitusopas*, Helsinki: Edita.

Tarasti, L. and Taponen, H. (1996) *Suomen vaalilainsäädäntö*, Helsinki: Edita.

Taylor, M. and Herman, V. (1971) 'Party systems and government stability', *American Political Science Review* 65, pp. 28–37.

Thompson, D. F. (2008) 'Deliberative democratic theory and empirical political science', *Annual Review of Political Science* 11, pp. 497–520.

Tiihonen, S. (1990) *Hallitusvalta*: Helsinki: VAPK-kustannus/Hallintohistoriakomitea.

Tiili, M. (2004) 'Hallituksen keskustelukulttuuri: kurkistus kollektiivisen ja kollegiaalisen ulkokuoren alle', *Politiikka*, 46(2): 137–42.

— (2008) *Ministers as Strategic Political Leaders? Strategic political steering after NPM reforms in Finland*, Helsinki: University of Helsinki, Acta Politica 34.

Toivonen, T. (2011) 'Perussuomalaisten nousun taustoista', in Wiberg, M. (ed.) *Populismi*, Helsinki: Edita, pp. 82–93.

Tuikka, T. J. (2013) 'Urho Kaleva Kekkonen – Kainuusta Kekkoslovakiaan', in Tiihonen, S., Pohls, M. and Korppi-Tommola, J. (eds) *Presidentti johtaa. Suomalaisen valtiojohtamisen pitkä linja*, Helsinki: Kustannusosakeyhtiö Siltala, pp. 190–212.

Upton, A. F., (1980) *The Finnish Revolution*, Minneapolis: University of Minnesota Press.

Valkonen, T. (1985) 'Alueelliset erot', in Valkonen, T., Alapuro, R., Alestalo, M., Jallinoja, R. and Sandlund, T. (eds) *Suomalaiset. Yhteiskunnan rakenne teollistumisen aikana*, Porvoo: WSOY, pp. 201–42.

Van Biezen, I., Mair, P. and Poguntke, T. (2012) 'Going, going … gone? The decline of party membership in contemporary Europe', *European Journal of Political Research*, 51: 24–56.

Van der Brug, W. (2010) 'Structural and ideological voting in age cohorts', *West European Politics*, 33(3): 586–607.

Vartiainen, J. (2010) 'Sverige – Finland, del 2', *Hufvudstadsbladet* 21 February 2010, p. 11.

Venho, T. (2008) *Piilotettua julkisuutta: Suomalaisen puolue–ja vaalirahoituksen avoimuusintressi normeissa ja käytännössä*, University of Turku, Department of Political Science: unpublished doctoral dissertation.

Verzichelli, L. (2008) 'Portfolio allocation', in Strøm, K., Müller, W. C. and Bergman, T. (eds) *Cabinets and Coalition Bargaining: The democratic life cycle in Western Europe*, Oxford: Oxford University Press, pp. 237–67.

Vihavainen, T. (1991) *Kansakunta rähmällään: Suomettumisen lyhyt historia*, Helsinki: Otava.

Vloyantes, J. P. (1975) *Silk Glove Hegemony. Finnish–Soviet Relations, 1944–1974*, Kent State, OH: Kent State University Press.

Von Beyme, K. (1985) *Political Parties in Western Democracies*, London: Gower.

Warwick, P. V. (1994) *Government Survival in Parliamentary Democracies*, Cambridge: Cambridge University Press.

Wass, H. (2007) 'Generations and socialization into electoral participation in Finland', *Scandinavian Political Studies*, 30(1): 1–19.

Webb, P. (2002) 'Introduction: political parties in advanced industrial democracies', in Webb, P., Farrell, D. and Holliday, I. (eds) *Political Parties in Advanced Industrial Democracies*, Oxford: Oxford University Press, pp. 1–15.

Wiberg, M (2008) 'Puolueet eduskunnassa ja hallituksessa', in Paloheimo, H. and Raunio, T. (eds) *Suomen puolueet ja puoluejärjestelmä*, Porvoo: WSOY.

— (2009) *Hallitseeko hallitus?* Sastamala: Kunnallisalan kehittämissäätiö.

— (2011) 'Mitä populismi on?', in Wiberg, M. (ed.) *Populismi*, Helsinki: Edita, pp. 11–21.

Internet sources

https://manifesto-project.wzb.eu
http://www.worldvaluessurvey.org
http://thedata.harvard.edu/dvn/dv/jwjohnson/faces/study/StudyPage.xhtml?globa
    lId=hdl:1902.1/17901
http://idea.int
http://nesstar.ess.nsd.uib.no/webview
http://laborsta.ilo.org
http://www.defmin.fi/?663_m=3335&l=en&s=270
http://www.finlex.fi/sv/laki/alkup/1969/19690391
http://www.eduskunta.fi
http://www.tilastokeskus.fi/til/evaa/tau_en.html
http://www.eduskunta.fi/thwfakta/hetekau/hex/hxent.htm
http://www.finlex.fi/en/laki/kaannokset/1999/en19990731.pdf
http://www.government.fi
http://government.fi/tietoa-valtioneuvostosta/hallitukset/vuodesta-1917/tulokset/
    en.jsp?report_id=V2
http://www.ssfindex.com/cms/wp-content/uploads/indicator8.pdf
http://www.stat.fi/til/evaa/2011/evaa_2011_2011-04-29_kat_001_en.html
http://www.transparency.org/research/gcb/gcb_2010
http://www.transparency.org/cpi2012/results
http://www.vaalitutkimus.fi/en/vaalitutkimus_suomessa.html
http://www.valtioneuvosto.fi
http://www.wvsevsdb.com/wvs/WVSAnalizeQuestion.jsp
http://svenska.yle.fi/artikel/2014/01/29/partikartan-oforandrad
http://www.oecd.org/eco/surveys/economic-survey-finland.htm

Data provided by the Finnish Social Science Data Archive (FSD). Available through http://www.fsd.uta.fi

FSD registration number	Name of dataset
FSD0152	World Values Survey 1996; Finnish data
FSD0153	World Values Surveys 1995–1997
FSD0157	European Values Survey 1999–2001
FSD1002	Finnish Party Barometer 1975
FSD1003	Finnish Party Barometer 1976
FSD1004	Finnish Party Barometer 1977
FSD1005	Finnish Party Barometer 1978
FSD1006	Finnish Party Barometer 1979
FSD1007	Finnish Party Barometer 1980

FSD registration number	Name of dataset
FSD1010	Finnish Party Barometer 1982
FSD1011	Finnish Party Barometer 1983
FSD1012	Finnish Party Barometer 1984
FSD1013	Finnish Party Barometer 1986
FSD1014	Finnish Party Barometer 1987
FSD1015	Finnish Party Barometer 1988
FSD1016	Finnish Party Barometer 1990
FSD1018	Parliamentary Election Survey 1991
FSD1029	Finnish Party Barometer August–September 1992
FSD1030	Finnish Party Barometer 1994
FSD1031	Finnish Party Barometer 1995
FSD1032	Finnish Party Barometer 1996
FSD1033	Finnish Party Barometer March 1992
FSD1034	Finnish Party Barometer 1997
FSD1037	Finnish Party Barometer 1998
FSD1038	Finnish Party Barometer 1999
FSD1042	Parliamentary Election Survey 1999
FSD1260	Parliamentary Election Survey 2003
FSD2024	Follow-up on Parliamentary Elections 2003
FSD2263	Parliamentary Elections 2007: Small Constituencies
FSD2269	Parliamentary Election Survey 2007
FSD2274	Finnish Party Barometers 1992–2005; combined datasets
FSD2276	Finnish Party Barometers 1973–1990; combined datasets
FSD2653	Parliamentary Election Survey 2011

Index

Page numbers in italics refer to Tables and Figures.

33–7, 89–90
1961 'Note Crisis' 34, 35
presidential power of 79, 84, 87,
   88–90, 91, 93
social democratic/conservative
   challenge 35–6, 38, 45, 90, 146
Khrushchev, N. 34
Kiviniemi, M. 77, 92
Koivisto, M. 15, 37–8, 77, 79–80,
   84–5, 89
cabinet politics and stability 79–80,
   89, 90, 103
electoral support of 37, 110
leadership style of 84–5

labour-union movement 20, 32, 33,
   38–9
consensus politics, move to 39, 40
Incomes Policy Agreement (1968)
   38–9
industrial disputes, level of 38, 39
organisational split (1969–74) 39
Left Alliance (*Vasemmistoliitto*) 18,
   20, 21 n.12, 38, 46, 55–6, 91, 147,
   152
candidate profile 64
electoral alliances, use of 67
formation of 38, 46, 147
membership analysis 55–6
2011 elections, effect on 19, *25*, 46,
   82, 118, 147
left parties 21 n.12, *25*, 147
decline of 147
Left Party 21 n.12, 25, *55–6*, 65, 66,
   78, 90, 93
Liberal Party 19, 24, 151
liberalism 19, 21, 24

Manifesto Research Group (MRG) 5,
   48
left-right scale of 48
see also western European
   comparison analysis
mass parties 6, 50
organisational structures in 50–1

nationalism 151
NATO 15, 20
Niinistö, S. 134

Paasikivi, J. K. 145
parliament and parliamentarism 6–7,
   15, 16, 17, 39–40, 69–70, 79,
   105–6, 143
cabinets in 36 n.2, 39–40, 69,
   73–106
   bureaucratic influence, growth of
      104, 150
   conflict resolution, pattern in 98,
      100, 150
   decentralisation of 98, 99, 101
   discipline/code of conduct in
      95–6, 150
   elitisation in 104, 150
   legislative process, role in 94–8,
      100
   majority backing (post 80s)
      39–40, 78–81, 96
   party-leader meetings role in 98
   types 1950–2009 *40*
   stability of 8, 39, 40, 79–80, 95,
      100, 104, 105, 149, 150
   standing committees of 94, 97–8,
      104
   see also coalitions and cabinet-
      formation
democratic changes in 105–6, 143
   accountability, problem of 105
   consensual politics 105, 143,
      149–51
legislative turnover 69–71, 87
   cross-national comparison
      analysis 70
   patterns of (Finland) 70–71
   political protest, role in 71
ministers and ministries in 94, 98,
   100–1
   civil servant power/relations
      99–100, 104, 150
   decision-making power of 98,
      100–101, 104

www.ingramcontent.com/pod-product-compliance
Lightning Source LLC
Chambersburg PA
CBHW072132020426
42334CB00018B/1763